Journalism in Context

Journalism in Context is an accessible introduction to the theory and practice of journalism in a changing world. The book looks at the way in which power flows through media organizations influencing not only what journalists choose to present to their audiences but how they present it and then in turn what their audiences do with it.

Using examples from across the world, as well as from her own research, Angela Phillips explains complex theoretical concepts. She invites readers to consider how news is influenced by the culture from which it emerges, as well as the way it is paid for and how different countries have approached the problem of ensuring that democracy is served by its media, rather than being undermined by it.

Journalism has always been an early adopter of new technologies and the most recent changes are examined in the light of a history in which, although platforms keep on changing, journalism always survives. The questions raised here are important for all students of journalism and all those who believe that journalism matters.

Angela Phillips is a Professor in Journalism in the Department of Media and Communications, Goldsmiths, University of London. She spent the majority of her career as a journalist working for national newspapers, magazines, TV and radio. She is the author of *Good Writing for Journalists* (2006) and co-author of *Changing Journalism* (2011).

Communication and Society

Series Editor: James Curran

This series encompasses the broad field of media and cultural studies. Its main concerns are the media and the public sphere: on whether the media empower or fail to empower popular forces in society; media organisations and public policy; the political and social consequences of media campaigns; and the role of media entertainment, ranging from potboilers and the human-interest story to rock music and TV sport.

Journalism in Context

Practice and Theory for the Digital Age

Angela Phillips

LONDON AND NEW YORK

First published 2015
by Routledge
2 Park Square, Milton Park, Abingdon, Oxon, OX14 4RN

and by Routledge
711 Third Avenue, New York, NY 10017

Routledge is an imprint of the Taylor & Francis Group, an informa business

British Library Cataloguing in Publication Data
A catalogue record for this book is available from the British Library

Library of Congress Cataloging in Publication Data
Phillips, Angela.
Journalism in context : practice and theory for the digital age / Angela Phillips.
pages cm -- (Communication and society)
Includes bibliographical references and index.
1. Journalism--History--21st century. 2. Journalism--Technological innovations.
3. Online journalism. I. Title.
PN4815.2P47 2014
070.9'051--dc23
2014010179

ISBN: 978-0-415-53627-1 (hbk)
ISBN: 978-0-415-53628-8 (pbk)
ISBN: 978-0-203-11174-1 (ebk)

Typeset in Baskerville
by Taylor & Francis Books

MIX
Paper from
responsible sources
FSC
www.fsc.org   FSC® C013056

Printed and bound in Great Britain by
TJ International Ltd, Padstow, Cornwall

Contents

Acknowledgements

This book is the summation of 20 years of lecturing to students at Goldsmiths, University of London and reading essays that very often told me things that I didn't know or pushed me into considering new directions. I am grateful to all of them and very conscious of the extraordinary privilege of working with the young people who will develop the journalism of tomorrow. I salute them for their intelligence, clear-sighted realization of the momentousness of the changes underway and dedication to being the best that they can. Particular thanks go to Lawrence Dodds who read and commented on early chapters and Chiara Rimella who checked the bibliography. Also to Nick Couldry, Mirca Madianou, Sarah Kember, Justin Schlosberg, Omega Douglas, James Curran, Glenda Cooper, Rachel Sturrock and Rodney Benson who read through drafts and commented. Your remarks and encouragement were invaluable. And finally thank you to Mike for debates about structure and agency and for love and support throughout.

Introduction

This book starts with the assumption that journalism is important, and that it is worth our while to consider how it could be improved. As a journalist and a teacher of future journalists, what I write is firmly embedded within the culture and practice of journalism, but it goes beyond a concern with intros and stand-firsts to consider what many decades of academic research can teach us about our profession and to what extent it is relevant to the everyday work that we do. In writing it I hope to open up the doors between theory and practice, to sift through the work that academic researchers have done and to consider what is useful to practitioners.

For too long there has been a stand-off between theory and practice. Practitioners have regarded academic researchers with suspicion as out of touch and unable to understand the complexities of their world. The study of journalism has been seen, at best, as a necessary means of imparting craft skills, at worst it has been completely ignored. This reaction is largely defensive. For too long critical journalism studies has felt like an attack rather than a dialogue, or a spur to action. Academic researchers have too often been guilty of approaching journalism from above and failing to see either its complexities or the pressures ordinary journalists have to deal with daily. But as more journalists move into the academy and more students enter the profession with a background in journalism studies, this defensive barrier is starting to crumble. Indeed, as the profession continues to be assailed by an almost continuous barrage of technical and economic shocks, the insights of critical outsiders and more reflexive insiders will be vital to the way in which it renews and rebuilds itself. Journalism can no longer ignore its critics. It needs to understand them and indeed learn from them.

Critiquing the critiques

The study of journalism is a deeply contested field. Indeed the stand-offs between different theoretical approaches have often seemed as deep and damaging as those between the academy and the profession. During the 1980s and 1990s, political economists and those taking more cultural approaches found it hard to find common ground. Political economists felt that cultural approaches failed to recognise the importance of economic structures and the way power flows through them. Cultural theorists criticized political economists for seeing only structures and failing to see that audiences had agency and could 'resist' power. Those approaching journalism from a liberal pluralist position might have been on a different planet – or at least a different continent.

Entering the academy from a career as a freelance feature writer, working across print and broadcast media, I was well aware of the impact of structures. It was clear to anyone working in the UK that the print media was profoundly partisan and largely represented the interests of the white, male, conservative elite. Studies of the public sphere (Jürgen Habermas) and the political economy of the media were persuasive in their explanations of media power, and the work of James Curran clearly traced the development of and consolidation of the UK news media into the conservative force that it is today. But it was the burgeoning field of cultural studies, represented by Stuart Hall, my colleague David Morley and American academic John Fiske that (even with its profound limitations) began to explain the failure of these powerful institutions to entirely capture their audiences. The writing of Antonio Gramsci, on the one hand and Michel Foucault on the other, opened up new possibilities. In the slippage between the sender and receiver of messages, lay the possibility of resistance and change. But, although audience studies demonstrated the possibility of a disobedient public, it failed to offer explanations for differences between media organizations, or the possibility of dissident journalists working within them.

As a feminist, with no prior media connections and no training, my own experience told me that the voices of women were easily marginalized and usually strictly confined to those spaces reserved for 'women's interests'. But I was also aware that it was still possible to provide an oppositional voice within the existing structures. It was this sense that something very important was being missed that drove my interest in researching journalists' decision-making in 2002 and then 2007/8. In my earlier work, interviewing ethnic minority journalists in mainstream newsrooms, I had the evidence but lacked an interpretive frame, so I am grateful to Rodney Benson and Erik Neveu whose book, *Bourdieu and the Journalistic Field* (2005), helped me to focus my later research using field theory as a framework.

Field theory will be encountered throughout this book because its explanation of the way in which occupational fields create their own pressures is helpful to anyone trying to understand how a fairly defined occupation such as journalism, both reproduces itself and is changed by pressures from within and outside. What is important for practising journalists is to be able to survey the field and to see where light has been thrown onto the practices that are too easily taken for granted and how the insights of academic researchers can be used to make more 'reflexive' practitioners capable of examining and improving what they do. Theory is not a straitjacket, nor should it be seen as a reproach but as a tool that helps us to see more clearly what we are doing when we work.

The structure of the book

Chapter 1 'News Defined' asks the fundamental question: 'What is news?' The simple answer is that news is a mix of what we need to know and what we are curious about. The work of journalism is to find information that is likely to be considered important, or curious, to a specific group of people, and to package it so that it is received and understood. But this is not a process that happens in a vacuum. Journalists do not wander in a forest of information and simply pick the juicy titbits off the trees. They are under pressure to pick particular fruit and present them in specific ways, so that they emphasize one aspect of what is considered important, rather than many others. It is this process of packaging that determines what is available to be consumed. News, in other words, is what is presented to audiences as important or curious and it is the process of picking and packaging that this chapter starts to address.

Chapter 2 'News Interrupted: Ownership and Control' addresses the structures within which journalists operate. It begins by asking, not what is news, but why is it important to be informed. In a sense this chapter is the heart of the book because it argues for a journalism that should be the life force of a democratic system. This is why its health is of vital importance to all of us. Without information that can be trusted it is impossible for ordinary people to take part in the governance of their country. However it doesn't suggest that we need to protect what we have so much as look for something better because we have not, as yet, evolved a means of providing trustworthy channels of information that do not over-represent the views of the most powerful to the detriment of the rest.

Chapter 3 'Journalists and Their Sources' takes a closer look at what journalists actually do and the way in which power operates in their everyday work. It takes apart the crucial relationships that largely determine which information is passed on and which is passed over. It considers why source relationships are not equal and how very difficult it would be to make them so. It considers the importance of trust and just how the simple requirement to verify information militates in favour of the known, as opposed to the unknown, source and while it argues for greater vigilance in source selection, it recognises that news reporting will inevitably prioritize the powerful, because it is their actions that require the greatest scrutiny. The question for journalists is therefore not so much about whether to approach elite sources but about how to do so critically.

Chapter 4 'The Making of Journalists' asks who journalists are, what drives them and whether there is any need for them in a world of interactivity in which (we are informed) anyone with a smartphone can be a journalist. It then goes on to consider the way in which the changing work environment is affecting the jobs they do. This chapter uses 'field theory' to situate journalists and considers the way in which power struggles in the field have manifested themselves in changing workplace practices that have little to do with improvements, or even with technical change and a great deal to do with the need to minimize the impact of unfortunate business decisions. It then discusses the way in which the players in the field jockey for position and attempt to protect themselves by invoking law and regulation; protective activity that is regarded by some as an attempt to insulate the profession from incursions by an active audience, and by others as an attempt to maintain standards in the face of growing commercialization.

Chapter 5 'Audience, Networks, Interaction' brings the audience more clearly into focus and discusses the growing body of media theory and research that sees the 'pro-sumer' as the saviour of journalism in an interactive age. This chapter questions many of the often un-examined assumptions of 'net-enthusiasts' who argue that the Internet would put ordinary people in charge of news production and dissemination. This chapter looks at the growing evidence that, far from emancipating audiences, where companies have opened up their sites to their audiences, it has mainly been to undercut wages and threaten jobs. It also addresses the suggestion that amateur journalists would do the job better than people who are trained and paid. It finds that audiences don't, on the whole, do research, but they do like to comment on the research done by others. While this is a perfectly valid way to bring the audience into the picture, it cannot replace work done by reporters.

Chapter 6 'The Business of Journalism in the Digital Age' brings the underlying questions raised in the earlier chapters into sharper focus. Here we look at how the business of journalism has adapted to the digital age. It explores the suggestion made by some researchers that journalists are directly responsible for the failure of some news organizations to adapt to the disruptions of the past ten years. They have been accused of being unwilling to embrace technology; of being greedy and afraid of change; of unreasonably trying to protect their jobs and refusing to embrace interactivity. This chapter focuses instead on the failure of news managements to understand how the Internet would change their funding base; on the greed of news organizations that bled their news operations dry in order to maintain profits; and on the failure to explore a joint approach to the collapse in advertising revenue. It then goes on to trace some of the new shoots that are beginning to emerge and raises the possibility that government action may be required to protect news from the destructive potential of an unstable market, as it does in parts of Europe and has done elsewhere in the past (McChesney and Nichols 2011, Benson 2011).

The final chapter 'Ethics in Practice' is where we bring the story full circle and consider the needs of journalists as ethical and active agents rather than cogs in the wheels of the media machine. It argues that the discussion of ethics has a place in media theory and that it certainly has a place in the training of the journalists of tomorrow. Clearly journalism cannot thrive if it is subject to state censorship, but nor can it thrive if it becomes too closely tied to commercial interests. A space needs to be made, between pure commercial interest and the interests of the state, in which journalists are able to exercise their conscience free from editorial pressures. Most attempts to protect journalists have been construed as (and have often become) attempts to erect barriers against newcomers. If journalism is to be protected, without becoming protectionist, then more imaginative solutions are required.

Chapter 1

News defined

In this chapter we will consider how news choices are made. What is reported as news, and why, has been a major preoccupation of academics interested in the field of journalism. Here we will look at the operational and cultural factors that determine what ends up as headline news, what is relegated to a more lowly position and what gets left out altogether.

Ideology and the news

There is no objective matter that can be described as 'news'. The stories that end up on the pages and in the bulletins don't arrive there by chance but through a set of decisions constrained by practical, structural and ideological factors. Some decisions are taken because of time constraints, and others because access is limited. But while these practical constraints are clearly important (and I will discuss them further), there are also deeper questions of culture, ideology and power, which underlie which events in the world journalists choose to select and amplify.

Part of a journalist's training is about learning how to determine what counts as news. Trainee journalists may at first find it hard to work out what is considered 'newsworthy'. Gradually they learn how to sort the stories that will make headlines from the ones that are destined for relegation to the bottom of page 20. This process of learning is part of professional training, but it is also a means by which ideological bias is transmitted from one generation to another. French sociologist Pierre Bourdieu (1977) refers to the complex rules that journalists (or any other professionals) learn to employ in the course of their work as 'doxa' – which we discuss further in Chapter 4 'The Making of Journalists'.

When political economists and cultural theorists study how these rules are made and implemented, and how they ensure that messages in society conform to particular norms, they often invoke Antonio Gramsci and his concept of 'cultural hegemony'. Gramsci was looking at the ways in which power flows through ideas as well as through economic control, and observed how it can be maintained without the overt use of force by winning the consent of those who are ruled over. He claimed that achieving and sustaining this hegemony was necessary to maintain power, but he also argued that this is a process, not an end; far from passively accepting ideas that have been fed to them, people need to be continuously won over and through this natural resistance to power, Gramsci saw the seeds of change (Gramsci 1971).

For most followers of Gramsci, news choices develop as a means of policing social norms. Journalists, guided by editors (who in most newsrooms make the major decisions about what is to be reported), search for examples of human behaviour that should be either punished or applauded, and thereby limit the allowable areas of debate to those that reflect the prevailing view of the world. 'The hegemonic sense of the world seeps into "common sense" and gets reproduced there; it may even appear to be generated by that common sense' (Gitlin 1980: 254).

As the Internet has ushered in a more 'open' form of journalism, in which audience feedback seems to take centre stage, some researchers see the collapse of a hegemonic model of news production, with audiences becoming more involved both in interacting with news and in authoring news reports (Beckett 2008, Jarvis 2006, Russell 2011). Certainly editors and reporters are more aware today of what audiences are actually reading. It is easy to find out what the audiences like because they click on what they like. Most newsrooms today display trending topics from Twitter and various news sites as an endless digital 'ticker tape' to help determine what subjects need to be covered in order to attract audience attention.

The success of the UK's *Daily Mail* in attracting a massive international online audience is entirely predicated on giving readers whatever they are most likely to click on. The result is a right-hand column of captioned celebrity pictures which critics have dubbed the 'sidebar of shame' (Collins 2012). But the *Mail*'s normative 'common sense' still comes through loud and clear: younger men are 'toy boys', all women are 'fighting the flab' (or they should be), and any single person in the news for any reason must be either looking for love or recovering from a split. It seems unlikely that this form of audience 'participation' in news choices would constitute what Gramsci had in mind by resistance to hegemonic ideas. It seems clear here that, although audiences appear to be more involved, it is more as consumers than as shapers of news ideology.

Some ideological approaches to news construction move in the other direction and come close to seeing a conspiracy at work, in which all editors and journalists are a part of, or are controlled by, the 'power bloc'. Teun Van Dijk suggests:

> Journalists often identify not only with a language but also with a nation state, and in nationalist ideologies, the positive self-image is in terms of *Us* in our country, on the one hand, and *Them* in (or from) other countries, on the other hand, as we also have seen for racist ideologies, with which nationalist ideologies are closely related.
>
> (Van Dijk 2009: 201)

I start from the assumption that journalists are as much subjects of ideology as their readers. They are overwhelmingly likely to be well educated and middle class and that will inevitably affect their view of their world. In most Western countries (and most news agencies) they are also likely to be white (Thanki and McKay 2005: 8, Guskin 2013) and they are usually under pressure to conform to an editorial line (this will be discussed in more detail below), but they need to be seen not as subjugated agents of the 'power bloc' – nor indeed as indistinguishable from it – but as individuals constrained by structures of power and ideology: as indeed we all are.

Bourdieu theorizes that individuals are shaped first by their social environment (family, education, class, gender, etc.) and each person defines themselves in relation to their peers. But this is not a fixed state. Individuals define their own position in relation to other people who share their family, educational, or occupational group. He describes this as Habitus (Bourdieu and Wacquant 1992: 133). Journalists are then also constrained by the operation of the 'field' in which they work. These constraints are partly internal to that field: occupational groups establish rules of behaviour and standards of quality, which members of the group learn to adhere to. But there are also external pressures.

The field of journalism is constrained by commercial interests and Bourdieu (2005) recognizes that there are big differences in the level of autonomy enjoyed by journalists depending on where they are placed within their field. Journalists working for non-commercial organizations are more autonomous in that they are mainly constrained by the internal pressures of the field and its rules, including notions of public service and neutrality, while those working for highly commercial organizations are less autonomous in that they are largely constrained by external commercial considerations and the need to attract audiences. Rodney Benson argues that the field is in turn influenced by an over-arching field of politics and the state, which uses law and regulations to influence the field (Benson 2006:198).

Journalism also provides one of the key means by which competing social and political groups magnify their own position by attempting to take control of the popular narrative (or as Bourdieu (1989) describes it: 'symbolic power'). Journalists and journalism organizations are always at the centre of battles for 'symbolic power' and therefore subject to attempts by more or less powerful organizations to win their attention and approval. The question that we will discuss further in chapters to come is the extent to which news organizations are captured by that process or are in fact shaping it. Or do they move from one position to another depending on their relative power in the field?

News choices in practice

Framing

Robert Entman, making use of the work of Erving Goffman (1974), looked at the ways in which ideological approaches are 'operationalized' by 'framing' issues and stories to reflect certain views.

> Framing essentially involves selection and salience. To frame is to select some aspects of a perceived reality and make them more salient in a communicating text, in such a way as to promote a particular problem, definition, causal interpretation, moral evaluation, and/or treatment recommendation for the item described.
>
> (Entman 1993: 52)

In newsrooms, 'framing' manifests as the very conscious process of finding an 'angle'. Every journalist understands that stories need angles, because we don't just report events in chronological order but also shape them into a narrative. Indeed, the art of news writing is largely the art of selecting and ordering events so that they are easy to read and to understand. That means journalists must always take a view on what is the most important piece of information, with other facts arranged to illuminate this key item of news – prioritizing certain facts over other ones and thereby encoding ideological assumptions.

Frames change according to where journalists position themselves, or (more often) are positioned by the editor. Where the appearance of objectivity is a culturally sanctioned requirement for journalism (particularly in the USA), alternative views will be incorporated, but the structure will always give primacy to the views endorsed by the editor. In countries where political bias is expected (such as southern Europe) there may be no attempt to put the other side of the story. It is assumed that the audience will recognize the framing of their information for what it is and adjust their own perceptions accordingly (Donsbach and Patterson 2004).

In order to get a story accepted that is a little outside the norm, it may be necessary for a reporter to write it within a pre-existing script that fits into the schema in the editor's head. One senior journalist said:

> I try and use the same news values that people have, the same news criteria. But I try and fit the stories that I want in the paper into those criteria and I try and show them why they fit the criteria. I find it then makes it very difficult for them to argue that they shouldn't be in the paper. Occasionally you have to go to the editor and say: 'If these people were white and lived in Cobham, would you run this story?'
>
> (Interview, senior reporter, regional newspaper, 2002)

One function of 'framing' is the tendency to give more (or more sympathetic) coverage to people who editors perceive to be 'like us' or related to us in some way (Nossek 2004). Research into the coverage of European Union elections found that most was about national rather than Europe-wide issues (Kevin 2003, Williams 2005). The same rationale governs stories about trade, which is only relevant if the trade is with 'us'. A Muslim country is more likely to take a sympathetic interest in other Muslim countries; a Francophone country will notice events in other French-speaking countries. Entman says:

Framing in this light plays a major role in the exertion of political power, and the frame in a news text is really the imprint of power – it registers the identity of actors or interests that competed to dominate the text.

(1993: 50)

Frames are effectively internalized as the 'mainstream view'. In terms of American politics, the mainstream lies within: 'the region of electoral contests and legislative debates, of issues recognized as such by the major established actors of the American political process.'

(Hallin 1986)

But of course 'mainstream' changes depending on where you happen to be standing. Consider, for example, the different ways in which the story of Hurricane Katrina, which devastated New Orleans in 2005, was told. A research paper (Robinson 2009) looked at the coverage as it unfolded in the local news-papers and websites. It found the local press producing a narrative of city officials defending civilization from overwhelming natural disaster. Local people writing on the websites saw officials and bureaucrats as part of the problem and characterized themselves and their friends as the heroes of their personal narra-tives of struggle against the odds. National newspapers, slightly further away from the action, fell back on familiar tropes about individual heroism that chime in with an archetype of plucky, rugged, all-American individualists who operate according to their own personal morality. This story in the *Wall Street Journal* could be describing the members of a posse in an old Western:

> He's a cop back in Mobile; Mr. Ellison a contractor there. Never mind that Mr. Churchville had the roof torn off of his own home by Katrina and Mr. Ellison's home also suffered damage. As soon as they started hearing the dire reports from New Orleans, they lit out, two of an estimated 1,600 such volunteers who have come in with boats to search the still flooded ramparts of the city for Katrina's trapped and dead.

(Wells 2005)

Move further away from the scene and the narrative structures are chosen to fit in with pre-existing assumptions about America. In this extract most of the material comes from Reuters but it was mainly used in India, Australia and New Zealand. The chaos was emphasized and the stories were shot through with a rather grim schadenfreude; India has so often been depicted by the Western media as unable to look after its own people perhaps this felt like payback time.

> The refugees, waiting to be taken to sports stadiums and other huge shelters across Texas and northern Louisiana, described how the convention centre and the Superdome became lawless hellholes beset by rape and murder.

(*Telegraph India*, 5 September 2005)

In the UK, the *Daily Mail*'s right-wing populist editorial line came up with a rescued maiden narrative. Mark and Gretchen were tourists who were trapped, with thousands of other victims of the hurricane, waiting to be rescued. In an interesting twist, the *Mail* casts the other victims of the Superdome as the villains, with Gretchen as the fair maiden and her boyfriend as the 'white knight'.

> Mark's father John, 56, from Stanford-le-Hope in Essex, said: 'The gangs looked on Gretchen as a typical American middle-class girl and they didn't like that at all. Mark had to really protect her because she was threatened with rape and violence.'
>
> (Yapp 2005)

In the rush to create a fitting narrative, myths are created that are later hard to shift. No doubt these stories were based on fragments of true information, but little attempt was made to verify the more lurid stories. The rape allegations were never subsequently traced to any specific victims and there seems to be no evidence of a rash of murders associated with the hurricane (Berger 2007, Younge 2005).

News routines

While ideological influences are clearly in play, other researchers (including Gieber 1964, Fishman 1980, Tuchman 1978, Gans 1979, Golding and Elliot 1996, Deuze 2010) have concentrated on the way in which the very routines used by journalists tend to influence what stories they choose and how they use them. The structure of work, the pressure of deadlines, access to relevant people, and financial constraints all have an impact on the kind of material which will be covered most frequently and the sort of stories that achieve prominence.

Speed

From celebrity gossip sites through fashion glossies and all the way to the front page of a daily newspaper, the major common denominator is novelty. For news organizations, there is enormous pressure to be first with the news, and this imperative is the overriding factor behind both the way in which newsgathering is organized and the industry's adoption of new technologies. The need for speed meant very early use of the fastest forms of transport and early adoption of the telegraph, radio, the Internet and social media (Rantanen 2009, Phillips 2012a). The most recent manifestation of this tendency has been the growth of 'live-blogging' as a way of reporting live events as they unfold. In the economy of news, being first brings with it a premium: the first to report a story has a major advantage in attracting an audience (Allern 2002: 145).

But very little reported news is completely unexpected or exclusive; most is planned and routine. A more important issue for most reporters is not to be first but to avoid being last – or, worse still, missing the story altogether (Schlesinger 1987: 51). The fear of failing to get the news is probably more pressing for the majority of journalists than the surge of adrenaline that comes with the publication of a true exclusive (Phillips 2010a: 91). Indeed, the degree of organization required to ensure that an outlet is 'first' often militates against the unexpected. Planned stories are far easier to organize: a big event like the Olympics can be covered in minute detail because the news organizations have had time to get reporters ready well in advance (Golding and Elliot 1979). Moreover, totally unexpected events tend not to happen in front of cameras and may take time to surface as 'news'. If they have been filmed by an amateur, without a large following, they may never surface at all, or may stay submerged for many days as reporters look for ways to verify them (see 'Access', below).

'New' news is by definition the information that news organizations are able to find and transmit within the necessary time-frame, and the vast majority of that comes from known sources that have alerted them in advance to events. Research in 1973 found that about two thirds of *Washington Post* stories came from press conferences and news releases (Sigal 1973). A report in the UK 35 years later, found that between 54 and 58 per cent of news stories in their sample were informed by PR (Lewis *et al.* 2008).

Likewise, features, comment, and analysis may deal with themes that are as old as human society, but unless the events being discussed have occurred within the necessary time-frame they are unlikely to be reported. On a monthly magazine there is a different pressure; coverage of live events is avoided because the stories would always appear to lag behind 'the news'. In order to appear new, monthly magazine editors look for recurring anniversaries and planned events, such as film releases, fashion shows or product launches that coincide with publication dates three months ahead.

Access

People and places that are easier to access tend to get more coverage. At the simplest and most practical level, journalists avoid writing about anything they cannot verify. If you were not actually there yourself to ensure that an event has taken place, or to check that words have been said or deeds have been done, then you have to verify the information by some other means. If you don't do this then you may publish something that is damaging and you could be legally liable for your mistakes. But there is something more important here than the threat of being sued. If journalists do not report accurately what they see and hear then they have nothing to offer which sets them apart from the continuous stream of rumour and counter-rumour available online.

The need to check usually means talking to someone you trust. As we discuss in Chapter 3 'Journalists and Their Sources', when journalists are seeking people to verify their stories in a tight time-frame, they are more likely to go to an established source. Such sources tend to be elite sources, partly because they are easier to contact: their press officers can whisk them to an interview at very short notice. But there is another reason that is often overlooked in critical analysis of news. If the job of journalism is primarily to interrogate power, then we should expect that government organizations would appear more often than individuals who have no power. Indeed, it is a matter of great concern when elite sources disappear from the news, because it implies that they are operating without scrutiny. Given that a high percentage of news stories involve government agencies it is also likely that the same organizations will be asked to comment. It is inevitable that in a simple count of news stories these 'elite' sources will be massively over-represented compared to ordinary members of the public.

The other question of access involves simple problems of geography and distance. This is changing with the impact of mobile technology. In the New Orleans floods of 2009, people on the ground had cameras and mobile phones, and the world's press were hovering above in helicopters waiting for the disaster to strike. In the Iranian presidential election that same summer, local people got information out via blogs and mobile phones after the big guns of the media had been shut out. In 2011, as events in the Middle East developed into what became known as the 'Arab Spring', coverage in the world press leaned very heavily on YouTube footage, Facebook and blogs (Ray 2011). Although there are still major events that get little coverage because they happen outside the gaze of new, wired witnesses, the problem of accessing information is generally being superseded by the problem of authenticating it. It is easy to fake material online, and even easier for others to spread it without checking (see Chapter 3).

Types of news

Very broadly, news can be divided into four categories:

- news of, about or against the state (including government, the judiciary and foreign affairs);
- news for and about business;
- news for consumers (health, fashion, sport, new products, reviews, etc.); and
- news that is titillating or sensational – which includes grisly murders as well as celebrity gossip.

These categories are usually organized quite separately. The first three are primarily referred to as 'hard news' (they are the stories that used to be on the front pages of newspapers and leading news bulletins), while the second two categories are often dismissed as 'soft news' or 'infotainment' (Thussu 2009, Franklin 1997). Even social trends and news from civil society (NGOs, charities, research organizations, political organizations and lobby groups, etc.) tend to be covered in relation to these four categories. Important academic research, for example, may be ignored completely unless it fits into a news agenda which is pre-structured by these divisions.

Of these four categories of news, many would argue that the first – 'of and about the state' – is the most important, because it feeds directly into the democratic role of the news media. It is the category that ensures that citizens are sufficiently well informed to be able to participate in the democratic process. Indeed, it is this function that in most democratic countries is deemed so important that some form of assistance is provided to ensure that it survives. This will be discussed in more detail in Chapter 2 'News Interrupted'.

In recent years, 'soft news', particularly in the form of personal stories, has seeped increasingly into the sections (and news outlets) formerly kept aside for hard (democratic) news. This process of 'popularization' or 'commercialization' is sometimes also referred to as 'feminization' because it has been ushered in by attempts to appeal to female audiences adjudged more interested in personal stories and 'consumer' issues (Bird 2003). At the same time, it has opened up new possibilities for advertising of consumer goods, and – initially, at least – brought new income streams into the popular press. This gave newspapers a new lease of life after the advent of television as the major news source for the majority of people (Phillips 2012a).

For many media scholars this popularization is a major cause for concern, because it appears to detract from the democratizing role of the news media (Franklin 1997, Thussu 2009). It can certainly be negative when it takes over the news agenda entirely (as we shall see in the next chapter), but it could also be argued that it has had the effect of dragging concerns that were once deemed to be 'private' into public view. Arguably, by making 'the personal political' this 'popularization' and 'feminization' have had a significant impact in shifting news agendas around issues of gender, race and sexuality (Fiske,1992, Bird 2003, Phillips 2008, Curran 2010b).

The mix of these four categories varies according to news outlets and audiences. Soft categories tend to be used to attract the attention of casual buyers and visitors. Editors in all media, aware that they need to woo audiences with an enormous range of information to choose from, are careful to balance the serious and alarming with the light and entertaining. That eye-catching picture, just to the right of the main headlines, did not get there by accident. By diverting you from a story about the economy to a silly piece about talking dogs, editors ensure you're going to click on another link – and keeping you on the site clicking links is how news organizations make money (see Chapter 6). Even at the most serious end of the spectrum, elite publications and professional journals will have a small amount of soft news, which is usually aimed very specifically at the cultural niche assumed to be occupied by their audience.

Titillating news in particular has grown in volume (Harcup and O'Neill 2001) and continues to do so largely as a function of news sharing. Stories most likely to be passed on via Facebook are overwhelmingly in the fourth category and they tend to be funny or unusual (Newman 2011: 24). Twitter sharing is more about hard news categories, but it is Facebook rather than Twitter that drives traffic (Phillips 2012c). News organizations such as the *Daily Mail* and the

Huffington Post, both of which have dominant online positions, tend to factor this into their news choices and the way in which they write headlines or introductions to attract users (Filloux 2012b).

Specific news factors

We will now go on to consider the more specific qualities that turn an event into a news story – and pull apart the process by which editors decide what is news to be published and what is just background noise to be ignored or relegated to the inside pages of a local newspaper. Whatever the cultural and political background to their choices, journalists are doing a job that requires rapid decisions to be taken about what aspects of their world they should be writing or talking about.

The process of news selection has been analysed via participant observation (e.g. Tuchman 1978, Gans 1979, Fishman 1980, Entman 1993, Golding and Elliot 1996), through investigation of relationships between journalists and their sources, and through analysis of news coverage (Galtung and Ruge 1965, Schlesinger 1987, Harcup and O'Neill 2001). Johan Galtung and Mari Holmboe Ruge isolated twelve 'significant factors' from their study of foreign reporting: Frequency (whether a story could be covered in a news shift); Threshold (size); Unambiguity; Meaningfulness; Consonance (predictability); Unexpectedness; Continuity (connected to an ongoing story); Composition (whether it fits in well with the daily 'mix' of stories); Reference to elite nations; Reference to elite persons; Personalization; and Negativity. They suggested that the more of these factors were present in any story, the more likely it was that the story would be covered.

When the same topic was revisited, by Tony Harcup and Deirdre O'Neill in 2001, some of these factors were still important, but others less so, and some new angles had been introduced. The original research had concerned three important events covered on the foreign pages of Norwegian newspapers, whereas the new study focused on the celebrity-obsessed British press. The researchers found that interest in 'people' had leapt up the news agenda. They also found that 'humour' was in itself a news value in the British press, and that stories might well be covered for their humour alone. Moreover, in the age of television, the importance of pictures was far greater than it would have been in 1964 when the Norwegian research was carried out. The authors refer to pictures of puppies and celebrities, but pictures are now important for every story: one disaster, in a clear example of structure creating content, will make the front page on the strength of a picture alone, while another one goes virtually unreported because it lacks illustrative material. Finally, the two researchers found that unexpectedness was of less importance than predictability.

Harcup and O'Neill looked at whole newspapers over a short period of time, rather than focusing on specific stories. This meant that they inevitably focused on the process of newsgathering as much as the qualities of individual stories.

Over a period of days, where no big exciting story breaks, this can involve sifting through masses of press material generated by press officers hungry for coverage. Local and national coverage, focusing on a multiplicity of events close at hand, will inevitably be more concerned with the banal and everyday than will foreign reporting, which scans the world for events big enough and important enough to be included in the daily news diet. The fact that unexpectedness did not loom large might therefore have been down to sampling: unexpected events don't happen every day. The diet of daily local or national journalism may be routine, but that doesn't mean that unexpectedness is no longer important.

Using these studies as a framework, let us try to get inside and pick apart the processes – conscious or unconscious – of story selection. We have already dealt with novelty and the unexpected, so will now go through the other qualities in turn.

Frequency and unambiguity

News coverage (as opposed to features and analysis) is dictated by time, technology and human attention span, which together ensure that it is episodic. As news has moved from the once-a-day deadlines of newspapers and evening news bulletins to 24-hour rolling news, its episodic nature has, ironically, become even more pronounced. Audiences are fed tightly written news 'bites' capable of being read in the 140-character world of Twitter or via a news feed on the screen of a smartphone.

Journalists and sub-editors, meanwhile, are expected to write expanded headlines, which will capture the essence of a story in the ten words that tell people enough to encourage them to click. They must also include a range of 'key words' that can be picked up by the search engines that constantly crawl the web for new material. Getting to the top of search results has become a key strategy for news organizations, because some 70 per cent of the audience arrive via a search engine and few bother to look beyond the first page of results (Currah 2009: 14). If you are not 'up there' you will not exist (Hindman 2009, Filloux 2012b, Webster 2011: 52).

Pressure to be succinct and unambiguous has never been stronger, but it is not new (McChesney 2000: 49–50, 110). The trend for keeping it short and simple was dictated by the invention of the electric telegraph in the mid-nineteenth century. Transmission costs were paid for by the word so reporters were encouraged to keep to the point (Phillips 2012a). Laying out newspapers in the era of lead type was laborious. Sometimes a few lines needed to be cut at the last moment to make room for an advertisement or a more important piece, so reporters arranged their copy in descending order of importance so that they could be cut, fast and from the bottom, without losing their main points.

Broadcast media exacerbated the need for simple, short pieces of information. News was also competing for attention with entertainment for audiences. The result was the news bulletin, in which information is broken down into little more than a series of headlines that can be swiftly ingested in half an hour.

This need to be short, simple, and clear in turn dictates what it is possible to report. Long complex background, or nuance and debate, give way to a short assemblage of basic information. Reporters break down each story into a series of clearly comprehensible episodes. The need to give each of the episodes a narrative shape ensures that we are introduced to a kaleidoscope of villains and victims, victories or failures, tragedies or triumphs, in which more subtle shading must be eliminated (Silverstone 2006, Phillips 2007b, Lule 2001).

Press offices play to this need for chunks of information and events that fit neatly into a news schedule by producing stories in bite-sized nuggets ready for consumption. Unexpected events are more challenging, and anyone watching live coverage of a disaster will be exposed to the news media operating outside its comfort zone. The desire to turn a live event into a series of stories that can easily be consumed is overcome by the reality that life doesn't really unfold that way. It is full of boring bits and hard to interpret as it happens.

The net result of producing short, comprehensible, and above all novel pieces of information – as Galtung and Ruge discovered 45 years ago – is that we tend only to read about ongoing events as they reach a crisis point. A famine is covered only when refugee camps are overflowing and babies are dying. The global warming that might be causing it is a slowly rolling situation that doesn't lend itself to being encompassed in a 300-word story. News therefore presents us with a drip feed of episodes in an unfolding drama. Each episode does, however, offer up an opportunity for a features and analysis 'hook'. It is here, in the inside pages, or the documentary slots in broadcast media, that the longer story can sometimes be told – though these items are also expected to fit in with the more commercial agenda of the 'features sections'.

Meaningfulness and consonance

As Peter Golding and Philip Elliot (1996) observed: 'in attempting to reach widespread, anonymous audiences, news draws on the most broadly held common sense values and assumptions, in other words the prevailing consensus, in establishing common ground for communication with its audiences'.

A story that steps outside the consensus has to be particularly well researched and, if possible, substantiated by an established authority. Where activities are not recognized, authenticated, and culturally labelled in this way, they are unlikely to be published. This process of consensus creation was described by British cultural theorist Stuart Hall thus:

> Things are newsworthy because they represent the changefulness, the unpredictability and the conflictful nature of the world. But such events cannot be allowed to remain in the limbo of the 'random' – they must be brought within the horizon of the 'meaningful'. In order to bring events

'within the realm of meanings' we refer unusual or unexpected events to the 'maps of meaning', which already form the basis of our cultural knowledge.

(Hall *et al.* 1996: 646)

As part of the process of consensus creation, journalists will explain a new event by comparing it to something similar that we have already experienced. This means that events that are similar are often linked, with the first event operating almost as a metaphor that explains, or at least illuminates, the subsequent events in the chain (Galtung and Ruge 1965). A gunman walks into a cinema in Aurora, Colorado, and shoots at random, killing and wounding many people (July 2012). The news reports look for ways of taking this random act and finding a place for it. They compare it in scale and location to similar outrages – Columbine (1999), or Virginia Tech (2007) – and then start to look for common threads. The need for speed and to fill 24-hour rolling news bulletins means that these commonalities may be extremely crude, operating on baseless stereotypes and assumptions. At Columbine, the student shooters were said to be 'depressed' and on antidepressants; to have been bullied, and to have targeted specific groups. None of these 'facts' were borne out by subsequent research (Cullen 2009).

This need to make sense of events happens at every level. It is how human beings process information and make it useable to them. By linking the baffling and frightening to the known and understood we 'tame' our world and make it comprehensible, reinforcing a sense of connection and normality. Journalists operate in the same way. Their process of sense-making provides audiences with ready-digested narratives already inflected towards an agreed behavioural norm (Bird and Dardenne 2009, Phillips 2007b).

The impulse towards consensus operates as a disciplinary process. Editors look for understandable patterns and then look to other journalists for confirmation. Scoops are important but they still have to fit within known conventions that signal the information is important and believable. As it becomes easier for news organizations to monitor one another's coverage in real-time, this anxious process of watching what other journalists are producing has speeded up. Reporters are continually under pressure to 'get the story' and, if they have missed it, they are likely (at least in British newspapers) to be expected to 'lift' and rewrite the work of other journalists (Davies 2008, Phillips 2010a, Boczkowski, 2010).

This cultural consensus creation operates in every culture – but always within the terms of that culture (Chaudhary and Gabriëls 1974, Nossek 2004). This is not to suggest that media perspectives are unchanging, or subject only to technical change and editorial fiat. In the search for meaning journalists are as important in enabling social change as they are in maintaining the status quo. In any society undergoing radical change, some journalists find themselves at the forefront of creating and defining the new cultural landscape. Al Jazeera, for instance, was an important force in establishing what became known as the

'Arab Spring'. The journalists picked up the changing mood and realized that isolated outbursts of anger were representative of a deeper shift. In choosing to report these acts as an uprising, rather than individual acts of disobedience (which the current leadership would have preferred), they defined the narrative for millions of people across the region (Howard and Hussain 2011: 45).

Negativity and conflict

In both major studies of news values, and also in Golding and Elliot (1979:115–23), negativity is seen as an important news value in itself, although in the Harcup and O'Neill research it was only marginally more important than positivity. A high percentage of the stories *they* analysed contained 'good news'. These stories often related to 'cures' of some kind and may also be related to the so-called 'feminization' of the news agenda (see above) – a term which James Hamilton (2004) uses to describe the increasing percentage of stories about such issues as 'health and education'.

Surprisingly, neither the Galtung and Ruge nor Harcup and O'Neill studies mentioned above included conflict as a news value, although Golding and Elliot include it in the broader concept of drama. This omission is hard to explain. Journalists in Western democracies learn that news stories containing a conflict, however small, are far more likely to make it onto the pages than those that are simply reports of the status quo. Possibly this doesn't show up in quantitative research, which is simply looking at the numbers of stories and their content. That method is unlikely to pick up information about why one story will be prioritized even if it is less common.

In UK newsrooms, conflict may be inserted by a journalist who deliberately seeks out people who disagree with a news event or press release. This device is often seen as providing the necessary 'balance', but by introducing an opposing voice it also introduces an element of conflict. Beyond making the account more lively, this convention acts to allow for minority voices to be heard, so it can also be an important way of broadening the number of voices in a story. Some newspapers also go out of their way to make events appear negative. A news editor working on a British mid-market national newspaper in 2008 described it like this:

> [The paper] works on the presumption that negative news sells – always go for the negative line even if it isn't typical. There is nothing untrue but it isn't a balanced representation. It's been twisted to conform to an idea.
>
> (Phillips 2010a: 57–58)

This search for conflict and negative stories, however, is not universal. In Singapore and China, for example, conflict is played down and reporters look wherever possible for the positive in a story. There was a time when even big disasters such as earthquakes and floods would be ignored, or put on the inside pages of Chinese newspapers and covered mainly in terms of how well the authorities were managing the crisis. In 1976, for example, the Tangshan earthquake in China killed hundreds of thousands of people, but was hardly reported domestically. Nevertheless, growing use of the Internet and Twitter means that it is increasingly difficult to filter out information in this way. In 2008, the Sichuan earthquake was being reported across the Internet, via live blogs and photographs, as it happened, and the news media inevitably followed suit.

Despite this, conflict is still kept to a minimum. In an August 2012 search for transport stories on the websites of Singapore's *The Straits Times*, the *China Daily*, the UK's *Daily Telegraph* and the USA's *Washington Post*, the main stories in Singapore concerned improvements to services while the top story in China was about higher wages for transport workers. The top stories in the UK and USA were about 'rows' and job cuts.

Proximity and size

Size is always important. The bigger the disaster the more likely it is to be reported, but proximity trumps even size. A disaster at home will attract more detailed and longer coverage than a bigger one far away. The UK was trans-fixed by a rail crash in London in July 1999 in which 31 people died and 400 were injured; it covered many pages of most newspapers over many days. A flood in Mozambique earlier the same year had a death toll of 800 and 70,000 people were affected; it took almost a week to make the front pages and only made it onto TV news bulletins because of the spectacular pictures. And it works the other way too: a car crash in which one person is injured is unlikely to be covered in a national newspaper, but could well be news in a local one, because readers may have witnessed it, or know people involved.

Surprisingly, proximity is another news value that appears only on the Golding and Elliot list. For the Norwegian researchers, proximity was not an issue, because all the stories they looked at were foreign, but for the British researchers it is an unexpected omission. There are moments, sometimes weeks, when the eyes of the world are all fixed on the same event, but on an everyday news day the vast majority of news concerns events happening at home. The British researchers alluded to the lack of foreign news coverage in British newspapers but did not seem to see this as worthy of analysis in itself.

The focus on our own backyards has increased over the last 30 years in UK newspapers (though not on TV where there are legal obligations governing content). Research from the Media Standards Trust found that the percentage of foreign stories in the front pages of four British national newspapers had plum-meted between 1979–2009, halving in the *Telegraph* and *Daily Mail* and dropping by a third in the *Guardian* and *Daily Mirror* (Moore 2010). Many reasons are suggested, mostly connected with declining budgets for foreign reporters; the *Daily Mirror* and the *Sun* (two UK tabloid papers) no longer have a dedicated foreign desk at all (ibid: 31). Author and foreign correspondent Alan Phillips, however, thinks this change in direction is a policy decision rather than simply lack of funds. He believes that editors are 'under pressure to provide something jollier and more attractive or risk losing their readers' attention' (ibid: 41).

Audience research by Ofcom in 2007 appears to back this. It found that 97 per cent of people polled (in the UK) want the same or more coverage of current events in their region (Ofcom 2007). Research in 2010 into local news needs found that, for most people, local means the area they can walk around. Information that might seem in the broad sweep of geo-political events to be trivial really matters to the people it directly affects. If the trash cans are not emptied, the schools close, the buses don't run, or the shops are not supplied, then the impact is felt right there in the neighbourhood (Fenton *et al.* 2010). It is not just that people need information about their services; they also need to be included in the conversation. As one elderly participant in the Fenton local research put it: 'Because it [local news] makes the community, doesn't it? It makes it all feel like you belong somewhere, I mean you're part of something' (ibid).

Resonance, personification, and continuity

To make it to the top of page one in a national paper, or onto network TV news, a story has to have relevance to millions of people but small stories can have extraordinary resonance if they seem to outrage community norms or resonate with our most primitive fears. These small stories are almost always about people. Human stories are so important in attracting attention that 'case studies' and vox pops are increasingly used to 'humanise' even the most complex and apparently unexciting issues. But quite often it works the other way around: it is the human story that captures the public imagination, challenging them to think about something that they have been able to ignore. Kira Agass, Senior Features Writer at *Woman* magazine believes passionately in the power of human stories to change behaviour. Talking to a group of students, she said:

> I believe a story about a woman battling cancer – and the emotional upheaval she's going through – is far more likely to encourage people to get tested or to be aware of symptoms than a leaflet or an article on policy.

When journalists speak of having a 'nose for news' it is these small stories that they are mainly concerned with. Recognizing a story that will 'resonate' with the audience is also about constructing a story so that it will do so. It is the manifestation of an editor's cultural assumptions about the audience, usually grafted on to a rudimentary set of predetermined narratives about good and evil. It is in the context of this 'resonance' that personification becomes so important. Reporters look out for the 'human angle' in a story because it creates a point of identification with the reader or viewer. It is far easier to comprehend complex information when it is illustrated with examples: understanding how it happened to a particular person or family helps us to understand how it might affect us.

Reporters are often criticized for this way of telling stories; it is referred to as 'dumbing down'. In fact, finding ways of communicating complexity through simple stories could also be seen as a form of democratizing and opening up news, so that audiences hear from ordinary people like them – rather than only from experts – in a way they can understand (Phillips 2007b, Bird and Dardenne 2009).

Stolen or murdered children tend to get a lot of coverage, not because such crimes directly affect the majority of people – in fact the murder of a child by a stranger is a rare event (NSPCC 2013) – but because they lock into the most basic fear that every parent has of losing a child. Resonance here is all about identification. The disappearance of three-year-old Madeleine McCann in Portugal in May 2007 was a case in point.[1] This was a hard-working middle-class family on holiday at just the kind of beach resort that a journalist might frequent. They had left their child asleep in her room a few yards away from them and she was stolen from her bed. It resonated because every journalist covering the story could identify with them. This was a random event, but in its randomness lay the fear. If it could happen to a family who had done nothing wrong, then it could happen to any member of the imagined audience: people who are law-abiding and respectable. People like an imagined 'us' rather than an imagined 'other' (Riggins 1997: 9).

Perhaps it was this fear of contamination that drove the subsequent negative coverage in a number of British tabloids and in the Portuguese press, which sought to implicate the parents in the child's disappearance. There was never any evidence to back this up but by demonizing the parents, some journalists became part of a crazy ritual of purification. It is easier to split off and condemn that which you fear, rather than to confront your own anxiety. This process of 'splitting off' things that are difficult to deal with can be seen in the press coverage of almost anything that seems threatening to the security of the majority community thus homosexuality, feminism and immigration are 'trigger' issues that very often elicit hysterical responses from the conservative media as they 'circle their wagons' to keep out any offending matter that might threaten their imagined solidarity and purity (Spivak 1985).

The press coverage of the murder of black teenagers Stephen Lawrence (in April 1993) and Anthony Walker (in July 2005) by white racists also had resonance, but these cases are particularly instructive because they seem to crystallize a moment when the narrative shifted in the UK. Knife crime is the most common method of killing in the UK and young black males are over-represented amongst victims of knife crime (Gov.uk 2012). When these crimes are reported it is usually in the context of a narrative about black crime. But, like the McCann story (in its early stages), these were cases in which the victims were blameless. It was not possible to distance oneself from the crime by assuming that they were implicated in their own deaths. They were 'us' not 'other'. Perhaps the deaths of two young black men at the hands of white thugs, and the dignified demeanour of their grieving parents, created a sense of guilt by association for the white-dominated news media. Here personification worked to counter previous narratives as the editors elevated the sons into symbols both of collective guilt and of the possibility of reconciliation (Phillips 2007b).

Sometimes, an event that would otherwise have passed unnoticed will be reported because of its similarity to other events that have also been highlighted. This is what Galtung and Ruge refer to as 'continuity'. For example, in autumn 1994, a group of Norwegian children murdered a child. It is unlikely that this story would have been spotted at all by British newspapers if it hadn't been for the murder in Britain of 2-year-old Jamie Bulger by two older children, the previous year. Resonance may also be conjured up by the newspapers themselves, by the creation of a 'moral panic' – the artificial amplification of a relatively minor event into a major social issue that requires government intervention (Cohen 1972). We discuss this in greater detail in Chapter 7 'Ethics in Practice'.

Reference to elite nations and elite people

Powerful countries and powerful people have more access to the media than ordinary people, and the news media re-enforce their power by privileging the information they offer and amplifying it. As Karl Marx put it: 'The ideas of the ruling class are in every epoch the ruling ideas' (Marx and Engels 1845).

A glance at any newspaper or news bulletin would seem to bear this out. The more powerful a person or country, the more likely their doings are to be reported. The power of a country dictates the level of international coverage given to what would otherwise be seen merely as 'local' stories. The destruction of the World Trade Center in New York on September 2001 was a prime example of an event that had relevance all over the world – not just because of the numbers who died but because of the possibility that it might have global repercussions. It is America's power that gave the attack such particular resonance.

However, the floods in New Orleans in August 2005 were also reported across the world, and these had no global significance. The number of people who died there – 700 – is dwarfed by the 73,338 who are estimated to have been killed by earthquakes in Pakistan in October that year. While there were reports of the Pakistan earthquakes in the international media, there was far less coverage, partly because of problems of access (see above) but also because, on the Western news agenda, Pakistan is only relevant in relation to the 'war on terror'. Other news stories are rarely reported.

Celebrity lives are also amplified. In this case it is not about power but about familiarity. People feel they 'know' those who appear on their screens. The trivial events of their lives are followed as though they were friends whose lives we are intimately attached to. Soon, through familiarity and repetition, these people achieve a certain level of status that does confer on them a level of power: the power of making the invisible visible. Thus charities and companies with products to sell are keen to get 'celebrity' endorsements, figuring that the familiarity of these people will bring into public view matters that might other-wise be overlooked. News organizations help to create this cycle. By promoting otherwise unremarkable people into household names, they produce a steady flow of material that will in turn attract a steady flow of clicks, as audiences check in each day to read the newest gossip.

Changing the news agenda

This chapter has provided a broad look at the criteria editors use when they are deciding what they will cover. As new entrants to the industry, young journalists are expected to internalize these 'rules'. As in any field of work, part of the requirement for getting in and getting on, is the rapid internalization of the rules, but that doesn't mean blind obedience to a higher power (see Chapter 4). Jour-nalists who remain critical, and hold on to the sense that their job is to interrogate power, can change the way we think about the world in quite important ways.

Frames can be changed when new people enter the field, bringing with them a fresh set of assumptions that challenge the established norms. In the steeply hierarchical world of journalism, such change can be very slow, as new entrants are forced to conform to the assumptions established by those higher up the ranking. An editor with an extremely conservative world-view will ensure that stories are framed in a way that is consistent with this world-view. Since editors (in the UK and USA) are usually hand-picked by the company CEO or board, they will usually reflect the world-view of those who have picked them (Greenslade 2009).

Occasionally, however, a new group of journalists with a different perspective reaches a position of relative power, or a journalist with a different vision is given sufficient autonomy to change the frame. These moments of disruption are rare but can have a very powerful effect. In June 2000, during the pre-election period in Zimbabwe, the *Guardian* sent a black reporter, Gary Younge, to the country, rather than relying on a white stringer. Until Younge arrived, reporting had centred exclusively on the fate of white farmers whose land had been taken from them; their families were interviewed, their funerals attended and reported.

The day after Younge arrived there was another funeral on the front page, only this time it was the funeral of a black family: Younge had chosen to focus on the fate of the opposition party. By changing the focus and selecting different facts, he told the story of a country bitterly divided along political lines, with a leader who had chosen to divert attention from his own shortcomings by staging a battle over race. Frames are 'plastic'. They are set from above but may also be contested from below.

Note

1 Three-year-old Madeline McCann disappeared from her bed in 2007 while her parents were having dinner nearby. The story, after initial sympathy, had extensive sensational coverage and became one of the major cases triggering Lord Leveson's 2012 enquiry into the British Press.

Chapter 2

News interrupted

Ownership and control

This chapter will look in more detail at how the economic structure within which news is produced can shape what kind of news we consume. It will consider whether the liberal pluralist concept of a field of competing voices is capable of providing the varied news media necessary for a healthy democracy; whether pluralism is an impossibility within a market structure; or whether there are ways in which social interventions in the marketplace could ameliorate the affects of a market homogenization that militates against plurality. Before entering this debate, however, it is necessary to establish clearly why any of this matters.

If news were merely a commodity, like socks, then difficulties around supply, pricing and quality would be abundantly clear to us. Unlike socks, which are either there or not there, either rough and scratchy or soft and comfortable, the quality of news is rather harder to determine through the direct experience of our senses. If your socks scratch that is a fact that you can entirely appreciate. If you see a plane crash into a tower with your own eyes, that is also a fact you can accept – but, if you do see it, you still have trouble interpreting its meaning without recourse to additional information that you cannot directly verify yourself. Most of what we know has been passed on to us second-hand, and whether we believe it and use it to build up our understanding of the world depends partly on our own experience and partly on our relationship with the source of our information. It matters where it comes from because we are forced to take it on trust. Hannah Arendt, one of the most important political philosophers of the post-war years, wrote:

> [C]onsiderably more than the whims of historians would be needed to eliminate from the record the fact that on the night of August 4, 1914, German troops crossed the frontier of Belgium; it would require no less than a power monopoly over the entire civilized world. But such a power monopoly is far from being inconceivable, and it is not difficult to imagine what the fate of factual truth would be if power interests, national or social, had the last say in these matters.
>
> (Arendt 1968: 7)

A few pages earlier, she had written: 'The sacrifice of truth for the survival of the world would be more futile than the sacrifice of any other principle or virtue' (1968:1).

However, for critical communications theorists, the very idea of truth is contested. Michel Foucault (1981) refers to a 'regime of truth' and suggests that 'truth is linked in a circular relation with systems of power which produce and sustain it, and to effects of power which it induces and which extend it'. To misuse a remark attributed to Winston Churchill: history is always written by the victor, and the victor will, in any given situation, be the group that is powerful enough to ensure that their version of events is accepted. We will look more closely at these ideas in future chapters, but for the purposes of this one we will take the view that it should be the aim of journalism in a democracy to question, rather than blindly reinforce, power wherever it arises. This is because, if powerful interests are able to dictate uncontested the way in which events are described, then we may find ourselves in the world that Orwell described in the book *1984*, where trust has evaporated completely because nobody has any sense of what is true and what is a story made up by the powerful to keep everyone else under control.

Liberal democracy and public communication

The way that liberal democracies have chosen to facilitate this attempt at truth telling, in spite of its inherent difficulty, has been to try and ensure that events can be examined from a multiplicity of points of view. Only when all views have been taken into account, it is argued, is it possible for rational people to make judgements and take action. English philosopher John Stuart Mill put it thus: 'If opponents of all important truths do not exist, it is indispensable to imagine them, and supply them with the strongest arguments which the most skilful devil's advocate can conjure up' (Mill 1859: 37).

The belief that ideas should be contested in order to find the truth lies at the centre of Enlightenment thinking and science. The systematic testing of ideas in a science experiment may have very little in common with the often impassioned and blinkered exchange of views in an election campaign, but the principled desire to inform people, so that they can be involved in their own governance, is one of the defining differences between a despotic and a democratic society. However flawed our democracies may seem, it is only through an informed populace, capable of keeping power in check, that they exist at all. That is why underwriting freedom of expression – and its corollary, freedom of the press – has been of interest to democrats. Thomas Jefferson, a principal author of the American Declaration of Independence was clear that, without an informed populace, America would soon be ruled by despots (though his concern to inform seems paternalistic by modern standards).

[U]nder pretence of governing they [European governments] have divided their nations into two classes, wolves and sheep ... Cherish therefore the spirit of our people and keep alive their attention. Do not be too severe upon their errors but reclaim them by enlightening them. If they once become inattentive to public affairs, you and I, and Congress, and Assemblies, judges and governors shall become wolves.

(Jefferson 1787)

Four years later, in 1791, the right to press freedom was written into the American Bill of Rights. It said: 'Congress shall make no law ... abridging the freedom of speech, or of the press; or the right of the people peaceably to assemble, and to petition the Government for a redress of grievances.'

Despite the general agreement of democrats worldwide on the need for a free press to uphold democracy, there is little agreement on what a free press is and how we could create it or protect it if we had it. On the one hand there are those who believe that press freedom is a fantasy dreamed up to reassure a populace already in thrall to the narratives of the 'power bloc' (Fiske 1992: 115). On the other, there are those who see a free press as a necessary product of a free market and believe that any public intervention in that market is an encroachment on press freedom and a threat to democracy. In between lie those who feel that a free press is an ideal to be fought for even though it may never be achieved. At the crux of this debate lies the question of who owns and controls the news, and whether public intervention in the form of regulation or subsidy enhances democracy or undermines it.

The public sphere as a concept

German sociologist Jürgen Habermas looked back to the period of the eighteenth century as a golden age of free debate. In his view, the growth of capitalism provided an alternative power base with enough financial backing to ensure a space between the private realm of the home and the established power of the state, in which free people were able to engage in rational debate about the organization of their society. He claimed that 'citizens act as a public when they deal with matters of public interest without being subject to coercion' (Habermas 1996: 92). In acting as a public they are able to articulate 'public opinion' and criticize and curb the authority of the state. It was precisely this form of informed and rational public that Thomas Jefferson aimed to produce by encouraging a thriving and independent press, though it is clear from his contempt for European governments that he did not believe that anything resembling an independent public sphere existed in Europe at this time.

The eighteenth century was a period of communications fecundity not unlike the early years of the Internet, and just as the Internet appeared to provide an unparalleled opportunity for the circulation of unmediated and uncensored debate, so too did the salons and coffee shops of the older era. Of course neither of these two similar 'moments' constituted a perfect public sphere in which 'rational debate' could take place. Just as the Greek forum (usually considered the birthplace of democracy) ignored the voices of women and slaves, only those with money, time and education were able to participate on equal terms in salons and coffee shops. In the same way, the early adopters of the Internet blogosphere were hardly representative of the society at large but were largely professionals with technical knowledge and access to computers (Curran 2011). Twitter users, for example, are still heavily biased towards professionals and city-dwellers (Newman 2011: 13).

Habermas, however, merely took this moment of flux as a starting point for an analysis of the media that was anything but rosy. Indeed, it is the destruction of this 'bourgeois public sphere' and what he referred to as the 'refeudalization of society' that most concerned him. He argued that liberal democracy and the free exchange of information that must accompany it, was destroyed by the very forces that gave birth to it. As society grew more complex, the free association of citizens gave way to organized interest groups, and free debate was replaced by negotiations behind closed doors. These organizations then asserted their right to speak 'for' the people, jockeying for space in the pages of newspapers that were now owned by wealthy businesses concerned mainly with increasing circulation or viewing figures and maintaining the status quo.

This process of refeudalization, according to Habermas, started in the mid-nineteenth century – roughly the moment when, according to many British historians, the press finally became free, with the lifting of the last taxes on newspapers. Ivon Asquith (1975) wrote of the British press: 'It was the growing income from advertising which provided the material basis for the change of attitude from subservience to independence' (Curran and Seaton 2003: 3). James Curran, in common with Habermas, saw a very different picture, in which small independent news organizations suddenly found themselves locked into a death struggle against well-capitalized publishing organizations that attracted very large amounts of additional advertising funding. Indeed, Curran described Asquith's version of press history as 'political mythology': a convenient story that successive press barons have used in order to justify their ownership of the press. A parallel story is now unfolding about the Internet, which has paradoxically destroyed the very advertising funding base upon which the bourgeois press had built its supposed 'independence' (McChesney and Nichols 2011, Curran and Seaton 2003, Phillips and Witschge 2012, Freedman 2012).

Free markets and free press

The differences between those who believe that advertising liberated the press and those who believe that it sowed the seeds of its destruction provide the axis around which much public debate on the role of the news media turns. Asquith's 'mythology' underpins the free market approach to the news media; it is based on an understanding of the market as the only guarantor of freedom, and it sees state intervention of any kind as a threat to that freedom. Free market approaches to the press are most pronounced in the United States, where the

First Amendment is regularly interpreted to mean that the government should leave the private sector to deliver news without interference from the state. As a result of fierce protection of the private right to own and control the news media, America, alone amongst democratic countries, did not nationalize the telegraph in the late nineteenth century, nor develop a public broadcasting sector in the twentieth (National Public Radio has little public funding and is mainly supported by donations) (Starr 2004, McChesney and Nichols 2011: 144).

In Europe, where the concept of press freedom arises more from the concept of plurality of voices than freedom of trade, the telegraph was nationalized at an early stage to prevent the development of a monopoly, which was thought likely to inhibit access to information (arguably, in some European countries, this was also a move by the state to take control of what was clearly going to be a vital asset in times of war). In Britain, nationalization was a later intervention and the result of a vociferous campaign by businesses (including the press) concerned about monopoly practices and the establishment of a 'cartel' amongst telegraph companies (Kieve 1973: 144–45). Equal access to the telegraph was deemed more important than private rights to control trade. There were similar legislative attempts in the USA to curb the power of the telegraph companies, but they failed, and Western Union went on to own 90 per cent of the market – a position not dissimilar to that of Google today, with almost 90 per cent of world search traffic (Karmasnack 2012, Crawford 2012).

Similarly, while Europe, Australia, New Zealand and Canada, took the rights to scarce broadcast spectrum into public ownership, American broadcasting rights were given to a handful of large companies by a process that John Nichols and Robert McChesney describe as 'by any standard corrupt and secretive' (McChesney and Nichols 2011: 144). The broadcast companies were thus handed, without charge, a near-monopoly interest in a public utility. In return they promised to operate in 'the public interest'. Huge fortunes were made from this benefit, but with the advent of cable TV, spectrum scarcity became a problem of the past, and the media organizations asked to be released from their obligations to produce fair and balanced news. In the absence of scarcity they believed that they had a right under the constitution to broadcast whatever they wanted without state interference. Indeed, Fowler and Brenner (1982) argued that public service obligations were an infringement of the First Amendment rights of the broadcasters and pushed for the repeal of any public interest obligations. They said:

> For a variety of reasons, the Commission [the FCC] has traditionally refused to recognize the undeniable fact that commercial broadcasting is a business. But it is a business, one that faces increasing competition in the years ahead for the eyes and ears of its audience.
>
> (Fowler and Brenner 1982: 210)

During the 1980s, the US public interest obligation was removed, and also the 'Fairness Doctrine', which ensured that TV stations had to give a fair hearing to all points of view, was also lifted. For the first time TV stations were free to take sides, or to avoid discussing politics at all. Outside America, meanwhile, commercial TV now operated alongside publicly funded TV, with a similar deregulatory mood taking hold. In many countries, funding was cut or a mixed economy of direct funding and advertising was introduced. In some cases (Canada, New Zealand, Australia and the Netherlands) public funding was sharply reduced. In the Scandinavian countries, the UK and Germany, public funding has maintained its position – and its audiences (Nordvision 2005).

James Murdoch, son of Rupert Murdoch and at that time presumed heir apparent to the News International media empire, addressed the Edinburgh TV Festival in 2009 with an attack on what he referred to as the 'state sponsored' BBC. It was his contention that, because the BBC provides a free news service across TV radio and online, it had somehow caused the financial problems that text-based news services were experiencing.

> The expansion of state-sponsored journalism is a threat to the plurality and independence of news provision, which are so important for our democracy. Dumping free, state-sponsored news on the market makes it incredibly difficult for journalism to flourish on the Internet. Yet it is essential for the future of independent digital journalism that a fair price can be charged for news to people who value it. We seem to have decided as a society to let independence and plurality wither. To let the BBC throttle the news market and then get bigger to compensate.
>
> (Murdoch 2009)

Murdoch went on to ask the conference to accept 'the simple truth that the ability to generate profitable return is fundamental to the continuation of the quality, plurality, and independence that we value so highly'.

Free trade, consolidation and homogenisation

The assertion that a free market is the only guarantor of a free press is often made. The evidence suggests on the contrary that free market capitalism will always move from plurality to monopoly. Economists observe that, in the early stages of an innovation cycle, the market is usually fluid; if the costs of entry are relatively low and numerous and competing organizations are able to enter the field, there is a period in which a free market can be a genuine guarantor of plurality. It is in the very nature of capitalism that this brief window is quickly closed. And where there are news organizations with overwhelming power they are capable of undermining democracy – either because they are too close to government, or because they use their power to intervene in government policy.

The early part of the eighteenth century in England was a moment of inno-vation and news plurality. Democracy was young and there were literally hundreds of competing publications delivering a multiplicity of views. Newspapers were relatively expensive, but were often shared among a number of people, so the cost of their production and delivery was covered directly by readers. In this period, radical newspapers with dissenting views were popular and had large circulations (Curran and Seaton 2003). That position changed with the introduction of advertising (Garnham 2000: 44).

Advertisers were happy to subsidize news in popular mass-market newspapers with stories about gossip and crime, but less interested in subsidizing more serious and lower-circulation newspapers unless they were aimed directly at high-spending business and professional audiences (Curran and Seaton 2003: 43). There is always a built-in tendency for the biggest advertising subsidy to go to the most popular product in the market. The combined effect of subsidy and popularization has meant that the most popular news organizations had the funds with which to employ more staff and seek out and pay for more sensational stories. For a recent example of this tendency, see this item published in 2004 in the British tabloid the *News of the World* (at the time the UK's largest circulation newspaper, owned by News International). It asked readers effectively to stalk celebrities with their cameras:

> We pay big money for sizzling shots of showbiz love-cheats doing what they shouldn't ought to. A-listers looking the worse for wear or Premiership idols on the lash the night before a crucial game.
>
> (Dale 2012)

A similar process is currently under way in South Africa and India, both countries where the number of newspapers is increasing. As these markets grow, fuelled both by local companies and by global media companies searching for new opportunities, we are seeing a similar story emerge: a market in which popular newspapers and television are all jostling for the same audience, all producing a similar diet of sensation with very little political content (Thussu 2009: 104, Wasserman 2008).

An opinion column in the *Hindu*, India's largest English language newspaper, highlights the impact of commercialization and popularization:

> The ABC of Indian media roughly translates as Advertising, Bollywood and Corporate power. Some years ago, the 'C' would have been cricket, but that great sport is fast becoming a small cog in the large wheel of corporate profit ... And, of course, everything but everything, has to be bollywoodised. To now earn attention, issues have to be dressed up only in ways certified by the corporate media. They have to be justified not by their importance to the public but by their acceptability to the media, their owners and sponsors. The more entrenched that ABC gets, the greater the danger to the language of democracy the media so proudly claim to champion.
>
> (Sainath 2010)

Some newspapers quickly grow in circulation as a result of this popularizing agenda. More serious publications then also try to popularize in order to grab some of the advertising subsidy, but with lower budgets to spend on buying up gossip and paying for pictures, they struggle to compete (Curran and Seaton 2010, McChesney and Nichols 2011, Wasserman 2008). Some move from mass market to niche and sell to a smaller but more select group of consumers. Others depend on rich benefactors who use them to gain influence in political circles. In some countries (particularly in Southern Europe) serious newspapers were until recently dependent on a degree of subsidy from political parties. Even where direct subsidy is declining political allegiance is still the norm (Hallin and Mancini 2004). These newspapers are clearly being used 'ideologically' – their purpose is to promote a particular view.

Inevitably, some fail and go bankrupt, some do reasonably well, and one or two manage to hit the jackpot. Typically, commodities compete on price as well as product 'differentiation': the company that can drop the price lowest will benefit, and that company will usually be either the biggest and most able to make economies of scale or the most ruthless at cutting corners and trimming costs. At this point the biggest players start to gobble up the smaller ones – because the less competition there is within a market, the more money can be made. Price cutting can be very effective as a means of squeezing out competitors who are less financially secure. Those organizations that are part of large conglomerates where it is possible to share losses as well as profits are in a particularly good position to simply undercut the opposition (Phillips and Witschge 2012).

News International, a multinational conglomerate with news businesses across the world, deliberately dropped the price of the UK *Times* below cost price in 1996, in order to try and squeeze out the competition. The *Independent* (which entered the market when new computer technologies dropped the price of entry in the late 1980s) had been doing relatively well, but was unable to compete on price and soon lost readers. Three years later, in 1999, News International was found guilty of 'predatory pricing' by the Office of Fair Trading. But the *Independent* had already been wounded and managed to survive only by selling out to a larger company and more recently to a Russian oligarch capable of coping with short-term losses in the hope of longer-term gain or influence. The other newspapers that had taken advantage of lower entry costs, and entered the UK national newspaper market at the same time as the *Independent*, all failed. They could not attract enough advertising revenue away from the incumbents to compete with them in this highly competitive market.

The process of market attrition has been particularly stark in America, where, in 1910, the biggest cities had (on average) 16 different daily papers. By 1930 the number had halved, and by 2006 there were an average of three newspapers in these great cities, one of which generally catered specifically for ethnic minorities. In most other cities there was only one newspaper, and in some there are now no newspapers at all (McChesney and Nichols 2011). This decline in the numbers cannot be blamed on the coming of TV or the Internet (though both technologies have certainly sped it up). The biggest drop happened before the birth of network television. It was simply a casualty of the way capitalism functions.

It was this process of monopoly formation that, in the USA, consolidated the move to a self-conscious attempt (supported by proprietors) at professionalization, the rise of journalism education, and the birth of 'objectivity' as a norm in American journalism (Schudson 2005: 94). The adoption of journalistic objectivity in the USA, Michael Schudson argues, was primarily a means of creating a profession that was capable of independence from politics. Nevertheless, there is no doubt that this norm also allowed the formation of monopolies without too much political interference; only an apparently neutral press could seek to replace a marketplace of ideas and retain any form of political legitimacy (Emery *et al.* 1996).

The professionalizing agenda was not adopted in the same way in Europe. While most European commercial and public broadcast media is regulated to ensure that it is professional and 'balanced', things are different in the print media. In Northern Europe plurality was protected to some extent by public subsidy to ensure that monopolies did not develop. In the UK the press was left far freer because an unusually large number of competing national newspapers gave the appearance of plurality (Curran and Seaton 2003). But competition is not the same thing as plurality. It is possible to have many competing news organizations without necessarily ensuring plurality of opinion. In the UK, national newspaper editors competed for readers with sensational content, but continued to ensure that newspaper coverage was inflected towards the requirements of the proprietor. Apart from a brief flirtation with Labour under Tony Blair, that meant the majority of British national newspapers have traditionally supported the Conservative party. Indeed former Conservative Minister Ian Gilmour said of the press in the 1980s: 'It could scarcely have been more fawning if it had been state controlled' (Gilmour 1993: 23).

Though the objectivity norm is strongest in American newspaper journalism, it has been exported, alongside the free market, as part of the democratizing agenda in emerging democracies. However, as we discussed in Chapter 1 'News Defined', objectivity does not itself guarantee plurality. It usually lends itself more to a reinforcing of the status quo. The fear of appearing 'biased' militates against bringing in voices from outside the mainstream.

In spite of rapid consolidation and dropping circulations in the second half of the twentieth century, there was no sense in which newspaper companies were dying. The existing monopoly newspapers in the USA made staggering profits because they sucked up all the available advertising for the metropolitan areas they serviced. It was this economic success that set the scene for the collapse that came with the arrival of online news (this is discussed further in Chapter 6). Over the previous 20-odd years, privately owned newspapers had been steadily bought up at high prices by large conglomerates eager to cash in on advertising revenue and high profits.

Most of these purchases had depended on loans, on the assumption that over a relatively short period of time the loans would be paid off (Phillips and Witschge 2012). It soon became clear that this wouldn't happen. The newspaper businesses had understood the value of putting news online, but they hadn't grasped the fact that the advertising revenue would not follow it or that, even when it did follow, they would now be competing with every other form of media on the shared online platform. The monopoly metro papers were now faced with competition from a newly emerging market with very low entry costs. Their own profits collapsed, shareholders ran for the hills, and the newspaper conglomerates started frantically cost-cutting – in some cases closing whole newspapers and in others cutting staff to the bone (Phillips and Witschge 2012, Paper Cuts 2012).

Now, we are seeing the same effect occurring – at an even greater pace – online. News organizations cannot find a way to fund news other than by getting bigger and bigger, managing thereby to take advantage of huge numbers of hits and clicks which each net only minute amounts of money (Phillips and Witschge 2012). The much-vaunted freedom of the Internet is following exactly the same pattern as we have grown used to with every cycle of innovation. To begin with, a thousand flowers bloomed, and some commentators saw this as the dawn of a new age of democracy (Elmer-Dewitt 1994, Nerone 2009), but economic realities soon started to blow through those fields. Sites must now be either wildly popular to succeed in what may now be a global market or very specialized (see more on this in Chapter 6).

As news sites compete for audience share (and advertising), they start to move towards the safe middle ground. This tendency towards size and homogeneity (Bourdieu 2005) is helped by search systems that always favour the most popular sites and thereby help them to become even more popular (Hindman 2009). People now have a mass of information at their fingertips, but they tend to go back to the same few sites that they trust. This often means those that are attached to already existing news organizations – the very organizations forced into a cycle of popularization by the fiercely competitive online advertising market. As Chris Anderson and Michael Wolff, writing in *Wired* magazine, pointed out: 'The top ten websites accounted for 31 per cent of page views in 2001, 40 per cent in 2006, and about 75 per cent in 2010' (Anderson and Wolff 2010).

This classic cycle, described by Marx in *Wage Labour and Capital* (1847), is the inevitable consequence of competition in a market: each company racing to outdo the other by increasing scale or employing new technologies to push down costs until the biggest beasts always end up guarding the biggest bones. The cut-throat competition between Apple and Samsung for control of the mobile technology market is an object lesson in how this process works to squeeze out competitors. For free market economists, following Joseph Schumpeter's concept of 'Creative Destruction' (1943), this cycle should not be resisted because it will force renewal and growth. However, as Pierre Bourdieu (2005) observes, competition in the field of journalism seems always to push news organizations further into the populist centre ground and to force out media diversity.

The global news market

One way out is to look for new markets. While news usually deals with matters of local concern, it often arrives via 'pipes' and processes dominated by a small number of very large global players. These companies can't dictate local events, but may still influence what local people consider important and the way such topics are covered (see Chapter 1). Ten companies dominate the world of media ownership, and most of them are US-based; their concern now is to move out from the stagnating news markets of the old democracies into newer, growing markets where there is still money to be earned.

This move has been much aided by American and European-backed efforts to 'modernize' emerging economies, which included advice on establishing media systems and have been seen by some as direct attempts to achieve global US domination (Schiller 1969, 1976, 1996). In addition to this, the structure of the flow of information – via news agencies in the field to the news hubs of London, New York, Paris and Atlanta, and then out again – means that international news arriving in Lagos, Delhi and Jakarta will have passed through the hands and minds of European or American journalists before it ever arrives at its destination (Thussu 2000).

The idea that America has been engaged in a form of 'cultural imperialism' is contested by those who point to the local nature of most news bulletins and to the counter-currents of culture moving back in the opposite direction in the form of telenovelas from Latin America to Europe and Bollywood movies from India. In news also there is a growing counter-flow, in particular from Al Jazeera, which now has 65 bureaus – many in the global south – and is able to put a different spin on stories (Al Jazeera 2012, Figenschou 2013).

Nevertheless, as Edward Herman and Robert McChesney (1997) point out, there is a more insidious aspect to the Western domination of media space. Global media companies, searching for pastures new, may not be operating directly as 'the new missionaries of corporate capitalism' (ibid) or deliberately using 'soft power' to make the world into a place where American global companies can safely trade. But what they are certainly interested in is making money, and the experience from Western markets is that entertainment, rather than news in the public interest, makes money for shareholders. Herman and McChesney rightly feared that vast global media companies interested only in their return on investment might 'erode the public sphere and create a "culture of entertainment"' (1997: 9).

Popularization and public knowledge

Giving people what they appear to desire makes sense in commercial terms: there is no economic point in wasting time and space researching and publishing stories in which the audience has only a passing interest. If South Africans prefer the *Daily Sun* to the *Sowetan* and British people prefer the tabloid *Sun* (circulation 2.5 million) to the *Guardian* (print circulation 200,000), then, some theorists argue, they are making a rational choice. Former *News of the World* journalist Paul McMullan told the Leveson Inquiry into the British Press:

> I see no distinction between what the public is interested in and the public interest. Surely they're clever enough to make a decision whether or not they want to put their hand in their pocket and bring out a pound and buy it? I don't see it's the job – our job or anybody else's – to force the public to be able to choose that you must read this, you can't read that.
>
> (McMullan 2011)

McMullan's old boss, Rupert Murdoch, is with him on this. He said: 'Anybody who provides a service which the public wants, at a price it can afford, is providing a public service' (Murdoch 1989).

Some critical cultural theorists endorse neither the free market view of press freedom nor the Habermasian view of idealized rational debate. The way they see it, the mass-market news media are simply imposing class values that completely bypass the needs and desires of any group outside the power bloc, which runs society in its own interests. They see the news media purely in terms of its ideological function, and suggest that there is little point in trying to change the way in which it operates:

> The motor for social change can come only from a sense of social difference that is based on a conflict of interests, not a liberal pluralism in which differences are finally subordinated to a consensus whose function is to maintain those differences essentially as they are.
>
> (Fiske 1990: 115)

For John Fiske, then, there is a rational basis to the refusal of working-class people to participate in what they see as an empty ritual of democratic debate. He suggests that they do not read or watch news programmes because they are alienated from them, and are perfectly capable of accessing the news that they need from a melange of available sources (Fiske 1992). Research in the UK seems to endorse his concerns about alienation. In an Ofcom survey, 55 per cent of people said that news wasn't 'relevant' to them, and 37 per cent said that the news 'put them off politics' (Ofcom 2007: 9). Such arguments have also been made about the rise of tabloid journalism in South Africa, where the establishment in 2002 of the highly commercial tabloid newspaper, the *Daily Sun*, was so successful that it spawned a number of competitors. These newspapers are aimed squarely at 'the man in the blue overall' (Wasserman 2008: 787, Steenveld and Strelitz 2010):

> [They] eschew formal political coverage, sensationalize news and publish excessively lurid or graphic pictures (including portrayals of violence). There

is a strong focus on sports and entertainment and through the avoidance of controversial political or ethnic positioning they ensure that as large an audience as possible is delivered to advertisers.

(Wasserman 2008: 790)

Wasserman argues that these newspapers are in fact more in touch with the lives of their readers than the political apartheid-era news organizations, which are seen as the mouthpieces of a regime that has lost its connection with the people it governs. At least the new tabloids, he argues, are aware of the issues facing the mass of South Africans and in touch with their aspirations. When the *Daily Sun* asked its readers to write in about the failings of local government, it claimed to have received 10,000 responses in a month (ibid: 792). Even as the *Daily Sun*'s circulation rises, the sun seems to be setting on the *Sowetan*, the newspaper launched in 1981 as the voice of the liberation struggle (Milne and Taylor 2006). Now owned by media group Avusa, it has increased its coverage of sport and crime in order to compete, but the *Daily Sun* still has a circulation some four times higher.

For political economists there is a flaw in this argument. Tabloid newspapers still reflect a hegemonic view of the world, which services the requirements of powerful commercial interests; worse, they argue, they do so in a way that is so compelling that audiences stop questioning the messages passed down. In the popular newspaper's view of the world, governments are usually corrupt, and collective action (unless orchestrated through the pages of a newspaper) is doomed to failure. The message continually pumped out by tabloid journalism is of a world in which everyone is on their own, struggling for themselves and their families, in which any attempt to change the status quo via political action is therefore pointless. Deon du Plessis, publisher of the *Daily Sun*, described his imagined reader thus: 'This guy was on the move. He now owned his house, he was starting to decorate it, worrying about his kids, rather than manning the barricades. The politics of struggle were over' (Du Plessis 2006: 49).

While the elite press may be out of touch with the aspirations of ordinary people, it is hard to see how the popular press could be seen in any way as a news of 'resistance'. Sensationalized and socially prescriptive news pages feature 'dog whistle' stories that pander to existing stereotypes and fears. Those who favour the market approach to plurality look to the Internet to provide alternative points of view, but research by the International Broadcasting Trust found that it is of limited help. 'Those who already have an interest in the wider world use the Internet to deepen their understanding,' it found; 'the rest of the population rarely read anything online which tells them about the lives of people in other countries' (Galloway 2010). It appears that the less people know about a subject, the less interested they tend to be, and the less they will then try and find out. It is therefore unlikely that the average American, fed stories about the horrors of socialized medicine or gun control, will have sought out alternative views online.

News: between the market and the state

Curran *et al.* (2011) conducted three separate studies on public knowledge in a number of countries. They were looking at the state of public knowledge in the USA (with its entirely free market news media) and comparing it with other mature democracies in Europe, where there is a mixed economy of private and publicly funded news media. They found that the lack of public service news media, and the reliance on commercial media, is tied to a lower level of public knowledge, particularly amongst those people who do not have a university education. In two successive studies, the gap between the level of news knowledge among those with a high level of education versus those with a low level of education was found to be very much greater in the USA than in Europe. In the USA, those with high educational attainment had a 'hard news knowledge' score twice as high as those with low educational attainment. The study also compared news knowledge by ethnicity and gender and found that the gap in the level of knowledge between the white majority and ethnic minority respondents in the USA was over twice that of the UK (the only other country where it was measured). Similarly, the gender gap in hard news knowledge was higher in the USA than in Europe. In Sweden and the Netherlands there was little gender difference.

It is therefore hard to argue that working-class people (or women) in the USA are better served by a news media that presumes to pander to their 'interests' than are those in Denmark, who get a large percentage of their news from a publicly funded service that is geared to informing as well as entertaining. In Denmark, the researchers found that those with the lowest level of education were actually marginally better informed than their college-educated peers (ibid: 57). In the UK, although the gaps in knowledge between the most and the least educated were not as steep as in the USA, there was still a bigger gap than researchers found in the Nordic countries. Britain's national newspaper market (with attendant websites) is particularly competitive, and sensational popular newspapers are read by more than three quarters of those consuming news, whereas Denmark exhibits a greater balance between sensational, populist newspapers and more serious ones.

Competition amongst national newspaper organisations in the UK has arguably also led to a lowering of ethical standards across the popular press (Phillips 2013). British tabloid journalists have consistently pushed at the boundaries of what is acceptable in terms of privacy (as the Leveson Inquiry of 2011–12 demonstrated), leading the way in promulgating a form of prurient celebrity journalism that thrives on the use of private detectives and (until it was stopped) illegal tapping of private telephone messages. Veteran journalist John Dale (2012) was concerned to find that it is now relatively commonplace to pay for stories and it is considered irritating rather than unacceptable when chunks of original reporting are simply lifted and reproduced without acknowledgement in a way that US reporters would consider to be plagiarism (Phillips 2010a).

Against this background it seems that the only thing keeping levels of public knowledge at reasonably acceptable levels is the fact that 81 per cent of British people use regulated television (with 65 per cent specifically mentioning the BBC) as their primary source of news (Ofcom 2012: 8). If news is meant to enlighten, as Jefferson felt it needed to, then most evidence suggests that an unregulated free market is not the best way to do it.

The idea advocated by the Murdoch clan and by News International – that a publicly funded news service is by definition a government-controlled news service – founders when news services are evaluated on the basis of their plurality and freedom from state interference (Benson 2011). The American organization Freedom House produces an annual press freedom ranking. In 2012, of the top ten countries with the freest news media, nine have publicly funded broadcasters; the other is tiny Luxembourg, where the company that owns the TV franchise there has a legal obligation to demonstrate 'neutrality' and to provide public information.

The top three countries in the list not only have publicly funded broadcasters, but also provide subsidies to the printed news media to ensure 'plurality'. The United States, with its commitment to a free market, is number 23 on the list. It is this far down the rankings largely because media consolidation and closures have left too many people without any choice in news delivery – though also because of police treatment of journalists covering demonstrations (Freedom House 2012: 5).

Of course public funding doesn't on its own produce a freer press. The worst three countries in the press freedom index are North Korea, Turkmenistan and Uzbekistan, where the government controls the news media and prevents dissenting voices from being heard. Clearly state intervention in news content is not in the interests either of press freedom or public knowledge. In all the countries topping the Freedom list, regulatory bodies have been established to ensure independence from government interference (Hallin and Mancini 2004, Benson and Powers 2011). Of course this remains a tricky balance to keep and public vigilance is required to ensure that governments do not interfere by threatening to cut public funding (as happened in Greece in 2013) or by intimidation as has been witnessed in Australia in 2014 when Prime Minister Tony Abbott attacked ABC, the public broadcaster (Ireland 2014), or in Argentina where public advertising is used as a lever to keep news organisations on side (Di Tella and Franceschelli 2009).

However, where free market economists look to commercial competition as a means of improving output, as we have seen above much of the evidence suggests that purely economic competition tends to homogenize content as news companies attempt to reach the same very large audiences (Bourdieu 1998, 2005). When the commercial sector also has to take account of a well-funded public sector, then the whole field is likely to shift towards the 'autonomous' pole where the standards set by journalists themselves have greater sway. Michael Grade has experience at the highest levels of both the public and commercial television sectors, as Chairman of ITV, Chief Executive of Channel Four, and first controller and then chair of the BBC. He said: 'When I was at Channel 4, I was fond of saying: "It's the BBC that keeps us honest." I stand by that still.' He went on:

> As commercial competition continues to intensify, and commoditisation continues apace, there is an overwhelming case for an independent and adequately funded sector of British broadcasting with a lot more on its mind than simply winning every time period and maximizing returns to shareholders. Some economic theorists believe the BBC stands in the way of a free market in broadcasting. A market that, left to itself, would offer viewers and listeners pretty much everything they could possibly want. Those who run this argument should get out more. Go to the USA, the biggest, richest, most developed free media market in the world. Ask yourselves, is this what we want to swap the BBC for? Is there a more depressing spectacle in broadcasting anywhere in the world than American PBS on radio and television passing round the begging bowl during pledge weeks? Is this a risk we're prepared to take?
>
> (Grade 2004)

Of course, this could be seen as special pleading, but James Murdoch's assertion that the BBC 'makes it incredibly difficult for journalism to flourish on the Internet' by 'dumping free, state-sponsored news on the market' needs to be contested. There is no large public broadcaster in the USA, and its level of news subsidy is amongst the lowest in the developed world (McChesney and Nichols 2011). Yet, while its news organizations dominate the global market, carrying with them the message that it is only the market that can modernize and provide news in emerging economies, the state of its domestic commercial news industry remains extremely fraught. In recent years even the vast news markets of India, which had hitherto been protected from foreign media influence, have opened up first to partnerships and then (more recently) to wholly foreign-owned publication. Yet at home, American commercial news has been brought to its knees by a system that is intent on milking every penny of profit for its shareholders, often at the expense of the journalism jobs on which any system of news production depends (Copps 2014).

Chapter 3

Journalists and their sources

If there is one thing that distinguishes the liberal model of news journalism from other forms, it is the reliance on fact-centred discourse (Chalaby 1996). Across the USA, Britain, Australia, New Zealand and Canada, the production of fact-centred news is the ideal against which the success of liberal journalism is measured. This requires an approach in which opinion is separated from fact, which is then presented to the audience in an apparently neutral form. All information is tied to a verifiable source and some attempt is usually made to provide more than one viewpoint.

Of course not all journalism is news. Features, interviews and opinion pieces depart from the requirement for balance and live blogs may stretch the notion of verifiable sourcing (we discuss this in more depth later) but for liberal, professionalized journalists, the gathering of facts, obtained via a range of identifiable and verified sources, is the ideal and any departure from this standard is frowned upon as a professional failure. Indeed it is the key factor that, according to journalists, separates what they do from unpaid amateur bloggers (Fenton and Witschge 2011, Pew 2006).

Not all journalists operate along these lines. In the Southern European model (Hallin and Mancini 2004), they are as likely to see themselves as interpreters, or power brokers. In China and Singapore, journalists may bow to the authority of the state but will still use similar sourcing techniques when reporting on other matters (Zhao 2012: 165). Those working in features, rather than news, might see themselves more, as Silverstone (1988) suggests, as storytellers re-aligning cultural ties and allegiances through establishing and reinforcing cultural myth. However, in all cases, it is through their choice of relationships and prioritization of information, that journalists determine what news their audiences will receive. So the question of who they speak to, how they obtain information, how they evaluate it, whose stories they choose to repeat and how they use that information is critical both for understanding how to 'do' journalism and for understanding what journalism is. Broadly speaking, research into source relationships focuses on three aspects of this exchange.

Adversarial

The first approach suggests an adversarial relationship in which the doughty reporter harries officialdom for the truth. This tends to be the version favoured by journalists in the liberal tradition. It fits with enlightenment and pluralist ideas of a marketplace of ideas, and of the press holding power to account. It provides the central trope by which liberal journalism understands itself and the key conceptual dividing line between good journalism (independent and investigative) and bad journalism which is improperly sourced, possibly driven by public relations materials and described by journalist Nick Davies (2008) as 'churnalism'. This approach starts from the assumption that pluralism would be better served if journalists just did their jobs better (Davies 2008, Kovach and Rosenstiel 2007, Lloyd 2011).

Reflective of power relationships

The second approach sees source choices as inevitably reflective of existing power structures. By these accounts, news is 'constructed' according to a series of routines (Golding and Elliot 1979) and rituals (Tuchman 1978). The decision to report, rather than ignore, the choice of who to speak to and the sources who are chosen as authoritative and therefore given precedence, is a process which produces power as well as reflecting it. This approach recognizes the routines and structures used for producing news reports under pressure, but also critiques the way in which the methods pre-structure the contents, in a way that almost inevitably reproduces power relationships.

Later, post-modern or cultural studies approaches look beyond structure and work routines, suggesting that even the attempt to produce neutral news is flawed. In the words of Michel Foucault: 'discourse is not simply that which translates struggles or systems of domination, but is the thing for which and by which there is struggle, discourse is the power which is to be seized' (1981: 52–53). In this conception of news, reporters and editors are part of a process of sense making which is inevitably also a process of domination.

Stuart Hall and his colleagues (1978) looked at how this process of reproducing dominant narratives works in practice. They traced the way in which particular views of unfolding events tend to take precedence over others. 'Primary definers' are those sources whose voices are always listened to. They are the movers and shakers whose actions define the way we live. These sources control the flow of, and access to, important information and through that, they effectively control the news agenda. If they are not the source of a story they will be the people to whom a journalist turns for an authoritative quote. They tend to be (relatively) elite sources whose power, social position or knowledge gives them an elevated status in the news hierarchy. They define the way in which information is delivered by virtue of their place in the way a story is ordered (important people tend to be quoted at or near the top of the story) and by the amount of space devoted to their views (Ericson et al. 1989).

The idea that journalists simply reproduce the views of the elite has been contested by those who point out that it isn't only recognizably 'elite' sources that lead a story and that there is often competition between sources and journalists for the dominant version of events. Philip Schlesinger and Howard Tumber (1994) for example suggest a shifting struggle for power between source and journalist or, as Herbert Gans (1979: 81) describes the relationship, 'a tug of war' in which sources compete for the attention of the journalist and for the right to define events. Daniel C. Hallin (1986) saw this struggle more from the perspective of the sources themselves and noted that many apparently revelatory stories are produced from the flak caused when elites fall out. The off-the-record political briefing is quite often the source of newly emerging narratives that break away from the dominant one. More recent research (Manning 2001) shows that a primary definer can be a person with apparently relatively little economic or political power, but the process of seizing the narrative is often temporary or limited, and always subject to contest by more established views.

Journalists as interpretive communities

A third approach sees journalists not so much as individuals, competing for the attention of sources, or as arbiters, deciding between varying versions of the same narrative, but as a 'pack' (Crouse 1973), or more politely as an 'interpretative community' (Zelizer in Berkowitz 1997, Berkowitz and TerKeurst 2006) in which interpretations of events are massaged into recognizable shared narratives (see 'Framing' in Chapter 1). Barbie Zelizer sees this as a function of the way in which journalists constantly reference each other, partly competitively (the need to get a story first) but also retrospectively as they check to see what they might have missed.

This approach is also rooted in journalists' ways of working; but rather than seeing journalists only in relation to external power, it looks at the way in which journalists operate in relation to one another: a process which tends to reinforce the status quo rather than challenge it. This approach has some similarities with the work of Pierre Bourdieu who recognizes that journalists are influenced by the internal rules and practices of their field (doxa) which are passed on from old to new members of the group (Bourdieu 1984: 471). Bourdieu's field theory also takes into account the external factors, in particular the degree of market competitiveness between organizations in the field (2005: 44, 1998: 23). He observed that such competition in fields of cultural production seems to increase conformity between organizations.

Research into the changing sourcing behaviour in UK national newsrooms (Phillips 2010a) seems to bear this out. In the UK during 2007/8, newspapers were undergoing rapid change and were under extreme financial pressure. Competition between organizations had been exacerbated by the impact of search engines. Whereas in the past people chose a particular newspaper and were unlikely to be aware of what was being read in any other newspaper, large numbers were now arriving at a list of news stories by entering a search term. If a news outlet had not got that story, or indeed that search term, in its headline, it would not turn up in the search and be out of the race for audience.

In the 2007/8 research, journalists reported a new hyper-vigilance, as they anxiously watched each other's top stories and rushed to ensure that they were not being left behind in the race to cover unfolding events (Phillips 2010b). One specialist reporter spoke of how this had affected the pack behaviour at conferences. He said:

> If your colleagues [from other news organizations] are going to do the story you've pretty much got to do the story. In the past you would be able to say to the news desk, look, my colleagues are doing a flaky story, we don't do flaky stories, let's not do this story. And that's gone.
>
> (Phillips 2010b: 96–97)

Berkowitz and TerKeurst (2006: 131) argue that relationships with key sources are often so close that they have effectively become a part of the 'interpretive community'. They found that, on those local newspapers in the USA where there was little competition, journalists were taught by both their editors and by key sources to temper criticism of local institutions on the grounds that it was not wise to cause trouble:

> During the early talks, we couldn't go public with it. This one young reporter, he decided he was going to write it up that we were keeping secrets. But we got him to understand. ... I nicknamed him 'The Big Investigative Reporter,' because of that incident.
>
> (Berkowitz and TerKeurst 2006: 131)

Such behaviour is explained away as a part of journalistic development rather than a departure from a professional norm. It is just what you have to learn to do, in order to get on. As Michael Schudson observes:

> The news, then, is produced by people who operate, often unwittingly, within a cultural system, a reservoir of stored cultural meanings. ... News, as a form of culture, incorporates assumptions about what matters, what makes sense, what time and place in which we live and what range of considerations we should take seriously.
>
> (1995: 40)

While these theories suggest the degree to which news, on an everyday basis, reflects the views of the powerful, they are less useful for explaining the fluctuations between upholding the status quo and the search for novelty and they don't all fully take into account the importance to individual journalists of breaking original stories. Bourdieu suggests that the need to differentiate oneself is essential to the way a field operates (2005: 40). For journalists 'a scoop' is the single most important way of demonstrating difference and standing out from the crowd. Journalists can make their names by standing up to power. A powerful news organization can differentiate itself by choosing to emphasize the voices of those without apparent power. People who find themselves in the public gaze, due to an accident or a crime, may be promoted to the status of 'primary definer' because their experience operates as a metaphor for a social change that is bubbling under the surface. Keeping these theories (and their limitations) in mind we will now look more closely at what sources are and how journalists use them.

Sources make stories

Sources come in myriad forms but essentially they divide into two: the information that initiates the 'story' and the means by which the story is either verified or augmented. Stories may be triggered simply by a date on a calendar (an anniversary). Many news organizations subscribe to news diaries to remind them of impending anniversaries, and other predictable or expected events (the first snowdrop, the weather, the birth of a particular baby). A major (and increasing) source of story initiation is other media. National news organizations monitor local and specialist publications and press agencies, TV and radio monitor 'the press', and everyone monitors each other (Phillips 2010b).

Stories may also be initiated by the launch of a product, or the announcement of a change of policy (usually via a press release), or by accidents, or acts of aggression (usually announced by the police). Blogs, Twitter, online forums, or the growing treasure trove of 'data' to be found online may also be sources of stories (Broersma and Graham 2013, Cision 2011). Some come from private tip-offs, (sometimes a whistle blower) and these are usually offered to a specialist reporter. They may also be initiated by diligent investigation or simply a reporter's hunch that things are not as they seem.

Selection, verification and follow-up

Having decided that a story needs to be told, journalists should then interrogate additional sources to verify or contextualize this initiating information. The journalist then needs to decide (or be told by an editor) how to tell it. The question for researchers lies in how this process of selection, verification, follow-up and ordering occurs. It is in these decisions that news outlets differentiate themselves and attempt to shape the way the initial news item is received by the audience (Reich 2006: 497).

In the newsrooms of the UK and Australia, the search for conflict in a story means that, wherever possible, journalists are inclined to look for oppositional points of views (Cushion 2012: 76). This means that there is a built-in requirement to provide space for secondary voices. This doesn't change the fact that in most cases the elite source is the first voice to be heard, and tends to be given more space and the final word, but it does mean that there is space for 'oppositional' reading to creep in (see Chapter 5).

In China and Singapore, there is less likely to be space allowed for alternative viewpoints but audiences are more aware that they are reading news that comes from a specific viewpoint. In India, public broadcasters in particular are more likely to look for voices that confirm the position of dominant (often government) sources (Cushion 2012: 76).

Selecting from the news blizzard

According to research by PR agency Twelve Thirty Eight, British 'national correspondents' have 300 emails waiting in their in-box when they arrive at work every day (Thompson 2013). This daily tidal wave of largely unsolicited information has grown in size since David Manning White, writing in 1950, first described journalists as 'gatekeepers' whose job is to decide which pieces of 'news' to allow through. Later Gaye Tuchman (1978) referred to a 'news-net', gathering in information from which journalists would select only the choice catch. A journalist interviewed in 2008 said: 'Being a ... journalist is rather like standing in the middle of a hurricane trying to pick out twigs. You're ... constantly looking around to see what's significant' (Phillips 2010b: 94).

It is in the process of selecting, or filtering information, that the journalist has the power to include or exclude voices, actions and operations. The final report may give the appearance of 'balance' or 'neutrality' but the journalist has the means of selecting and ordering information. That which is not selected is thereby rendered invisible. (The question of 'What is news' is discussed in more depth in Chapter 1.) Follow-up on an item of news is affected by a myriad of different factors: (1) the journalist's status, (2) the status of the source, (3) time, (4) access, (5) editorial bias and cultural assumptions.

It is worth making a particular note here of the role of news agencies and public relations, both of which are sources of large amounts of the information that makes up what is offered as 'news'. By some estimates these two streams of information are responsible for between 60 per cent and 80 per cent of news content (Franklin and Carlson 2011: 90–91). However in critical research about journalism, news agency material is often lumped together with public relations material (Davies 2008: 52) as though they were the same. They are different and should be treated separately.

Press agencies

Associated Press (AP), Reuters, Agence France Press and the Press Association are organizations that employ journalists. Journalists working for these agencies are doing the same sort of job as those working directly for a news outlet. Their material is paid for by news organizations via subscription and they exist to ensure that each has a wider reach than is possible with their existing core of paid staff. Journalists from subscribing organizations are free to use 'agency' copy as they wish. Sometimes it is simply used as an initiating source and

up. Sometimes the story is used in full. Ideally the publication should
it the news agency so that readers know where the material came from.
JK at least, agencies are rarely credited, which presents problems
of verification for audiences but is no reflection on the material itself (Petley
2011: 77).

As 'feeder' organizations, news agencies suffer from many of the same constraints as those directly employed by news organizations, which we will go into
below, but with one major difference: they are forced to make greater efforts to
be politically neutral because they 'feed' a wide variety of organizations of very
differing political persuasions using what I term 'vanilla news' which can then be
coloured and flavoured according to the particular interests of the news outlet
(Phillips 2012a). For the major news agencies, neutrality tends to mean conformity with a very broadly Western, liberal view of the world. In a sense they
are the embodiment of the 'liberal ideal' of journalism with all the flaws in that
model, in particular in relation to their coverage of non-Western nations and
political conflicts (Thussu 2000). However the material they produce is not, as is
sometimes implied, synonymous with PR material.

Public relations

Public relations personnel may also have been trained as journalists but their job
is entirely different. They are trying to sell a product, a person or a policy, or
trying to protect their clients from unwelcome scrutiny. They will always write
their material to ensure that 'oppositional readings' (see Chapter 5) are excluded
as far as possible. This health warning relates just as much to the press offices of
charities or NGOs as to the local council. Their job is to get a journalist to see
things from their point of view. They often have bigger budgets than the news
organizations they are feeding and their material will often include quotes, and
helpful statistics and possibly video shot by professionals. Given the dwindling
budgets in many newsrooms, it is very tempting just to take the glossy packages
on offer, and drop them, unaltered, into the news space.

To the unwary rookie, PR may proffer a plausible account, but it will always
try to avoid any references to material that might lead a journalist to criticize its
key message. To trained and seasoned journalists the relationship with PR is
fraught and often suspicious. Asked to provide information for a 'How Not To'
guide to PR, journalists were overwhelmingly scathing. These comments give a
flavour of the relationship from their point of view:

[comment from PR] 'We'd like to work with you on this.'
[journalist's response] '"Work with me?" I think not. You're on the other side of
   the fence, mate. Armed neutrality is the best you're going to get.'
[journalist] 'It infuriates our picture-desk when people ask if they can "book" a
   photographer. Request or invite, yes. Book, no.'

(Thompson 2013)

Research into the use of public relations material in news stories tends to the assumption that it is always an inferior source of information for news or at least less valuable than stories found entirely by journalists themselves (Lippmann 1922, Gandy 1982, Boorstin 1962, Davis 2002, Anderson 1991, Davies 2008). However this is an arguable point. A report on a government announcement about a change in the delivery of school meals or a planning decision that will completely alter the landscape is of no less value than the discovery that a Member of Parliament has fiddled his expenses, or that a rock star is having an affair. The fact that the information has been discovered via diligent searching (or by more nefarious means) does not necessarily make it more valuable to citizens than information that is delivered in public, by a representative of a public body. Press releases are often announcements of important information but, as with any source, private, public, exclusive or widely available, they need to be understood for what they actually provide: information which has not yet been verified or tested.

One of the reasons for the rather crude approach to the job of the public information providers is that researchers and commentators too often fail to separate investigations and regular news reporting. Public officials have a duty to inform the public of what is being done on their behalf and journalists have a public duty to reflect that activity, so the fact that press releases are noted in a large percentage of news stories is not really surprising. The day-to-day activity of a newsroom, as observed by generations of researchers (White 1950, Tuchman 1978, Gans 1979, Lewis *et al.* 2008), reflects this routine core activity of collecting information, checking it, interrogating it, simplifying it and then passing it on. So when Davies (2008: 52) expresses shock that only 12 per cent of stories are wholly generated by journalists, it is a bit like complaining that teachers only generate a small proportion of their teaching materials. The reality is that journalists and teachers are primarily employed to impart information generated by other people, rather than producing it from scratch. Virtually all stories originate somewhere other than the journalist. It is what is then done with the story that matters.

Status of journalists

All journalists are not equal, as Golding and Elliot appear to suggest in their study of television news (1979: 207). They operate within a 'field' (Bourdieu 2005) in which their news organization is competing with others and they are each competing with their peers, both for the attention of the audience and for the attention of those who can boost their career chances. Those just starting out in the job will usually be general reporters working under close supervision. The vast majority of stories will be assigned by an editor, so the question of searching for original stories will only arise in the scraps of time left between assignments (Phillips 2010a).

For journalists on the bottom rung of a British paper, it is speed, accuracy and obedience that are prized. (For more on this see Chapter 4.) So young journalists are conscious of two competing pressures: commercial and cultural

(Bourdieu 2005). Their editors are concerned to turn around news fast in order to get an edge on the competition, and they are themselves concerned to demonstrate their abilities to their peers and superiors, by following up and looking for stories that nobody else has found. Between the two sets of pressures it is easy to see that some stories could be skimped to make time for more complex ones carrying more prestige. Skimping usually means taking an item of news at face value and making little or no attempt to follow it up (Davies 2008: 113). The apparently less complex 'vanilla' stories are those that regularly get handed to junior members of staff, to be turned around in 30 minutes.

Journalists who have more status, usually have more autonomy (Gans 1979: 101, Tunstall 1993, Jacobs 1996, Manning 2001: 53, Phillips 2010a). Often they will be specialist reporters who have built up contacts in their area. They will know who to call and have the phone numbers of all their key contacts on speed-dial. They usually choose their own stories and work independently from desk editors, often not consulting anyone at all until the copy is filed. As one remarked, 'The trick is to be bossy with the news desk. You have to own your own time' (Phillips 2010a: 97).

For them the pressures are different because they need to constantly walk a tight-rope between 'burning' a contact (annoying them so that they don't pick up the phone next time) and becoming so involved with contacts that it is hard to write critically about them. On larger newspapers and national television news-rooms, where relationships are not so close, the specialist reporter will have more autonomy and often be a well-informed and vocal critic. Here there is a more equal power relationship. The sources need the journalist as much as the journalist needs their sources. It is at this level, in a study of CBS news, that Gans noted the 'tug of war' (1979: 81) between sources and reporters. The reporter is looking for stories he or she can 'sell' to the editor as 'newsworthy' and the source is trying to ensure that stories are taken up, but also that they are taken up the 'right' way. Sources are never neutral. They are always advocates for a particular point of view.

Source status

It is the status of the source that has received most intense research interest. Hall and his colleagues (Hall *et al* 1978) looked at the way in which elite sources dominated news coverage of policing. They argued that the very structures within which journalists operate means that they are bound to give greater credence to the police as 'primary definers' of meaning. There is no suggestion here that only the primary definers can be heard but rather that other voices (secondary definers) tend to be subordinated to the primary definers.

Primary definers

Journalists are trained always to look for 'authoritative' sources who will provide facts or opinions that can be trusted and will be credible to the audience. These sources tend to:

1 be powerful-and therefore more newsworthy;
2 be representative of particular groups or interests (which gives their comments more weight); or
3 have recognized and verifiable expertise.

They also look for eyewitnesses and participants in an event but these voices will typically be used later in a story, after the official version has been established. They are secondary definers and though their testimony may be compelling it is usually fragmentary. Each eyewitness presents a piece of the story and it is up to the journalist to piece the fragments together.

So, for example, when a train crashed in Spain on 24 July 2013, news stories put together the voices of witnesses (some survivors of the crash, others who lived near by). They spoke of hearing an explosion, of the sense that the train was going too fast, but these comments are placed in context as soon as the official version, from the primary definer, is obtained. In the case of the Reuters news agency report that day, the first line reported the death toll, the second paragraph described the scene and the third one used information from the government that the crash had been an accident. Only after that do we hear from the voices of people on the ground (Vidal 2013).

Primary definers are usually given the benefit of the doubt. They are only likely to come under close scrutiny if the story offered doesn't hold together, or if an equally powerful source provides an alternative version (Hallin 1986). However, the more powerful the source, the more careful the journalist needs to be that the evidence against is watertight and has been cross-checked from several different sources.

The story about the Iraq dossier, broadcast on 29 May 2003 on the BBC's influential *Today* programme exemplifies how a more powerful source can undermine the testimony of a less powerful source. In essence the source of this story, a UN weapons inspector, had told reporter Andrew Gilligan (in confidence) that information purporting to show the evidence on which the UK went to war in Iraq was not as clear as it seemed: that it had been 'sexed up'. In retrospect it seems fair to say that the source was making an important point, but Gilligan did not find any additional sources to verify his story and had promised not to name the inspector. Without corroboration, Gilligan, his editor and indeed the BBC as an institution were vulnerable to attack. They had probably not anticipated the ferocity of that attack, launched by the Prime Minister's press officer, Alastair Campbell. It culminated in the unmasking of the source (and his subsequent death), the resignation of the Director General of the BBC, and the sacking of Gilligan and his editor.[1]

This is certainly an extreme case, but it demonstrates just how careful journalists have to be when they are dealing with powerful people who have a range of weapons at their disposal for ensuring that their particular version of events holds sway. However it also, paradoxically, demonstrates that there is no simple equation between power and influence because arguably, the over-reaction of

Alastair Campbell, and the terrible consequences of that over-reaction, has fixed forever in the minds of the public the existence of a possibly 'dodgy dossier' that provided the evidence for taking the UK into a very unpopular war. Primary sources have 'symbolic capital' (Bourdieu 1986) at their disposal but audiences have to be won, they cannot be coerced into believing what they hear (see Chapter 5).

From object to subject – the journey of a source

There is a process by which otherwise less powerful sources can for periods of time, and often in fairly proscribed ways, change the way in which particular stories are framed. Manning looked at the relative success of Greenpeace, the environmental organization, in grabbing the attention of the news media (2001). Davis (2002: 180–83) looked at the way in which the Union of Communication Workers was able to defeat a government policy of post office privatization by means of a well-targeted media strategy using personal testimony. By focusing on the lives of individuals, the Communications Union was able to demonstrate the impact that privatization would have on ordinary people. It was hard for the government to be seen to ignore such individual stories of loss. Such personification, and its increasing importance in news (discussed in Chapter 1), is often seen as evidence of 'dumbing down', however it is arguably the single most important way in which ordinary people can, for short periods of time, break the rules on elite sources and find themselves with a role in defining events.

The death of Stephen Lawrence (also discussed in Chapter 1) is a useful example of the way in which a personal tragedy can become the catalyst for change in both the police force and the wider society. Stephen, 18 years old and the son of a plasterer and a bank clerk, was murdered at a bus stop in South London in April 1993. There were few initial press reports. The press assumption was that this was just another gang killing. But Stephen was not a gang member and his best friend had been with him at the time and lived to tell the tale of a vicious, racially motivated attack. There had been three such killings locally in the previous year[2] but this crime became a cause célèbre when police failed to charge the men who were thought to be his killers.

Brian Cathcart (2000) later suggested that the explanation for the extraordinary coverage of this case (which led to both a public enquiry and a change in the law) lay in the character of Stephen and his parents: 'This was a clean-living, honest young man with ambitions, from a well ordered and law-abiding home' (Peachey and Burrel 2012). The shooting of Trayvon Martin, another black teenager, in the USA in 2012 also led to world-wide press coverage. His parents suggested the reason why their son's story had been taken up by the nation's media: 'What touches people is that our son, Trayvon Benjamin Martin, could have been their son' (Stein 2012).

Both these factors fit with the earlier suggestion that, at the right moment, a single story can act as a metaphor for an unspoken social concern. A violent act, by pushing the story into public consciousness, becomes the catalyst that changes the discourse. However in both cases, there was an additional factor. The integrity of the parents was established beyond doubt when their causes were endorsed by people who themselves occupied elite positions. The Lawrence case leapt up the news agenda when Nelson Mandela, on a visit to London two weeks after the murder, spoke publicly of his concern about the inactivity of the police. The police quickly became the object of contempt rather than respect. In much the same way, the family of black teenager Trayvon Martin was helped by the words of President Barack Obama who said shortly after his shooting: 'If I had a son, he'd look like Trayvon' (Stein 2012).

It is usually only when their voices have been amplified by tragedy, that ordinary people are listened to on a level with more elite members of society, rather than as secondary definers, pushed to the end of a news story, where their witnessing may add colour and texture to a story that has already been defined by others. Even where there has been a tragedy, the status of those involved will be taken into account. Once celebrity endorsement had occurred, otherwise low-status sources are able to share the status of their protectors. Without the backing of an institution to give them protection, even the most apparently unimpeachable sources are vulnerable. It can take very little for today's victim to be turned into tomorrow's monster, as the parents of Madeline McCann discovered when they almost overnight morphed (in certain newspapers) from being the grieving parents of a lost child to number one suspects in her disappearance. There seemed to be no clear reason for this change of positioning but it took legal action, and a major commission into the ethics of the British press, to fully clear their names.[3]

Even when individuals are given the status of primary definers of an event, it can be difficult for them to avoid being taken up by one or other competing power interest. Elite sources have learned how to make use of the news media's interest in personal stories and routinely search for, and help publicize, stories that appear to give credence to a particular narrative. The UK Conservative government has been particularly adept at seeding personal stories that have undermined public confidence in welfare (Baumberg et al. 2012) and the National Health Service (see below). The combination of powerful supporters and compelling, personal testimony is impossible for news organizations to ignore, particularly when it is presented as part of a trend, rather than a one-off incident. Thus the 'interpretive community' of the news media pretty quickly find that they are helping to re-enforce the narrative of the primary definer.

Verification

In order for a source to become a 'primary definer' of a news event, they need to be credible and their relationship to the events they describe must be both direct and verifiable. In other words they must be able to discuss the matter under scrutiny with authority. Authority tends to be derived most easily from

institutional attachment: a rocket scientist is an authoritative source when discussing rockets but will not be called upon to discuss the state of education or
policing. At this first stage, public bodies and organizations or NGOs known to
the journalist have a massive advantage (Golding and Elliot 1996). This is not
simply some instinctive need to genuflect before power. If the local government
press office says that refuse collections are to be doubled, or halved, then people
need to know about it. If Apple has a new product launch, people will be
interested in it. If there is a famine in Ethiopia, the public should be alerted to it.
Joanna Bloggs may have something important to say as well but she will need to
compete for attention with the stories that have 'news value' (see Chapter 1).

After reading the primary report, journalists should then try to get comments
from other perspectives (this doesn't always happen – see below). To do this they
will turn first to their own list of contacts. These are people they have spoken to
before, who have a track record and who they feel they can trust (Reich 2011: 21).
They will prioritize those people who have authority. So if they are not already
familiar with a source, their first job is to check that the source really is who they
say they are and that their testimony can be relied on not to collapse under
scrutiny or cross-questioning. To describe this process as a 'strategic ritual'
(Tuchman 1972) may be reasonable, but only in the same way that 'triage'
(where a doctor or nurses rapidly assesses the condition of an incoming patient)
is a 'ritual'. Both are busy and working at speed, so they use a learned set
of practices to decide whether a source is likely to be reliable (Manning 2001:
68–69) or a condition is likely to be fatal.

Neither the doctor, nor the journalist wishes to be caught out making a major
error of judgement. In one case a patient may die. In the other, erroneous
information may be circulated that could end in a court case, or dismissal of
journalist or editor. It could also mean that lives are ruined. Mis-information
publicly circulated can do enormous damage. For Bill Kovach and Tom
Rosensteil, authors of *The Elements of Journalism*, the key American text book on
journalism practice, verification is the key to the integrity of journalism: 'In the
end, the discipline of verification is what separates journalism from entertainment, propaganda, fiction, or art. … Journalism alone is focused first on getting
what happened down right' (Kovach and Rosenstiel 2007).

The less well-known the source, or the more tenuous the information, the
more work the journalist has to do to check their identity and credentials. So a
single person complaining about institutional neglect may be ignored for lack of
corroborating evidence, whereas the same story, if taken up by a more powerful
organization, may be used without any checks at all. Faced with an unknown
source, journalists will look for common threads: Is this story plausible (it is
easier to believe if it is running with the dominant narrative rather than against
it – see Chapter 1)? Do I know anyone who knows this person? Do I know the
organizations that this person is affiliated with?

Where an unknown source has a story about a well-known person or organization, alarm bells will ring. However good the story, no journalist can afford to

base a critical story about a powerful person on an unreliable source. Here the hierarchy of credibility comes sharply into play. The higher the status of a person criticized in a story, and the lower (relatively) the status of the critic, the harder the work required to verify the information. Powerful sources are far more likely to complain if information they don't like is published. If the information published turns out to be inaccurate, there is always the chance of legal action. Comments made by powerful sources about less powerful people are less open to attack and complaints are less likely to be listened to.[4] People without means are also less likely to take legal action.

Verification has become even more important as sources go online where they cannot be confronted face to face. Journalists have been badly burned by spoof websites and Twitter streams that purport to come from a reliable or well-known person but turn out to be fakes (Broersma 2013). As a result of these mistakes reporters have become a great deal more cautious. If the contact is on Twitter, or a website, or the information comes in via an unknown email, there is already a series of tests that journalists employ to check them out (for more on this see Dick 2013):

1   Do they use their own name and display 'real life' contact details?
2   Have they got a history of commenting on this issue that can be followed up?
3   How new is this account? Does it appear elsewhere?
4   If there is a photograph in the email, is it possible to ascertain whether it really shows what it is alleged to show?

Social media contains its own history and it is usually possible to establish bona fides quite quickly through cross-checking online. A source with no history and no real life contact details is not likely to be followed up (Lyon 2012, Turner 2012). Some journalists are so anxious to avoid being hoaxed that they only follow tweets carrying a little blue tick that tells them that the account has been checked and verified by Twitter and really does belong to the person it appears to represent.

The death of Bin Laden provides a clear lesson in the way in which, even in the clutter and noise of Twitter, journalists who are focusing on verification can provide clarification for confusing events. Speculation started with an announcement by the White House of an imminent address by the President. In the Twitter chatter many people speculated that the address could concern Bin Laden but at that stage no one version of events had any traction at all. Half an hour later a Tweet was posted by @keithurbahn, former Chief of Staff at the office of Donald Rumsfeld. Urbahn had a small Twitter following but one of his followers was Brian Stelter of the *New York Times*. Stelter recognized the authority of the source immediately and re-tweeted. Reassured by the authority of the source, within a very short time all major news networks were running the story (Gilad and Devin 2011).

The imperative need to check sources increases the reliability of journalism but it also means that the open possibilities of social media are closed down. As

Zvi Reich discovered (2011), a journalist's most trusted resource is his or her own direct observation. Nicola Bruno looked at the coverage of the Haiti earthquake by CNN, the BBC and the *Guardian* and found that all three made significant use of social media in the first 24 hours of the disaster but, once the BBC and CNN had their own people in Haiti, they stopped relying on social media.

Bruno noted however that the *Guardian* (with far fewer resources): 'seems to have embraced an editorial policy more open and consistent with regard to the diversity of online voices' (Bruno 2011: 63). This is partly a positive embrace but it also reflects editorial necessity. The *Guardian* doesn't have the money to send teams to Haiti. At home it is also experimenting with 'social' but the experiment is largely confined to live blogs (see below) where there is an acceptance that verification of information is part of the construction of the story.

More generally, rather than using social media to expand contacts, journalists tend to be using it to follow existing, verified contacts. Or they use it to search for contacts who may have a comment to make on a running story. Journalists are far more likely to use social media to seek people they are looking for than they are to use it as a means by which unknown people can make contact with them (Phillips 2010a). Indeed so difficult has it become to sort out truth from fiction in social media that organizations such as Storyful have been established to help journalists filter out the unreliable sources and focus on reliable information.

This caution reinforces the power of the journalists in relation to their sources, but it also reinforces the power of the primary definers. They are not only more likely to be approached, they are also less likely to have their comments cross-checked. Those who are unknown to the journalist will be treated with scepticism and additional sources will be sought to back up both their integrity and their version of events (Reich 2011: 31). The need to be careful, added to the need to be quick, still tends to narrow source relationships (Golding and Elliot 1996, Phillips 2010a).

Speed

Speed is to news managers what verification is to professional journalists: the essence of the job (Gans 1979: 82). Unfortunately the need for speed tends to operate in direct contradiction to the need for verification (Manning 2001: 68–69). In a time-pressured environment, where daily deadlines have been replaced by rolling news deadlines, the urgency is not to meet a production time-slot but to get online and up to the top of Google faster than the competition.

A low-status journalist may find that even getting a press officer (of any kind) to speak, off the cuff, on the phone, can be difficult. Press officers are also working under pressure and trying to avoid saying something that might not please their clients or superiors. An email paper trail provides proof of an interaction and evidence of what they have said. So they would rather just stick a few quotes and a summary into an email and send it out. Very often a response will be delayed, or the final comment will prove to be irrelevant to the query. The time taken to find the unknown source of a breaking story may be prohibitive.

Under deadline pressure it is very tempting to ignore the chore of following up information from a trusted and known source altogether. Reporters may use the press-released quote and look through their contacts book for an established 'opposition' voice likely to be available at short notice to balance it. Under extreme time pressure the journalist might make do with a response cut and pasted from Twitter. The more considered response of a more thoughtful expert is unlikely to make the story because it will take too long to locate and because thoughtful people often want time to consider the story before speaking. Time is something that, increasingly, journalists do not have (Phillips 2012a).

An analysis of nearly 3,000 stories in four large-circulation UK regional dailies found that journalists often give up on trying to get any alternative view. Some 76 per cent cited only a single source (O'Connor and O'Neill 2008). This indicates that a journalist had taken the word of the initiator of a story at face value and done no follow-up at all beyond re-arranging the words on the page.

Given the importance of verification to a journalist's own sense of their professional worth (Fenton and Witschge 2011), one might expect that on larger newspapers follow-up would be rather more rigorous. It is certainly easier for journalists working on national news outlets to get an apposite comment because press offices prioritize their time so that journalists from the larger dailies are always dealt with first. However, in a 2008 study of the elite press in the UK, insistence on high productivity meant that some journalists were being asked to produce up to a dozen stories a day, a very high proportion of which were directly poached from another media outlet (Phillips 2010b). In most cases there was some attempt to follow up the stories but there was very little time. One journalist interviewed, commenting on a particular story said:

> They go: 'Can you do 400 words on this', and it's something from the Daily Mail or something. I'd read it through, find out who the people are, try and move it forward a bit. So I was doing that one day … and the news editor came over and goes, 'You haven't filed that thing. … ', and I was like, 'I'm just speaking to the mother now to get some quotes', and he was like, 'don't bother with that, it's been in the Daily Mail just rewrite it'.
>
> (Phillips 2010b: 140)

In this study, journalists covering breaking stories found that many of the sources they needed to contact had already contacted them with carefully worded and targeted emails ready to be dropped into the story. The Internet has certainly made it easier for ordinary people and campaigning organizations to send material to journalists. The trouble is that, since everyone can do the same, it becomes increasingly difficult for the journalist to handle the sheer quantity of incoming information. The difficulty then lies, not in finding relevant sources, but in deciding which ones to make use of. This is where news judgements are focused. And this is also where it is easy to make assumptions of reliability based on prior 'safe' contacts. Time spent searching for a new voice, or for someone with more relevant expertise, may feel like time wasted if there is a news editor breathing down your neck. It is easier to use what you already have or to ask a colleague for a contact.

Live blogs

Many newspapers have now started using live blogs as a way of handling both speed and verification. A live blog allows a journalist to start writing as soon as a story breaks and then to verify as the story unfolds, updating with information gleaned online, from a variety of known and verifiable sources, as well as linking to information that cannot be immediately verified so that the audience can refine the story as it unfolds. Such 'crowd verification' has become a useful adjunct to journalistic practices but it does rely on news organizations being prepared to link away from their own sites and correct as they go.

This form of transparent journalism, which allows audiences to see how a story is constructed and encourages participation from experts in real-time, does have the potential to open up source relationships but it still requires fast judgements about what material to include and exclude and that will, inevitably, tilt the power relationship in favour of known, trusted, verifiable sources. Andrew Sparrow of the *Guardian*, live-blogs regularly but he works 'by and large ... with a relatively narrow patch of usual suspects and I know who they are'. His colleague, Matthew Weaver agreed: 'I'll be doing Syria or Yemen, and I won't be looking at generic search terms, I'll be looking at lists of people who we know are there' (Thurman and Walters 2013).

Editorial and cultural bias

Casual cultural bias is likely across all news outlets because, working at speed, and often without much discussion, news journalists tend to filter sources according to their own unconscious, cultural assumptions. These are often clearest when journalists are writing about people who are different from them. Sources who do not conform to the majority culture of the newsroom may also find that they are only sought out to make comments within stories pre-structured according to the assumptions of the editorial line:

> [W]hen [Muslim women] do wish to speak out against anti-Muslim discrimination and harassment, they do so with the encouragement and support of Muslim communities, but are too often treated with hostility or indifference by those outside those communities. On the other hand, if they wish to speak about dysfunctional gender norms within Muslim communities,

they have little difficulty in finding an audience among non-Muslims, but their voices are appropriated and woven into anti-Muslim discourse, and they risk being labeled as disloyal by some members of their own communities.

(Dreher 2009: 4)

Unconscious bias plus the imperatives of speed and accuracy can mean, as Todd Gitlin observed, that: 'Simply by doing their jobs, journalists tend to serve the political and economic elite definitions of society' (1980: 12). He was looking at US print news outlets where a belief in 'objectivity' in news reporting operates as a professional norm. Similar structural effects have been noted in British TV news coverage (Golding and Elliot 1996) where regulation insists on political balance. But news coverage is not all the same and it is politically aligned news organizations that provide the clearest view of how conscious bias uses sourcing to create specific political and cultural narratives.

Deliberate bias

Where news organizations are politically aligned, all journalists will be aware of the political and cultural leanings of news outlets for which they work. So conservative news organizations such as Fox News in the USA and the *Daily Mail* in the UK tend to look for conservative spokespeople, whereas liberal news outlets such as the *Guardian* in the UK will look for people who represent liberal views on most issues. If the primary source for a particular story represents a position that is out of line with the news organization's worldview, an equally powerful alternative source will be found to refute it. This bias may not be overt. The news organizations may not mix comment with news coverage but the ordering of information, the points chosen for amplification and the spokespeople chosen to comment, will nevertheless follow a political line which is even more insidious because it appears neutral.

So, for example, in 2013 when the Conservative government was embarking on a programme of health service privatization, it chose to release a lot of statistics about poor standards in British hospitals. The *Daily Telegraph* (with a conservative political agenda) and the *Guardian* (with a liberal political agenda) led with entirely different interpretations of the same story. The *Telegraph* referred to 'NHS shame' and did not include a single source that was critical of the figures. The *Guardian* referred to 'TripAdvisor style ratings' and 'skewed' results and found several important sources who cast doubt on the figures or called for caution in interpreting them (Ramesh 2013).

In the same way, stories about 'benefit cheats' started appearing just at the point that the UK government wanted to cut back on welfare spending. A survey for the charity Turn2us looked at articles over the period 1995–2011. It found a particularly sharp peak in negative stories about people on benefits in the period up to and just after the elections in 2010 (Baumberg *et al.* 2012: 41). The researchers also found that conservative popular newspapers (the *Express*,

Mail and *Sun*) were considerably more likely to use negative stories about benefits (69–75 per cent of stories on the subject were negative) than was the more liberal tabloid, the *Mirror*, though even here 50 per cent of stories were negative (Baumberg *et al.* 2012: 38).

There had been no underlying change in levels of fraud, which might have provided a context for illustrative case histories, indeed the UK government's own figures (2013) put the level of fraud at 0.7 per cent of all claims, a figure which had varied little in recent years. It was clear that journalists had been specifically sent out to track down stories that would play well with an anti-welfare agenda. As the stories rolled out, the atmosphere did indeed become more antagonistic towards people on benefits, as later polling information attested (Baumberg *et al.* 2012: 7).

The sources for the case histories were usually people without status who had little idea how their stories would be told. They were just the evidence chosen to stand up stories in which the political line had been pre-scripted. However, as those cases demonstrate, it is not the politicians, however powerful they may be, who in the end determine the way in which the story is told. This formulation of how power flows through news reporting fails to take proper account of the newspaper's own agenda. It assumes that the newspaper is simply reflecting power rather than, in the case of the British press, actually shaping it – a fact which became abundantly clear during Lord Leveson's Inquiry into the Culture Practices and Ethics of the Press (Leveson 2012).

Whose power?

Sources who wish to use the media in order to make a particular point must always recognize that they are only part of a patchwork and that their voices are mediated via journalists and editors who may not have the same view of the story or the same interests in telling it. Sources who do not have a 'mainstream' message will only have an impact if their story is too big to ignore and preferably if they have backing and support from someone who is known to journalists and trusted by them.

Where news organizations have an obligation to try and produce politically neutral news coverage (for example the news agencies, regulated broadcast news in the UK and much of Europe, and in the professionalized newspapers of the US), they are still subject to the built-in structures described above. This ensures that they produce a narrative that is broadly supportive of the prevailing consensus, while giving a voice to those shades of opinion that vary around that centre ground. However, where newspapers have a political agenda and a mass audience, they hold the power in the relationship (Leveson 2012). They determine whose voices will be heard but they also situate those voices within a particular, usually pre-defined, narrative (see Chapter 1).

Nevertheless, in spite of these constraints, oppositional voices can be heard, even when the context is negative. (See more in Chapter 5.) A journalist explained how he used his position to open up channels for minority voices. He knew that their voices would be used negatively but trusted that minority readers would be able to read between the lines. He described his relationship with a local community organizer who was usually projected as a hate figure in the paper:

> He was a cold realist about the whole thing. He just realized that they needed a profile and he knew full well when he gave me a story what the editor was going to do with it. But he took the view that if there were two pars in the story that got his point across then he was quite happy with that. … , the people he wanted to read it would read it and they would take from it what he hoped they would take from it.
>
> (Interview 2002, senior reporter, national newspaper)

Notes

1 This celebrated case was the subject of the Hutton report of 2004. Available at http://webarchive.nationalarchives.gov.uk/20090128221550/http://www.the-hutton-inquiry.org.uk/content/rulings.htm (accessed 5 January 2014).
2 BBC News, (1998) 'What happened on Stephen Lawrence's last night alive?' Available at http://news.bbc.co.uk/1/hi/special_report/1998/03/98/lawrence/65060.stm (accessed 1 August 2013).
3 Three-year-old Madeline McCann disappeared from her bed in 2007 while her family was on holiday in Portugal. The story had extensive sensational coverage and became one of the major cases triggering Lord Leveson's 2012 enquiry into the British press.
4 The UK organisation MediaWise has a dossier of information about people who have been inaccurately reported and been unable to get a correction or apology.

Chapter 4

The making of journalists

In other chapters we have seen journalism broadly speaking from the perspective of political economy and cultural studies. While political economy approaches describe the way in which power structures operate to reproduce power relationships and cultural studies approaches recognize the active participation of audiences, neither of these approaches satisfactorily engage with the position of journalists. Thus we tend to see journalism and journalists as inextricably linked to power, rather than subject to it. In this chapter we will look at what happens to those people who become journalists, how structures limit their agency as individuals, and what alternatives are available to them.

Journalism varies in every country because it is a product of differing systems both political and commercial (Hallin and Mancini 2012). Values and professional norms have developed to reproduce the specific practices and behaviours that fit each system. While the professionalized 'liberal' model of journalism is often held up as a norm, it is in fact a minority trend in a world where politically aligned journalism is arguably more common than neutral 'objective' journalism and journalists are as likely to see themselves as commentators, as they are to see themselves as neutral information gatherers. Given these systemic differences, journalists also learn very different approaches to authority – minor law breaking and breaches of privacy are considered necessary to 'press freedom' in some places and taboo in others.

One of the very few things that seem to unite journalists globally, at least as an ideal worth fighting for, is autonomy from state control (Splichal and Sparks 1994). Even those journalists working in countries where they are not free to report what they see and hear, believe the freedom to do so is worth fighting for (Himelboim and Limor 2008). Where the state exerts power over journalists through the use of law, or business through the application of economic power, then that independence is inevitably constrained. Taking the freedom to report critically as the norm against which we judge the state of journalism in a democracy, this chapter will consider how changes in practices and structures are impacting the autonomy of journalism.

Who are journalists?

We have a wealth of material to draw upon which shows us what journalists do: memoirs, films, fiction and empirical research. Films and memoirs tend to be about investigative journalists working for national news outlets. Academic researchers tend to look at major newsrooms. Herbert Gans (1979) looked at the big beasts of networked news, NBC, CBS and Newsweek and Time. Golding and Elliot (1979) looked at British network television and Philip Schlesinger (1987) at the BBC. So when we read about newsrooms as factories 'manufacturing' the news (Golding and Elliot 1979: 119, Fishman 1980) we are seeing all of journalism through the experience of those at the top of the profession.

However, of UK journalists surveyed in 2002, only 11 per cent were employed in the national media (Skillset 2001). The other 89 per cent were employed across a vast range of outlets, from magazines to local newspapers, radio stations and online start-ups. A study by the International Federation of Journalists (Walters et al. 2006) found that, worldwide, 30 per cent of journalists worked freelance, as casual workers, or on short term or rolling contracts, and that doesn't include the interns and amateurs working without pay.

Ursula Rao is one of a few researchers who have focused on local, lower-status, journalists. Working in Lucknow, India, she found that '[a]lmost every man I met claimed to be a journalist. It took time to understand what the word journalist meant here.' Many of them are working on an informal basis; they 'fulfil the task of mediating between the local community and the newspaper'. The reward is that this activity 'turns them into key members of a network that produces publicity' (Rao 2010: 104).

Local newspapers in the UK also have a system of community reporters, often unpaid or paid a few pounds for a report, who, as one editor put it, 'cover every spit and cough' of the local scene. Like their counterparts in India, they are composed of people who take an active interest in their communities and are willing to act as mediators for very little reward. In the UK the information they produce is typically anodyne and uncontroversial and is knocked into shape by a small core of paid reporters working in a newsroom (Bew 1998: 204).

The existence of this fringe of people who are loosely associated with news organizations is more commonly noted online. The Huffington Post, for example, uses a large number of unpaid amateur writers, as does OhmyNews in Korea (see Chapter 5). Indymedia brings together the work of 'alternative' journalists keen to produce news from a different perspective from that of the mainstream. The Internet has made this informal journalism a great deal more visible but also more exploitable. News organizations increasingly see amateurs, not so much as additional voices adding variety to news coverage, but as a source of free labour, allowing them to lower staff costs. Though, as we discuss in the chapter on audiences (Chapter 5), this is not as easy as it appears. In order to maintain quality, the free material is usually 'processed' by trained journalists to make it conform to a set of common standards.

Added to this multiplicity of actors, all of whom see themselves as 'doing journalism', we can now add the independent bedroom bloggers or writer-gathers, as Nick Couldry has called them (2010: 139). These people are not attempting to add to existing news operations but to augment or critique them. Some see themselves as journalists, others as campaigners. As the work of 'publicity' become ubiquitous, it is easy to assume that we are, 'all journalists now' (Gillmor 2006, Shirky 2008), but in many ways that ubiquity makes the clarity of definition even more necessary. Activities of mediation are not all alike and power is exerted in different ways on journalists depending on where they stand. While bloggers working individually may appear to be independent, in reality that freedom is often compromised: they may have difficulty accessing information and they may be under pressure to accept gifts or payments from companies whose products they review. Organized journalism may often be ethically compromised, but at least there is a possibility of scrutiny. It is much harder to find out whether a blogger is genuinely independent or being paid to talk up one brand at the expense of its rivals.

Autonomy and the state

The freedom of journalism from state interference is widely agreed upon as a principle in most democratic countries and news organizations jealously guard their independence. The right to press freedom is written into the UN Universal Declaration of Human Rights and the European Convention on Human Rights and, where media organizations receive public subsidy, the Council of Europe recommends that it should be subject to 'strict rules prohibiting government interference' (Vike-Freiberga et al. 2013).

However these rights are also constrained by the rights and freedoms of others, including legislation to protect individuals from libel and hate speech. In addition, the Council of Europe spells out the other circumstances in which states may curtail press freedom:

> [I]n the interests of national security, territorial integrity or public safety, for the prevention of disorder or crime, for the protection of health or morals, for the protection of the reputation or rights of others, for preventing the disclosure of information received in confidence, or for maintaining the authority and impartiality of the judiciary.
>
> (Article 10 of the European Convention on Human Rights)

In other words, press freedom is in all places and at all times a matter for negotiation with the state.

Nevertheless freedom to publish is a right that is fought for. According to Reporters without Borders, there were 178 journalists imprisoned in 2013 for acts of journalism (www.rsf.org). Most imprisoned journalists are from non-democratic countries with dubious human rights records but intimidation of journalists is a growing problem. In the USA, journalist Barrett Brown was arrested in 2012 for investigating (and publishing a link to) leaked emails from Stratfor, a private intelligence company. In the UK between April 2011 and March 2013, 59 journalists were arrested (Turvill 2013). Most of these were charged with privacy-related offences – phone hacking and accessing the private messages of celebrities. In August 2013, the partner of *Guardian* journalist Glenn Greenwald was detained at Heathrow airport in London. Greenwald was working on material leaked from the US National Security Agency (Coddington 2013).

Maintaining editorial independence

While the need to guard against state interference is a principle that, in democracies, usually unites proprietors, editors and journalists, autonomy from government is not the only independence that matters for journalism. Individual editors and journalists may also be under both commercial and party political pressure (Örnebring 2012: 572) and even where proprietors, and the editors they choose, may be free of coercion, the same is much less likely to be true for individual journalists who often find that their independence is heavily constrained.

In Europe, political partisanship is the norm (Hallin and Mancini 2004) though direct party affiliation has declined as a result of increasing commercialization and consolidation (Hallin and Mancini 2004: 181). Some argue that this has benefited journalism because, where news organizations are owned by corporations, rather than parties or individuals, they are better able to stand back from party in-fighting and serve the common interest and are more likely to embrace the professionalization agenda that characterizes the US press. However there is a reasonable argument to be made that a partisan press, provided all parties are represented, is more representative of the political landscape than a commercial press that, though apparently neutral, tends only to represent a narrow centre ground which simply reproduces the status quo rather than challenging it.

> The French press has traditionally seen itself not as a neutral observer but as an active participant in the public sphere. For these reasons, paradoxically, less politically 'autonomous' journalistic fields, such as those that exist in France and other western European democracies, may actually be the most effective in facilitating a clash of opposing viewpoints and criticisms.
>
> (Benson 2011: 317)

Where commerce has broken the link with direct political control it has also ushered in the possibility of commercial influence. Where there is a reasonable balance in the broad political affiliation of news organizations (in Scandinavia and France encouraged by the use of press subsidies) journalists have the freedom to work for the organizations that reflect their views. In the UK, where the majority of journalism jobs in national newspapers are in organizations with conservative political affiliation, this is not necessarily the case and journalists find that their work is routinely rewritten to reflect the political inflection of the newspaper (Phillips *et al.* 2010).

In Norway and the Netherlands, the fear that editorial control would be exercised by proprietors from above led to controls on the rights of owners to influence editorial policy. In these two countries, economic subsidies (which are widespread) are only available if journalists have complete editorial autonomy (Hallin and Mancini 2004: 175). In the USA, where commerce is generally seen as the only guarantor of media plurality (McChesney and Nichols 2011), journalists have no similar guarantees. While the right of press freedom is written into the constitution, it is the freedom of the editor that is guaranteed; the freedom of individual journalists is upheld by nothing stronger than a widespread belief in the professional norm of 'objectivity'.

However, commercial activity is not completely unconstrained even in the USA, where the hidden influence of advertising was acknowledged more than a century ago with the introduction of the 1912 Newspaper Publishing Act, which decreed that any publication sent through the mail (and most newspapers were sent by mail) had to separate editorial content and use the word 'advertisement' to label paid content. Similar rules on the separation of paid-for content from editorial are enshrined in the UK Broadcasting Acts, and the Consumer Protection from Unfair Trading Regulations 2008.

While news organizations were thriving, this 'glass wall' between editorial and advertising was easier to maintain but, as news organizations look for new ways of attracting funding, the wall is becoming dangerously thin (Bærug and Harro-Loit 2011). In a study of journalists across the world by the International Federation of Journalists (Walters *et al.* 2006: 6), concern about the impact of advertisers on editorial independence was mentioned in Nicaragua, Peru, Taiwan, Pakistan, Serbia and Australia. A statement the same year from the American Committee of Concerned Journalists put the case bluntly:

> We are facing the possibility that independent news will be replaced by self-interested commercialism posing as news. If that occurs, we will lose the press as an independent institution, free to monitor the other powerful forces and institutions in society.
>
> (Kovach and Rosenstiel 2007)

It is only by understanding how structures work against autonomy that we are able to consider what protections journalists need so that they are indeed free to hold power to account rather than finding themselves forced to ignore transgressions of the powerful or flatter those who are paying their wages. As Champagne says (2005: 50): 'the history of journalism is: the unending story of an autonomy that must always be re-won because it is always threatened'.

Field theory

Pierre Bourdieu's field theory is a useful way of understanding how news media operate, particularly in those democracies where state support of media is not synonymous with state control (Benson 2011). Bourdieu's theory has much in common with the 'New Institutionalism' as described by Walter Powell and Paul DiMaggio (1991). Both are concerned with the ways in which institutions are formed and reproduced, recognizing that individual decisions are shaped by the environment and the history of the institution. In this they build also on Max Weber's work on structures and institutions (1947). These sociologists recognize that journalists are not individually responsible for maintaining press freedom, but nor are they indivisible from the power structures that that they represent. Bourdieu's approach (Bourdieu 2005: 42) is particularly concerned with the complexity of the relationship between economic and cultural power and between structure and agency. Rodney Benson and Erik Neveu explain in the introduction to *Bourdieu and the Journalistic Field*:

> Field theory positions itself precisely between those approaches (political economy or cultural) that commit the short circuit fallacy and link news production directly to the interests of broad social classes or the national society, and those (organisational) that focus too narrowly on particular news producers.
>
> (Benson and Neveu 2005: 12)

Bourdieu conceptualises a field across two axes. The horizontal axis lies between the autonomous pole and the heteronomous pole. The less an organization, or individual, is tied to the market and the need to appeal to populism, the greater the autonomy of thought and action. The more closely it is tied to audience ratings and advertising dollars, the less free are those who work for it. He sees journalism as a 'weakly autonomous field' because most people working as journalists are to some extent tied down by the need to increase audiences. The commercial imperative operates in all countries with a commercial media but, as Benson points out (Benson 2013: 21), it is tempered by the operation of public funding, censorship, regulation and employment laws. The more that news organizations are protected from the demands of commerce on the one hand and censorship on the other, the greater, according to this formulation, will be their autonomy.

Organizations and individuals in a field are always in competition with others close to them in the field. They need to stand out from the market. So news organizations appealing to the mass market will compete with each other for scandalous stories in order to attract audiences and increase economic capital. In the USA and India, television news is particularly commercially oriented, so any broadcaster entering the market with a more populist offering is seen as a competitive threat and the market keeps moving further to the heteronomous (commercial) pole in order to compete (Thussu 2009: 103–4). As companies compete for the centre ground of the market, they then become less differentiated and more like one another (Bourdieu 2005: 44, Fenton 2010a).

Television journalism in Northern Europe is dominated by publicly funded broadcasters, who are supported by license fee and are independent of government. In France, Germany and Ireland, license fee funding is also topped-up by advertising, All these organizations are hugely influential but they gain influence primarily through cultural (rather than economic) capital which is related to the degree of prestige attached to them and to individuals working within them. One might imagine then that they would not need to bother with providing the kind of programming that attracts popular audiences and advertising. They should be happy simply putting on serious late-night talk shows that demonstrate their cultural value. But publicly funded organizations cannot ignore ratings. They also need to maintain a relationship with mass audiences because otherwise they would rapidly became irrelevant, ceding audience share (and power) to their commercial rivals.

Keeping this balance of cultural power between the cerebral and the popular means that to some people, public service broadcasting may seem unduly 'populist' (Bourdieu 1998, Humphreys 2010, Lloyd 2004, Meyer and Hinchman 2002: 129, Thussu 2009), but journalists working for public broadcasters must engage as well as inform their audiences and arguably it is precisely the tension between the two poles that allows public service television both to thrive and to produce the competitive pressure for higher quality that the more commercial companies are then bound to follow. As long as they are big enough to compete, these publicly funded organizations have an impact on their commercial rivals and force them to consider the cultural demands of the field for quality and integrity as well as commercial demands for higher audiences (as Michael Grade argues in Chapter 2). Arguably then, any weakening of the publicly funded broadcasters would reduce autonomy across the field and further compromise journalism.

Both commercial and cultural capital are also connected to the 'field of power'. Powerful proprietors trade influence for political advantage. The degree of that influence in the UK was made clear when Sir John Major gave evidence to the UK Leveson Inquiry[1] into the press. Where there are no legal guarantees of journalistic independence, wealthy individuals such as Rupert Murdoch, whose company (News International) bought *The Times* in 1981, Jeff Bezos who bought the *Washington Post* in 2013 and the Lebedevs who bought the UK's *Evening Standard* and then the *Independent* in 2010, possess the means of intervening in the public narrative. As Evgeny Lebedev memorably tweeted after appearing at the Leveson Inquiry in 2012: 'Forgot to tell #Leveson that it's unreasonable to expect individuals to spend £millions on newspapers and not have access to politicians.'

Nevertheless, direct proprietorial control is blunted by the need to retain cultural influence, without which news organizations have little value to their owners. The balance between serving the audience and serving the proprietor does provide some measure of autonomy at the elite end of the field where there is a recognition of the need to distinguish themselves from the populist press. As Anne Spackman, then managing editor of the UK *Times*, said to the UK *Press Gazette*: 'If I wanted to play the traffic tart game, there are certain things we could write about all the time, like Britney Spears. But that's not really what the *Times* is for.'

But for those working for the steeply hierarchical UK popular press, there is very little independence. Journalists are expected to follow instructions (Phillips *et al.* 2010). Those working for the commercial press in Northern Europe are not quite so constrained because of the greater power of professional organizations (in particular trade unions) and the impact of public subsidy (Hallin and Mancini 2004:175) which has been able to tilt the field towards the 'autonomous pole'. Here the journalists' organizations themselves have more power in defining the field and norms of behaviour.

The vertical axis of the field describes the economic and cultural position of people and organizations. Those at the top have more power, whereas those at the bottom have little. Highly paid commentators appear to have independence because they are paid to express personal opinions that are, generally speaking, aligned to the editorial line of the organization. However, if they change their minds, they usually have to change their jobs – so that independence is still constrained. If they are sufficiently influential however, the cultural capital accrued will help them to change their circumstances by moving to a more congenial news organization with which they are more in tune.

Small fashion bloggers, on the other hand, who may be entirely dependent on being sent samples by big brand commercial organizations (Robison 2012), can be found somewhere on the bottom right hand side of field. They have very little economic power and their autonomy is also completely circumscribed because, if they say what they really think about a product, they may not be sent another one. Some bloggers attract audiences by virtue of their outspokenness and difference from the mass-market outlets, but although they provide a refreshing change from the mass-market media organizations, they often find it difficult to maintain financial independence and that in turn is likely to undermine their ability either to survive at all or to speak out. Without recourse to funding from an organization or individual, they often struggle financially (Knight Foundation 2013). The more successful voices may then be acquired by a company that is prepared to sustain them, which in turn may lead to commercial compromise and increasing homogeneity.

All the different actors in a field are organized in relationship to one another and have to define themselves by differentiating from others who are closest to them in the field. But the differences are small and there is the danger that, if one popular blogger, for example, accepts payment for editorial (without declaring it), others will follow and the independence of all bloggers will be compromised. Similarly, if one organization pays private detectives to find gossip about celebrities,[2] all the other comparable publications will have to do the same thing or lose in the race for readers. When organizations find themselves competing for 'popularity', ethical standards may be quickly eroded across the whole field unless other organizations in the field can act fast to underpin existing standards (see Chapter 7). This work of rule-making is the way in which a field maintains itself (Bourdieu 1996: 66).

For example, the efforts by the *Guardian* in the UK to prevent other organizations from using phone-hacking as a means of accessing celebrity gossip can be seen as just such an attempt to protect the journalism field from activities by more commercially driven rival organizations, who are thought to be undermining audience trust in journalism. Their coverage culminated in the Leveson Inquiry into the ethics of the press with its attempts (so far unrealized) to create a better regulatory system for non-broadcast media. The battle in the early twentieth century to regulate advertising can also be seen similarly as a fight to maintain the integrity of the field and prevent commercialization destroying journalism as a separate occupational sphere. Advertising is a useful means of subsidizing news production but, if audiences cannot tell the difference between editorial produced independently and advertising that is paid for, it will quickly undermine the integrity of all journalism. For journalism to survive as a separate field it has to ensure that regulation is in place to help police the boundary of the field.

Changes in employment practices

The news industry is used to the shocks caused by unexpected changes to the composition of the field. It has had to absorb big changes from a period in which newspapers were the dominant mass-market agents, through a period of disruption from radio and television followed by a series of technical innovations from computerised printing to the Internet. Digital transformation has yet to make an impact on news in countries with lower levels of access to broadband. Right across India and the continent of Africa, print journalism is healthy and growing as literacy rates rise. The Internet shock is not yet a world-wide phenomenon but it will come (Kilman 2012).

With each change there has been expectation that either the job of journalist will be engulfed by a tidal wave of mass market populism, or that the changes would unleash democratic engagement in ways unseen since the Greeks invented the term (Curran 2010a). Undoubtedly each change has been followed by a period of upheaval but it has then been followed by a further period in which relationships in the field are re-established and equilibrium returns. At no stage has the job of the journalist disappeared, although it keeps changing and adapting to new circumstances.

During the 1980s and 1990s, changes in technology, allowing faster, cheaper printing, were expected to decrease the high cost of entry into the business and allow a range of competitors to challenge incumbents and increase the range of views available. However the changes mainly allowed existing organizations to massively increase the amount of space available for advertising and thereby the number of editorial pages, increasing their profits and driving out the new challengers. One UK study found that the number of editorial pages had tripled between 1985 and 2006 (Lewis *et al.* 2008: 10–11) as advertising boomed.

In the UK, the number of staff jobs in journalism rose very little over this period. The expansion in pagination was made possible by a big increase in the freelance labour force. It was not just a time of technical change. It was also the period when the post-war collectivist consensus began to give way to a new, far more individualistic approach to social organization. In the USA it was called Reaganomics and in the UK it was dubbed Thatcherism and it ushered in a period of anti-trade union activity, which seriously undermined trade unions in the UK (Hallin and Mancini 2004: 171, Ursell 2012, Lee-Wright and Phillips 2012).

These changes were helped along by a rising number of young, highly educated people, keen to enter what are broadly termed the 'creative industries' and willing to help dismantle the carefully erected barriers that had protected journalists from competition from untrained and lower skilled workers (Örnebring 2012: 571). In the UK, an apprenticeship system had been founded in 1951 in response to a Royal Commission set up to look into press bias. Organized by the National Council for the Training of Journalists (NCTJ), it established a stately progression through an extended apprenticeship system on the local and regional press, punctuated by regular exams in shorthand, law and the operation of local government. Until the 1980s, it was almost the only way for an ambitious young journalist to 'make it' to Fleet Street and the national press. Similar systems provided training across Europe, much of it established by, or with the encouragement of, trade unions which, in the case of journalists, often stood in for the professional organizations that defend practices in other skilled areas of work (Stephenson and Mory 1990: 34).

The NCTJ still exists but it has been side-stepped by two generations of young graduates and post-graduates, skilled, flexible and impatient with a system that seemed to tie them in to antiquated and often uncritical ways of working (Carey 2000: 19). In the USA and across Europe and South America, degree or post-graduate level training was also producing young graduates with new skills. Instead of spending money retraining experienced journalists for the new flexible working practices, it was cheaper to bring in younger graduates, many of whom were already using new technologies and found it easy to adapt to a world in which the use of computers was now central.

For Bourdieu, the use of younger journalists to undermine the working practices of older journalists would not have been surprising.

> The overproduction of university graduates creates, around the fields of cultural production, a cultural reserve army equivalent to the old 'reserve army of labour' in industry. The pressure of this reserve army on the universes of cultural production facilitates a policy of precarious employment in which censorship can be exercised through political or economic control.
>
> (Bourdieu 2005: 42)

And if we look at the changes being made to working practices, we find that casual work was used as a way of trying out new staff and keeping the full-time work force relatively small. Competition was created for jobs and individuals were increasingly prepared to work on low salaries and on short-term (or no term) contracts (Stephenson and Mory 1990: 36, Walters *et al.* 2006). According to the International Organization of Journalists, '[i]ndividual contracts or short-term rolling contracts are now an issue for journalists in Australia, Argentina, Pakistan, Peru, Nicaragua and Greece. Precarious employment, unfair dismissals and working without any contract are problems in Mexico and Brazil' (Walters *et al.* 2006).

This new way of working is by no means confined to the news media. Zygmunt Bauman, in *Liquid Modernity*, sees it as a condition of life in the post-modern world: 'An individualised, privatised version of modernity, with the burden of pattern-weaving and the responsibility for failure falling primarily on the individuals shoulders' (Bauman, 2011: 7–8). While opportunities were plentiful, this slightly precarious way of living had its advantages. A young graduate, with highly prized technical skills, could quite easily by-pass the traditional methods of getting into the job. The newsrooms of commercial TV stations and later websites were staffed by young people who possessed skills that their seniors did not understand and were able to work at the boundaries of the new technologies with little supervision.

Things changed for journalists when advertising started to leak away from traditional news media to the Internet. The high profit margins that the media companies had got used to became unsustainable – stock-holders demanded cuts in expenditure (see more in Chapter 6). With lower profit margins, news organizations were faced with the need to explore a new medium online while at the same time starting to reduce staff numbers, centralize jobs and hold down wages (Walters *et al.* 2006). The problems for individual journalists have been particularly acute in poorly unionised countries where jobs were easier to cut back or de-skill.

New technology and cultural conflict

With the move online, many news organizations attempted a new technical revolution. Journalists were told that the future was multi-skilled and that they should all be ready to work 'across media' (Avilés and Carvajal 2008). Television reporters were to provide material for radio and TV and journalists were to learn how to use their mobile phones to capture video for multi-media websites. In a 2008 international survey of newspaper editors, more than 80 per cent expected that journalists would need to produce video (Zogby International 2008).

Where companies had cross-media operations already, they were most likely to take the opportunity to converge newsrooms. For single media companies, convergence required either wholesale retraining or the employment of people with new skills. Where converged newsrooms were established, editors were keen to embrace the challenge (Avilés and Carvajal 2008) but the journalists themselves struggled. TV editors were unhappy with the low quality video provided by hastily trained print journalists with no time to practise their skills and print editors felt that video journalists were skimping on basic research (Witschge and Nygren 2009). All were unhappy with the fact that they were paid no more to work in another medium in spite of the fact that it increased their workload (Singer 2004). Indeed, so unsuccessful was the move to multi-skilling that one Dutch newsroom subsequently de-converged (Tameling and Broersma 2013).

Truly multi-skilled journalists are still a rarity, even amongst the 'digital generation', because it is hard for any individual to work in two media simultaneously – they require different forms of attention (Quandt 2008, Lee-Wright and Phillips 2012). Research in Swedish newsrooms found that print journalists were using videos or cameras but they were ambivalent about doing so and worried about the quality of their work (Witschge and Nygren 2009: 44). In television, increasingly multi-skilled operators plan, shoot and edit their own work, but in general the jobs of writer and videographer are still distinct, because a trained camera operator, editor and writer are usually faster and produce better material than someone trying to do all three at once (Saltzis and Dickinson 2008: 7, Wallace 2013).

Certainly journalists on small operations are now expected to be able to stand up in front of a microphone, take simple photographs and use video if absolutely necessary (often on a phone). There have been some attempts to establish a more, informal kind of online video product, mixing simple sometimes unedited 'squirts' of material captured on a phone, with amateur material found online, but where video or audio of any quality is used it tends to be produced by specialists. Even at the UK *Daily Telegraph*, with its much copied 'hub and spoke' news desk, in which all forms of media were to be integrated, journalists are rarely asked to do more than sit in front of a video camera from time to time and answer a few questions (Lee-Wright and Phillips 2012). At the *Manchester Evening News*, a brave attempt at integration collapsed when the company was sold off and the new owners (Trinity Mirror) declined to buy the TV operation (Oliver 2010).

While digital means that everything can be used on the same platform, there is no intrinsic reason why it should all be produced by the same person. Indeed, far from moving towards a multi-skilled 'back-pack journalist', larger organizations, looking towards the future, started creating new forms of specialists. Sub-editors and copy-editors, once derided as entirely unnecessary in the new world of online media (Phillips *et al.* 2009), started to be re-invented as highly specialised production journalists working on copy, adding relevant links, sizing and adding photographs and video produced by reporters, photographers and videographers. Data journalism, with its sophisticated use of data mining and data visualization is also changing the way in which journalists use computers and providing new specialist jobs for highly trained people (Phillips 2010b).

The debates about multi-skilling have grabbed most of the attention but the bigger changes going on are related to the interlinked nature of the Internet itself and the new possibilities for searching, linking, interacting and disseminating information. For breaking news, the big change is not the back-pack journalists but the use of eyewitnesses' video (Andén-Papadopoulos and Pantti 2013). Given that so many people now have phones capable of capturing and publishing video, there is a high chance that whenever a big story breaks, there will be someone there to witness and to transmit images. A Pew Center report in 2012 found that almost 40 per cent of 'most watched' news videos on YouTube were from amateurs – most were of natural disasters where just 'being there' trumps everything else (Jurkowitz and Hitlin 2013). For online multi-media journalists, part of the job has become looking for suitable video material, checking rights to it, embedding or linking to it and writing posts to contextualize it. These jobs are technically different from the older ones of interviewing, analysing and producing a simple summary in video or text, but they have not obviated the need for the older skill-set. Both are equally important.

From multi-skilling to de-skilling

To begin with most news organizations experimenting with online working had simply employed a room full of young, badly paid people with basic computing skills and left them to get on with it (Quandt 2008). Young people entering an unfamiliar workplace usually learn quickly how to assimilate the habits and practices around them in order to 'fit in'. Transgressions of cultural behaviour may be 'punished' in many ways: by laughter, discipline or withholding of praise. The person who is 'quick on the uptake' is the one who assimilates the 'doxa' of the particular cultural 'game' (Bourdieu 1984: 170). Bourdieu describes doxa as: 'An adherence to relations of order which, because they structure inseparably both the real world and the thought world, are accepted as self-evident' (1984: 471). The uptake of learned behaviour in a specific, structured context produces a way of doing things that is guided by the power relationships in the field and then reproduces those relationships over time.

In the new online spaces there was often no older generation to learn from so young journalists in the start-ups and web operations of legacy news media evolved new ways of working, involving the creation of a whole new set of tacit understandings about the way in which news-work should be organised. Young journalists working online started to evolve their own 'doxa': a set of rules that grew out of the capabilities of the medium and involved rituals of linking to other sites and a particular etiquette in cutting and pasting copy (but giving credit to the original author). The need to verify information before publishing gave way to the concept of 'transparency' – the assumption that if you cite and link to your sources and they are wrong, someone in the audience will correct you. Above all, speed became the key value for all news (Friend and Singer 2007).

The new 'web' journalists marked off their territory by despising the traditional journalists on legacy news organizations. Researchers looking at Norwegian attempts at convergence found that:

> people in Nettavisen [the Internet section of TV company TV 2] thought that TV 2 people were some arrogant pricks who don't know the Internet, who have no interest … to do the simplest things that we should have done to help Nettavisen in their competition with VG Nett.
>
> (Konow Lund and Puijk 2012:76)

Established journalists, in turn, looked down on them as untrained amateurs.

This newly emerging world of young journalists, unencumbered by old methods or notions of professionalism, provided news managements with a useful opportunity for changing news-gathering methods and cutting costs at the same time as they moved operations online. By exploiting the different approaches of the 'webby' journalists and the traditionalists, it was easy to redraw boundaries. A report by the International Federation of Journalists (Walters *et al.* 2006:4) found that laying-off experienced journalists in favour of younger, cheaper ones was widespread. Just as, at the high end (the autonomous pole), jobs were becoming more specialised, something different was happening at the commercial end. In publications that are less bound by journalistic traditions, clear boundaries between editorial and commercial material were blurring and there were real concerns that inexperienced journalists, isolated from legacy newsrooms and suspicious of norms developed on 'dead tree editions', were eroding the divisions between commerce and editorial to the detriment of independent journalism (Bærug and Harro-Loit 2011).

A new kind of news writing had started to emerge (Witschge and Nygren 2009, Phillips 2010b, Williams and Franklin 2007, Anderson 2011: 555) which was relatively low-skilled and required little more than sourcing three slightly different versions of the same story online, and putting together a version with a different introduction and some search-engine friendly key words. Younger journalists (often trainees) were employed to produce this, working with little supervision and very little training (Williams and Franklin 2007: 17). Professionalism, concern for ethics and a sense of public responsibility could be bracketed off as 'old school'. Younger journalists, keen to get themselves into established positions in media organizations, made useful tools for management keen to de-layer the workforce and reduce costs by offering redundancy to older workers.

One idea for cost reduction was the use of amateurs to fill up online news spaces. For some theorists, the new technologies had held out the hope of a more democratic journalism in which audiences would have a direct relationship with news providers, increase plurality and provide a countervailing force to commercialism (Gillmor 2006, Beckett 2008, Deuze 2007). Media managers, on the other hand, saw amateurs as a means of filling spaces for free and cutting staff, a view which is rather closer to the one imagined by Bourdieu and the Frankfurt school sociologists, who saw the audience in a commercial sense as a means of bringing in advertising dollars rather than a source of greater democratic empowerment.

Journalists were, not surprisingly, unhappy about this development. Audience interaction seemed to offer little. They did not want to be tied to their desks processing copy sent in by amateurs; they wanted the independence that journalism had promised and they felt that amateur work was decreasing the value of the product they produced. As one editor put it when discussing the new amateur contributors: 'they think they can all be journalists, you know, and they can't – it's dire. Now I wouldn't put it in a newspaper. So why, just because I can, should I put this crap into the website?' (Lee-Wright 2012: 33).

Print journalists found that they were working harder and longer with less time to investigate and check facts. Rather than making journalism more highly skilled, the move online was, in many instances, making it less so (Witschge and Nygren 2009, Phillips 2012a, Deuze and Fortunati 2011: 118). The professional group perhaps most damaged by the use of amateur material has been the photographers. Where most newspapers used to employ a number of photographers, today there are few jobs left. In May 2013, for example, the *Chicago-Sun Times* laid off all its photographers. Much of their work is now covered by a combination of freelance and contract workers, easily accessed web-libraries, beat journalists equipped with smart phones and amateurs (Press Association 2013).

Some scholars have criticized what they see as journalists' refusal to 'democratise the process of journalism' and to embrace the 'citizen' as a partner as a bid by journalists to create false 'distinctions' in order to maintain the power to define their field (Hermida 2011). However, journalists are understandably concerned for their jobs, the quality of their work and for the quality of the product (Örnebring 2013). According to a Pew Center, State of the Media report (2009):

> Those journalists surveyed, who come largely from websites linked to legacy media, also believe the Web is changing the fundamental values of the journalism – mostly for the worse. In particular, they are worried about declining accuracy, in part due to the emphasis online that news organizations are putting on speed and breaking news.

Analytics take charge

While multi-skilling and audience interaction have been the changes most discussed amongst journalists and scholars, analytics and big data are arguably having a far greater affect on news production (MacGregor 2007, Anderson 2011). Analytics are now capable of discovering, in real time, exactly what readers are clicking on. It is possible to chase Google clicks simply by moving key words up into the headline or introductory paragraph of a story. Christopher Anderson, researching the use of audience analytics in Philadelphia, found that editors were making major editorial decisions on the basis of audience traffic numbers (Anderson 2011: 559) This new link with the audience means that journalists on the most commercially oriented newspapers and websites can serve up exactly what audiences seem to want just by watching which words are being searched for and producing stories relating to those words. The immediate result was a big increase in the numbers of stories that could somehow be linked to celebrities or to sex – the two subjects that are most searched for on Google. This in turn increased the number of readers who could be 'sold' to the advertisers to increase online ad-spend. Anderson found that the 'click culture' was changing the way the (mostly young) journalists thought about news.

> We're trying to be a real strong local news site that appeals to our audience and gets traffic. You just sort of get used to knowing what kind of news gets clicked. A story about the Middle East, a national story – no. We're trying to pick out strong local stories or strong state stories that we know will appeal to our readership. We're a news site, but we don't feel tied to the definition of news, as in breaking news. As far as the spotlight versus the biggie goes, it's intuitive, but we just put about anything we think will get clicked up there at this point. You just have a gut feeling about it. Like for an article about Michelle Obama: your gut instinct is that it's not going to get picked up, but if it's getting clicked we'll bump it up.
>
> (Anderson 2011: 562)

The rush for 'clicks' was in part at least a response to growing panic as profits drained away. Philadelphia Media Holdings (where Anderson did this research) filed for bankruptcy in 2009. Clearly the rush for popularity had not been enough to reverse the drift of advertising away from news (Associated Press 2012). But the need to shore up share-holder profits was not just affecting the American regional press. The International Federation of Journalists report (Walters *et al.* 2006: 4) found that the growing insecurity of journalism jobs was having an effect on editorial quality across the board. The main issues raised by the respondents were:

- insecurity of employment leads to timid reporting;
- employment changes dictate a decline in critical and investigative reporting;
- media concentration and government pressure lead to bland news;
- media have been tamed by advertisers and governments;
- low wages lead to a decline in ethical reporting.

Richard Peppiatt, a UK tabloid reporter who resigned rather than continue to work on at the *Daily Star*, a highly commercial British tabloid newspaper, said of his work:

Editorial decisions are dictated more from the accounts and advertising departments than the newsroom floor. The net effect of this is that stories which sell well (e.g. about Katie Price) had to be sourced on a daily basis whether there was a tale to tell or not. This naturally led to fabrication in order to fulfil an unrealistic quota. Much more insidious was when this same philosophy was applied to stories involving Muslims and immigrants, when yet again a top down pressure to unearth stories which fitted within a certain narrative (immigrants are taking over, Muslims are a threat to security) led to casual and systemic distortion.

(Peppiatt 2011)

Used in defence of good journalism, technical innovation has a great deal to offer, but when technical innovation is used not for editorial innovation but for de-skilling young journalists and undermining their integrity, it needs to be questioned. There is no challenge to be found in re-writing what others have written and there is no future in trying to find ways of replacing journalists with automatic computer-driven content harvesters (Hollander 2013). Data is, by definition, the imprint of past behaviour. It takes imagination and intellect to use it to go somewhere new.

Journalism and social change

Journalism has always had the dual (and contradictory) roles of reproducing the status quo while at the same time facilitating social change and it is in this interest in social change that autonomous journalism finds a way back in. New ideas may be treated derisively at first but, once they gather enough interest, they are rarely ignored because there is a constant tension in journalism between the maintenance of the status quo and the drive for novelty. Added to this built-in tension is the fact that journalism tends to be a young profession and young people are concerned with differentiating themselves and with re-defining the way in which society sees itself (Bourdieu 1990: 135). They can do this either by working from the outside, establishing their own organizations and generating their own media, or by joining the establishment and waiting until they are sufficiently powerful to make changes – but by that time they may have absorbed the doxa of the organization and simply end up re-producing the status quo (Bourdieu 1988: 128).

Working from the outside is usually precarious. Individually the pamphlets, publications and blogs produced by new thinkers appear puny compared to the power of the established news organizations. They are usually run by unpaid or very low-paid workers and have small audiences but they have the autonomy that is only available to those who have nothing to lose: no job, mortgage or pension. The emergence of Midia Ninja in Brazil is an example of the way in which people organize outside the mainstream in what has been described as 'subaltern public spheres' (Fraser 1992) and produce material that is then spread by orthodox news producers and becomes part of a wider debate.

Midia Ninja is an offshoot of an organization that promotes music. Most of its journalists are unpaid and have very basic training. They make their mark by getting material that is not accessible to the big broadcasters but then they work with 'big' media in order to take advantage of their wider influence and network. In July 2013, some of their footage was used by Rede Globo, Brazil's largest TV network. The Midia Ninja Facebook page jumped overnight from 2,000 to 160,000 fans (Spuldar 2013). The Internet also provides the valuable additional service of giving a platform to radical thinkers (Pussy Riot in Russia, Ai Weiwei in China) who may be silenced in their country of origin, but pose no apparent threat to the status quo in the countries where their activities are reported. By offering them a platform and amplifying their activities, global media organizations then help them to blast their messages back to the dissidents in their own countries.

This is not to suggest a revolutionary role for global news organizations. The circulation of ideas from the periphery to the centre is not new, it is simply the means by which news media renew themselves. Some individuals working in these alternative publications find that they are 'shouting into the abyss'. Others very quickly accumulate 'cultural capital' and media organizations, thirsting for novelty, appropriate the most articulate communicators among them so that, for a short time at least, they are able to create a cultural bridge across which new ideas flow into the mainstream (Phillips 2007a). For some this 'bridging work' is a means to a political end, for others it is an opportunity for self-promotion.

Looking back at the alternative media of the late 1960s and 1970s it is not hard to track the way in which new social movements, using their own media, propelled different ideas about women and gay people into the mainstream. UK feminist magazine *Spare Rib* was published for more than 20 years and *Gay News* lasted for 11 years. But on the whole, the determined autonomy of such publications is unlikely to be compatible with 'popularity', which means they are unable to gather audiences big enough to pay reasonable wages. They blaze and then burn out, but their influence, taken together, is considerable.

Such complete autonomy of thought and action is not reproducible in large news organizations with hierarchies, legal constraints and shareholders. Nor would it provide the daily diet of news that is necessary to provide citizens with the information they require. For journalism to function at a level where it is providing a service to democracy, it needs both the operating scale of an organization that can pay decent wages and also the level of autonomy that will allow journalists to make decisions that are not solely based on the number of 'clicks' earned by a story and the number of stories churned out per day. So next we will review some of the ways in which autonomy can be enhanced.

Autonomy, professionalism and statutory protection

As Bourdieu (2005: 43) points out: 'precarity of employment is a loss of liberty, through which censorship and the effect of economic constraints can more easily be expressed'. In other words, people who fear that they will be sacked, or will never get a job, are inclined to do what they are told, rather than risk losing their jobs. In order to protect independent journalism it is therefore necessary to try and create the circumstances in which the autonomy of journalists is protected.

Attempts at professionalization have been used as a form of protection from editorial interference, and a means of shoring up the autonomy of journalists, particularly in the USA where, in spite of the commercialization of the media, journalists are considerably less likely to report editorial interference in their work than in the UK (Donsbach and Patterson 1992). However the rapidly deteriorating commercial situation for news media is almost certainly eroding that autonomy (see Chapters 2 and 6). There are those, such as the Project for Excellence in Journalism, who see professionalization as the way of shoring up standards but, without the means to create the tightly drawn legal boundaries that protect other professions, journalists' assertions of professionalism and declarations of standards (Kovach and Rosenstiel 2007) can only provide a benchmark of what journalism can be; it does little to assist individual journalists who find that commercial constraints make it difficult to live up to those standards. It is noteworthy that in the USA it is the freedom of publishers that is written into the First Amendment, not the freedom of journalists.

The literature on what constitutes a profession is extensive but Örnebring (2013) suggests that two key areas are specialist knowledge and organizational boundaries. Certainly journalists are increasingly required to attain a high level of training, to be familiar with a wide range of software, with image use and with data, in order to get employment in a highly competitive job market. The majority now have degrees – though these are not necessarily degrees in journalism (Weaver 2005, Stephenson and Mory 1990) and (in the UK) over 50 per cent have further training (Skillset 2001). This tends to back up the suggestion that journalism is 'professionalizing'.

However, although it is clearly a practical necessity for any well-run news organization in this fast-changing field to employ a core of trained staff, training is not usually compulsory and there is also a contradictory trend towards de-skilling (see above) as work is routinized and more amateur material is used to fill news space (Lee-Wright and Phillips 2012). Indeed there is little to prevent individuals from setting out their stalls and simply declaring themselves to be journalists. Some would argue that there is no longer any need for a separate group of people known as journalists at all, because now everyone can find information without the help of mediators (Gillmor 2006). Against this contradictory background it is hard to identify a specific body of knowledge that a journalist needs, any more than we can identify a specific body of knowledge that a novelist needs. Journalism is a process; it requires time and the application of skills rather than a remembered set of texts (Örnebring 2013).

Some suggest that licensing could be a way of defining boundaries and protecting professional practice. Apprenticeships, qualifications and other forms of licensing are already used to control entry in some countries (Weaver 1998), but licensing those who can speak is a dangerous tool because it could be used to prevent access to media channels for those who challenge the status-quo (Örnebring 2013). This was certainly the case, for example, in Brazil, where licensing was established by the military rulers in 1969 (Albuquerque 2012: 83). It could also allow editors to hold individual journalists responsible for upholding ethical standards, rather than taking corporate responsibility for the content of their publications.[3]

Professional membership organizations are more likely to be effective in both protecting freedom of speech and establishing professional norms (Weaver 2005: 48). In Northern Europe, trades unions have been sufficiently powerful to protect against some of the excesses that have been seen in the UK and have been directly involved with debates on ethics, professional standards and the formation of press councils. In the UK, their effectiveness has been undermined by casualization, economic insecurity and the lack of statutory rights for people who wish to join trade unions. In a six-country study (Donsbach and Patterson 1992), 22 per cent of UK journalists said that they had been pressured by management to change work and in Italy the number was even higher. In the same study, German and Swedish journalists were the least likely to report that they had been pressured by an editor to change work.

There are also other ways of improving the autonomy of journalism that don't depend on dividing it off or making it difficult for people to 'do journalism' but they require the involvement of those who are outside as well as those who are inside the profession. If we take the conditions of autonomy to be freedom from direct commercial or political constraints then the only way that journalists will be free to represent people rather than power is if they can be assured of some degree of editorial independence from the influence of the companies that own them as they are to some extent in the subsidised press of Norway and the Netherlands (Hallin and Mancini 2004: 174). The principle of editorial independence is enshrined in the European Press Freedom Charter, which acknowledges that freedom from commercial pressure is just as important as freedom from pressure from the state. Article 6 states:

> The economic livelihood of the media must not be endangered by the state or by state-controlled institutions. The threat of economic sanctions is also unacceptable. Private-sector companies must respect the journalistic freedom of the media. They shall neither exert pressure on journalistic content nor attempt to mix commercial content with journalistic content.

In a world in which the freedom of markets is upheld as a social good, this aspect of press freedom gets insufficient attention. However if journalists are to be free to make ethical judgements in their own work then they must also be free of editorial interference by their proprietors. Legislation and regulation to limit the operation of the market has already been successful in a number of ways. It has, among other things:

- limited the incursion of advertising in the guise of editorial (although these boundaries are now clearly under threat and legislation needs strengthening);
- created some ethical boundaries, for example limiting hate speech;
- attempted (rather unsuccessfully in most countries) to prevent the formation of oligopolies and monopolies;
- allowed the creation of public service media that raise the standard and create a quality benchmark across the board.

Regulation can create a fairer field for journalism to operate within. It can ensure greater diversity of opinions and limit the level of populism. Unfortunately, it is under threat across the democratic world, as the rhetoric of free choice and the supposed abundance of news sources create a wave of enthusiasm for de-regulation, even though, as Chapters 2 and 6 demonstrate, much of this apparent abundance turns out to be just more of the same. Nevertheless, if journalists are to be able to operate with a level of autonomy from the market as well as the state, they will continue to need frameworks that are specifically aimed at protecting them.

Notes

1 Ex-Prime Minister John Major made clear in evidence to the Leveson Inquiry that he had been asked directly, by Rupert Murdoch, to change British policy on Europe and was told that the Murdoch press would not otherwise support him. The video of John Major giving evidence to the Leveson Inquiry can be viewed on YouTube at www.youtube.com/watch?v=qLQxz9WFZGA (accessed 8 December 2013).
2 Operation Elvedon was a police enquiry launched in the UK in 2011 into payments for information made by journalists to police officers. Source: police press statement, available at http://content.met.police.uk/News/Statement-from-Commissioner/1260 269177528/1257246741786 (accessed 8 December 2013).
3 The idea was floated by the editor of the conservative leaning *Daily Mail* in evidence to the UK Leveson Inquiry 2011–12 but it was rejected.

Chapter 5

Audiences, networks, interaction

This chapter looks at how audiences use, re-use, and interact with journalism. Much has been made of the audience's new power and the ways in which it will change journalism. We have considered this also in Chapter 4 'The Making of Journalists' and Chapter 3 'Journalists and their Sources', but here we examine the audience on its own terms. We will question some recent research which looks at the 'active audience', asking just how much the journalism/audience relationship has really changed – and whether technology has merely allowed us to redraw the boundaries around essentially the same divide.

The theoretical debate around journalism audiences follows roughly the same contours as other discussions in the field. Some researchers regard audiences as groups of concerned citizens involved to a greater or lesser degree in the governance of their country; others recognize that they may also be excluded or included according to their class position and relation to power. Some see audiences largely as commercial entities to be traded to advertisers, whereas opponents regard them as active and conscious consumers of cultural products. Each researcher then makes judgements about the audience for journalism within the context of these assumptions.

The view of citizens engaged (albeit imperfectly) with the political system has become an idealized reference point for liberal theories of journalism stretching back to the Enlightenment. In this view, audiences in a democracy are (or should be) free to choose between a diversity of different news sources, and, as rational, deliberating people, make up their minds about matters of public interest. Much of the public debate about the health of the news media in a democracy therefore revolves around the question of news diversity: do citizens actually have access to a number of different sources or do a small cabal of interest groups control the flow of information? Where information is controlled by the state or by other interests, the argument goes, it is difficult to come to a rational decision about the best course of action. Uninformed people do not make good judgements, either about their own personal lives or the governance of their country.

For Marxist theorists, this idea was hopelessly flawed because information is always controlled by those who have power. From this perspective, the audience of mass media is not so much a collection of rational individuals as a mass of eyeballs and eardrums, which are bought and sold by multinational conglomerates either for material or political gain. The possibility of a plural media and an informed electorate is fatally undermined by the grip of elites on the machinery that produces and disseminates information (see Chapter 2 for more on these arguments).

Theodore Adorno, a Marxist of the Frankfurt School, saw journalism as merely a part of the 'culture industry' in which undifferentiated audiences blindly follow the siren call of populism. In his essay 'Culture Industry Reconsidered', he condemns audiences for their passivity as surely as he condemns the industry for its manipulation. 'The concoctions of the culture industry are neither guides for a blissful life, nor a new art of moral responsibility,' he writes, 'but rather exhortations to toe the line, behind which stand the most powerful interests. The consensus, which it propagates, strengthens blind, opaque authority' (Adorno 1961: 55).

Jürgen Habermas (also discussed in Chapter 2) is often called in aid to concepts of a democratic pluralist media, but he was almost as pessimistic as Adorno when he wrote *The Structural Transformation of the Public Sphere* (1989). He described an ideal public sphere as something like that which emerged in eighteenth-century England, when a space developed between the private sphere of the home and the realm of the state in which rational 'public' debate could take place. For Habermas, however, this was unattainable in our segmented and consumption-dominated modern world. Once ordinary people are unable to interact directly in order to form public opinion, they cede their power to interest groups who rule in their name. The news media, which ought to facilitate such discussion at scale, was also, in his opinion, too caught up with serving these interest groups to enable adequate public debate.

Habermas was attacked both for his idealization of a society that excluded women and minority groups and for his assumption that all meaningful debate must happen in a single public sphere representing all interests (Fraser 1992, Benhabib 1992). His critics argued that democratic debate happens not only within recognized institutions but also in what Nancy Fraser refers to as 'subaltern' public spheres. Indeed these scholars say that assuming the supremacy of a single (exclusive) public sphere is by definition 'hegemonic'; such a centralized form of power could only ever be interested in reproducing power relations rather than challenging them.

Habermas moderated his arguments in response to these debates, and his older model gave way to a more benign view of informed democratic discussion which works via 'influence' (Habermas 1994: 8). 'Informal public opinion-formation,' he wrote, 'generates "influence"; influence is transformed into "communicative power" through the channels of political elections; and communicative power is again transformed into "administrative power" through legislation.' In this writing, he saw the news media as an important means of both formulating and transmitting public opinion, exercising 'communicative power' which in turn informs law-making. This opens up a role for an informed audience that is capable of transmitting influence, but it doesn't entirely deal with the problem of power. In order to influence, it is necessary to be heard. We will discuss below the degree to which minority voices, rather than constituting only a rather passive audience, can be amplified to the point where they are indeed heard in the corridors of power.

The power of oppositional reading

Cultural theorists have developed this debate in a different direction. John Fiske (1992), building on the Marxist view of journalism and power, arrives at a radically different view of the audience either from Adorno, Habermas, or his detractors (see Chapter 2). Fiske does not depart from the idea that news media is controlled by and reflective of the interests of power, but he does see audiences quite differently. In his interpretation, they also have power: not the rational communicative kind suggested by Habermas and Fraser but an oppositional power either to reject the messages that are beamed out at them or to make their own messages by repurposing the material made available through the mass media.

Fiske and Michel de Certeau (1984) are among a number of cultural theorists who, building on and departing from the work of Antonio Gramsci, Michel Foucault and Mikhail Bakhtin, began to see how people who had no direct power in society found ways of expressing it through resistance. Gramsci was writing in the 1920s and 1930s during the rise of fascism in Italy, and he developed his theory of 'Cultural Hegemony' to understand how those with power can 'seduce' people into consenting to be ruled by convincing them that their interests lie with those of their masters. But he saw also that the maintenance of cultural hegemony required vigilance: 'It has continually to be renewed, recreated, defended, and modified. It is also continually resisted, limited, altered, challenged by pressures not at all its own' (Williams 1977: 112).

Foucault was likewise interested in the instability of power – how it is exercised throughout society, not just from the top down (Foucault 1981), and how it is kept in place by cultural systems that order the way we think and behave. Media, and in particular the news media, help to circulate the meanings through which power is both defined and upheld. For Foucault, those who have power determine meaning, and therefore the way in which events will be interpreted.

De Certeau, however, writes of readers as 'poachers' and sees reading as: 'games played with the text'; readers, he says, borrow ideas and then co-opt them for their own ends (1984: 175). Fiske takes a similar view, regarding serious news journalism as a means of reproducing power relationships ('alliances formed by the power-bloc in white patriarchal societies'). Popular culture, on the other hand, can be more easily poached and then transformed:

> [P]opular culture is made by the people out of the products of mass media – it is not imposed on them by the media and their power-bloc allegiance.

The news that people want, make and circulate among themselves may differ widely from that which the power-bloc want them to have.

(Fiske 1992: 46)

The popular press, with its sensationalism and half-truths, is for Fiske less oppressive to ordinary people because it is less likely to be believed:

The last thing tabloid journalism produces is a believing subject. One of its most characteristic tones of voice is that of sceptical laughter which offers the pleasure of disbelief, the pleasures of not being taken in. This popular pleasure of 'seeing through' them ... is the historical result of centuries of subordination which the people have not allowed to develop into subjection.

(Fiske 1992: 46)

While Adorno has been accused of writing off the mass of people for not appreciating elite cultural products, De Certeau and Fiske can be criticized for their apparent assumption that 'the people' can simply overturn power through laughter – without needing to understand the nuances of what they are laughing at (Sparks 1992, Bird 2003). Nevertheless, both have useful things to say that should be kept in mind as we move further into this chapter. Fiske reminds us that the audience is not a 'passive lump' and that audiences create their own meanings, which are often very far from those intended by the author. Nor have Adorno's concerns about media power become any less important. Not for him the belief that the people, given a repertoire of 'choices', can simply select from what capitalism makes available and, by re-inventing them, mixing them together, or subtly transforming them, assert their own power. Indeed, his view can be summed up usefully in this sentence: 'The customer is not king, as the culture industry would have us believe, not its subject but its object' (Adorno 1961: 55).

This view of the industry as a process by which audiences are sold to make profits for media companies has even more relevance today. While much has been made of the counter-cultural potential of 'pro-sumers', who use a plethora of online tools to mash up and play with an unlimited supply of cultural products, some are beginning to question who is really running the online playground and for what purpose? Mark Andrejevic (2007) considers the way feed-back mechanisms, that appear to liberate the consumer, are harnessed as a form of surveillance by companies targeting us for their own purposes. Sometimes the targeting is organized on behalf of the state. We know, for example, that social media companies have been collaborating with security services (MacAskill 2013). Usually we are targeted to sell products. In a line attributed to Metafilter user Andrew Lewis (aka blue_beetle): 'If you're not paying for it, you're not the customer; you're the product being sold' (Lewis 2010).

These positions are the 'poles' in any debate about power and the media, and we will return to them as we debate the position of the audience in the digital age.

The thinking audience

At around the time that Adorno was formulating his concerns about the effects of the culture industry on the minds of the masses, sociologist Paul Lazarsfeld was investigating the relationship between audience and media by interviewing 600 people every month for seven months in the run-up to the 1940 US general elections. He did not find a direct relationship between publication of information and decision-making. On the contrary, he discovered that messages were taken up, interpreted, and circulated by influential people within communities, and that this personal and direct influence was far more potent than anything journalists could accomplish by themselves (Lazarsfeld *et al.*, 1948).

In 1973, Stuart Hall produced a paper that started to put together the theoretical Marxist view of media effects with the findings of Lazarsfeld and asked why audiences were not directly affected by the messages being beamed out to them. He concluded: 'if no "meaning" is taken, then there can be no "consumption"'. In other words, the successful transmission of a message lies as much in the way it is received as in the way it is broadcast. At a stroke, the audience takes on a new position within the circulation of information. Hall called the two ends of the process 'encoding' and 'decoding', and opened up a whole new strand of research into the way in which audiences use information (Hall 1973).

Hall was interested in the gap between producer and receiver as a site of 'resistance'. He recognized that there was slippage between what the author intended to say and the way in which those messages were read, but he was also aware that the greater power usually lay on the side of the sender. When producers set out to communicate they try to limit misinterpretation by the way they 'encode' the initial message. Hall refers to this as the 'dominant' or 'hegemonic' message. As we learned in Chapter 1 on news values, the attempt to limit misinterpretation includes simplifying news stories so that there is little ambiguity, ordering material so that the most important facts (as seen by the producer) are given prominence, and choosing stories that are 'culturally familiar'. This ordering allows the producer to encode a preferred meaning which will help the audience to interpret it in the way that the author intended.

But the audience doesn't always oblige. David Morley's research on *The Nationwide Audience* (1980) discovered that readers' cultural background and experience was critical to the way in which material was received. The dominant (or hegemonic) reading might be strongly encoded, but that did not mean that the same message was decoded. Much depends on the existing knowledge and cultural position of the audience. Some audience members may 'negotiate' their understanding – accepting part of what has been offered but questioning it where it conflicts with their own knowledge. Other groups entirely rejected the messages offered, bringing their own 'oppositional' readings to bear on the subject. Following Morley, a number of researchers (Liebes and Katz 1990, Gillespie 2003) looked at different audience groups and discovered that gender, race, and sexual orientation also coloured the way in which audiences understand messages.

Audiences use material in ways that are quite different from that intended by the author. Fiske sees in this refusal to conform to hegemonic readings the possibility of rebellion. He refers to 'knowledge gangsters' who steal information and rearticulate it so that it tells a different story (Fiske 1996: 191–92). Such rebellious interpretations have been aided by the massive increase in available information since Fiske wrote this text (as evidenced by the increase in websites devoted to a variety of conspiracy theories). Digital technologies have clearly increased the possibility for audiences not only to 'steal' information but also to post their own interpretations of events for everyone to see. John Stuart Mill (see Chapter 2) would have been amazed to see the range of arguments about 'important truths' that can be found online at the touch of a mouse.

Clearly the ability to argue and transmit dissenting views can unsettle the status quo. However, as we shall see, the news media have a variety of ways of dealing with unsettling incursions from the fringe: they can ignore them, they can denounce them, and they can co-opt them.

When audiences speak back

John B. Thompson, writing in 1995, claimed it a condition of mass communication that:

> the flow of messages is a *structured* flow in which the capacity of recipients to intervene in or contribute to the process of production is strictly circumscribed … The personnel involved in producing and transmitting media messages are generally deprived of the direct and continuous forms of feedback characteristic of face-to-face interaction.
>
> (Thompson 1995: 29)

It is this one-way traffic that has given mass media its hegemonic power. But in fact there has never been a time (as Fiske demonstrated) when mass media audiences have been completely silent. A minority have always wanted to engage: through tip-offs, vox pops and interviews, or more directly through letters to the editor or advice columnists. Indeed, it is the 'Agony' column that provides the best early examples of both oppositional readings and interactivity. Where letters to the editor tend to be declamatory – a demand to be heard rather than a desire for interaction – letters to the advice columnists demand an answer.

The earliest advice columns were written in the late seventeenth century in the *Athenian Gazette* (Kent 1979: 3). Three hundred years later, in the 1960s and 1970s, advice columnist Marjorie Proops was the most widely read writer on the mass-market British newspaper the *Daily Mirror* (Patmore 1993: 314). She was far better known than her male peers on the comment pages and was one of the first journalists to appear on posters advertising the newspaper she wrote for. Arguably this impulse to share and compare personal information provides mass-market tabloid journalism with its *raison d'être*. It often descends into sensationalism and populism; at its worst, it is responsible for breaches of privacy and persecution of individuals (as the Leveson Inquiry of 2011–13 attested). At its best, however, it can be liberating. Feminists in the 1970s coined the phrase 'the personal is political' to denote the fact that so much of what held women back was designated as 'personal' and therefore outside the reach of politics. Part of the potency of second wave feminism lay precisely in its refusal to keep silent about things that were supposed to happen behind closed doors.

Of course, in writing to an advice columnist the reader is appealing to the authority of the author/auntie. That author has the power to determine what is put into the public domain. Yet in a study of advice columns between the 1970s and 2003 (Phillips 2008), it became clear that the columnists were being directly influenced by their readers – who were speaking out about such things as rape, sexual harassment, domestic violence, unwanted pregnancy, and sexual orientation – and allowing space on their pages for the direct voices of women speaking for themselves.

The agony columnists were to some extent sheltered by the fact that they were not considered editorially important. They wrote 'stuff for women' and it was that very invisibility that allowed them to open up an almost subversive relationship with their audience. They became: 'The lightning conductors of social unease. They listen to what has been unsayable, and in listening and then re-producing these forbidden discourses, they bring them into the realm of the "normal" and sayable' (ibid: 97). These columnists (with the exception of Marjorie Proops) had very little power, but, even as the front pages were 'outing' prominent people for their sexual behaviour, the back pages were reassuring ordinary readers that such behaviour was normal and acceptable. Given the popularity of these pages, readers were regularly being offered very differing accounts of changing social mores from which to construct their own positions.

The TV equivalent, the talk show, started in the same vein: daytime programming for stay-at-home women where it was possible to talk about matters that would rarely be discussed in the corridors of power. The popularity of these pages and this programming did not go unnoticed. Very soon whole magazines were being published devoted to the first-person narratives of people who had rarely found their lives depicted in the pages of serious newspapers. The *Guardian* and the *Washington Post* may have talked about the working classes, but the pages of *Take a Break* or *Chat* were filled with the voices of working-class women, apparently speaking for themselves, though actually ventriloquized by skilled journalists.

While it would be a leap to suggest that the 'agony aunts' or women's weeklies directly affected the political status quo, they were certainly capable of translating what they heard into a form of influence which fed back into public attitudes. The sheer popularity of these forms of journalism ensured that new ideas about sexuality and gender were being widely circulated at a time when British social attutudes were changing very rapidly. The agony aunts and their relationship with the audiences may not have changed the public discourse on their own, but they were certainly part of the process.

Once it was clear that there was money to be made from the stories of ordinary people, these formats very quickly moved on from an extended kitchen table discussion, into a form of manipulated 'reality' in which personal agony was served up as entertainment and the audience provided only a disempowered backdrop to a manipulated drama (Shattuc 1997). This act of co-option also took place in magazines, and, where once stories found their place on the pages because their storylines seemed universal, they were gradually replaced by ever more manipulated, sensationalized stories about ever more glamorized subjects.

With the advent of the Internet, some of these negotiated and oppositional readings moved from the cultural space of the 'water cooler', or the curated space of the agony columns and editors' letters, into online venues. Forums sprang up to debate matters of common interest and comment spaces were opened up beneath (some) articles. To begin with, comments were usually provided on the same principle as letters to the editor – the assumption being that people will comment on what has been presented to them. It took a decade before it occurred to those writing the code that people might also want to talk to one another – and then to make the comment thread more of a conversation than an act of 'doffing the cap' to the author.

Research indicates that much of what is written 'below the line' is ignored by the news organization and also by readers (Wardle and Williams 2008). Occasionally, however, an oppositional reading online hits a nerve so hard that editorial intervention is attempted in an effort to restore the original, hegemonic reading. For example, when UK *Grazia* magazine produced a sneering article about feminism in October 2012, it was roundly attacked both on Twitter and in its online comments. A week later, on returning to copy the comments, all the links from feminist websites to the original article were broken. A newer and slightly less aggressive version of the article was posted in its place, followed by a slightly less angry set of comments including this one:

> The only thing relevant about this un-referenced re-hash is that a vibrant debate on feminism in the comments section has been deleted by Berlusconi's Grazia – A case in point for a media wash out on sexual equality.
>
> (Molphy 2012)

Grazia's editorial line, favouring a sexualized, gossipy, apolitical femininity, was not apparently changed by this incursion. But the fact that an exchange on the representation of feminism took place in its backyard – even for a few days – does suggest a new kind of poaching, in which minority audiences can move inside the territory of powerful media organizations and make use of their platforms to spread messages of a rather different kind. It suggests also, however, that this power will be circumscribed and heavily policed.

Audiences as co-creators

While comments and letters to the editor or advice columnists do provide an opportunity to 'talk back', many people saw the advent of the Internet as an opportunity for something rather more profound, in which the difference between audience and journalist started to disappear. Jay Rosen (2006) famously started referring to 'The People Formerly Known as the Audience' (TPFKATA), suggesting that audiences would change the way in which news was produced and consumed. Some saw this as a genuine move towards a far more open public sphere in which a multitude of voices would be heard, while others saw it more as a tactic of resistance – a means of destabilizing the power of the media companies. In the writing of Clay Shirky (2008), these are united: resistance by legacy media to the new networked 'everybody' is just institutional foot-dragging by dinosaurs.

In their 2006 book *Wikinomics*, Don Tapscott and Anthony D. Williams reintroduced the word 'Prosumer' (originally coined by Alvin Toffler in 1980) to discuss the idea of an active audience that creates, modifies, and participates in products online. They were not looking specifically at news but at the possibilities for co-creation in industry and entertainment. Henry Jenkins (2008) soon followed up with *Convergence Culture*, which looked mainly at fan behaviour online, but spoke of the web as 'a site of consumer participation' (Jenkins 2008: 137) allowing for deliberative networks of engaged consumers.

The same year, Shirky wrote in *Here Comes Everybody*: 'Individual weblogs are not merely alternate sites for publishing; they are alternatives to publishing itself' (2008: 66). But while any improvements in media diversity are welcome, it would be wrong to confuse the rise of successful blogs with a change in audience behaviour. The blognescenti created the assumption that anyone could start a blog and everyone was equally likely to be noticed. In fact the majority of successful bloggers are (still) male and well connected (Trammell and Keshelashvili 2005). In the early days, innovation and good connections were enough to stand out and draw followers. Jeff Jarvis, Andrew Sullivan, Guido Fawkes (in the UK), The Drudge Report, Mashable, BuzzMachine, The Huffington Post and Popbitch (the last two run by women) all came to notice because they featured individuals who were clearly well informed and stood out in a relatively small pond.

Just as the early bloggers generated massive press interest and a considerable audience, the new generation of what the *Guardian* dubs 'YouTubers' are being heralded as harbingers of the end of TV as we know it. In 2013, 1,000 of these 'vloggers' worldwide earned upwards of €100,000 per annum. Most of them are young men whose vlogs are being viewed by young women (Lewis 2013: 10). Some of them will, like their blogging counterparts, go on to professional careers. Their entry into the market may have been different, but they are no more TPFKATA than any new entrant into a professional career. Most will make nothing at all because advertising rates online are so low.

Today it is far more difficult to get noticed as an individual blogger than it was when the A-listers got started. If you Google 'style blogs', you get 2.5 million possibilities; if you check for 'technology blogs' you will be offered two billion (8 April 2013). Rosen (2006) cannot see a problem in 'too many speakers', and writes that: 'A highly centralized media system had connected people "up" to big social agencies and centers of power but not "across" to each other. Now the horizontal flow, citizen-to-citizen, is as real and consequential as the vertical one.'

As the number of entrants rises exponentially, however, only those who are most adept at using social media, most socially connected in 'real life', or already taken up by bigger media organizations are likely to stand out. Clearly, the ability to broadcast does not in itself ensure that there is an audience to broadcast to: if everyone shouts at once then nobody gets heard. The result is that now, in order to get any real traction, new online voices have to be backed by established news organizations, local or national campaigns, political parties, or PR agencies. In style blogging there is an additional factor. In an interview, fashion editor Frances Davison said: 'Disposable income is completely paramount in maintaining the high turnover of different items "needed" to post with regularity on a personal style blog and remain current or on trend.'[1]

So is any of this really about greater audience power? Alternative voices have always started at the fringe and then moved into the mainstream. Fawkes, a UK political blogger, is an irreverent voice, but not more so than the UK print publication *Private Eye*, which started in the 1960s and has barely changed in 50 years. Both have found an audience – one offline and one online – and neither of them have established a different relationship with their audiences. Bloggers reserve the right to decide what comments they will publish and when and how they will respond to them. Ironically it is the *Eye* that is doing best commercially, with a circulation of over 200,000 and an annual profit of £210,000 (Dowell 2011).

Participant audiences

The ability of the Internet to provide new spaces for a different kind of journalism will be discussed further in Chapter 6 'The Business of Journalism in the Digital Age', but online tools have also opened up mainstream journalism to the potential of more direct audience participation in the delivery of professional news services. Where comment sections and forums provide the opportunity for playfulness and for 'poaching', some journalists (and researchers) see new opportunities for a more collaborative relationship with audience members, which could democratize news organizations from the inside:

> The emergence of the alternative news media in the last decade has challenged the controlling posture towards the public established by Lippmann.

Journalists today can no longer ignore networked communication – largely because it has transformed the role of the news audiences from a mostly passive to an active force.

(Russell 2011)

This 'networked journalism' is what Charlie Beckett describes in *Supermedia* (2008). He looks forward to a time when journalists will be:

Connecting with the world beyond the newsroom; listening to people; giving people a voice in the media; responding to what the public tells you in a dialogue. But it has the potential to go further than that in transforming the power relationship between media and the public and reformulating the means of journalistic production.

(Beckett 2008: 43)

Jeff Jarvis had a similar vision:

In networked journalism, the public can get involved in a story before it is reported, contributing facts, questions, and suggestions. The journalists can rely on the public to help report the story; we'll see more and more of that, I trust. The journalists can and should link to other work on the same story, to source material, and perhaps blog posts from the sources (see: Mark Cuban). After the story is published – online, in print, wherever – the public can continue to contribute corrections, questions, facts, and perspective … not to mention promotion via links. I hope this becomes a self-fulfilling prophecy as journalists realize that they are less the manufacturers of news than the moderators of conversations that get to the news.

(Jarvis 2006)

In South Korea, this reality started to come into being with the arrival of OhmyNews in 2000. The site ambushed the existing commercial media which had been established after press liberation in 1987. It not only made full use of the interactive possibilities of the Internet but also took a very different political line from the establishment media. Moreover, it had a completely different structure, involving some 70,000 citizen journalists who are paid a small fee for work that is published. In 2009, the site was attracting 2.5 million page views per day (Woyke 2009). An additional 'tipping' system allowed writers to be paid a supplement by readers who appreciated their work.

OhmyNews combines a core of paid reporters and editors with a constant feed of public contribution – very much as Jarvis envisaged. In 2011, 83 per cent of the citizen workforce was under 40 and a third were students. The professional journalists provide around 30 per cent of the content, and work with contributors to check and rewrite their copy as it comes in so that the final product looks professional and readable. Unlike other news organizations,

OhmyNews is democraticaly structured and editors have to publicly justify rejecting a story (Nguyen 2011: 195–209). Still, according to the editor, the majority of stories generated by amateurs are opinion or lifestyle (Joyce 2007). Hard news stories are almost all generated by full-time paid journalists.

Interest in the OhmyNews experiment was keen, not only because of its democratic structure. Media companies saw the possibility of cutting costs by introducing free labour into the very labour-intensive news business (Deuze and Fortunati 2011: 170). Indeed, the UK government's plan for the future of local television in the UK recommended the use of amateurs as a means of creating affordable local media (DCMS 2010). The problem faced by news organizations is that amateur copy and information from citizens is not actually as free as Deuze and Fortunati suggest (2011: 170); it takes time and professional labour to process because not much of it can be used unless the information is checked, corrected and shaped for public use.

Journalists (particularly on local newspapers) have always worked with reader tip-offs. In India, where local printed newspapers are surging in popularity, Ursula Rao (2010) demonstrates that local political organizations do not need electronic media in order to participate. They only need a receptive publisher. At the local level, competition for space is not so intense as it is in national news outlets and any reasonably well-organized activist can find a way of getting publicity. If the 'story' is good enough they may then engage national interest so the incentive for local politicians, or would-be politicians, to get their name in the local paper is high, with or without electronic means of making contact.

However mass access to the Internet has massively increased the amount of material that journalists in more wired cultures have to deal with and this has created problems. In 2008, the BBC employed 29 staff members just to monitor user generated content (UGC), and they dealt with 12,000 emails per day (Wardle and Williams 2008). The BBC is a large, publicly funded organization capable of dedicating a substantial staff team to this job. OhmyNews, on the other hand, struggles to survive because the job of producing news (as well as monitoring and supporting citizens) is extremely expensive (Joyce 2007). Its attempts to move into other countries have failed.

The sheer cost and difficulty of working with amateur newsgatherers has held back many others from plunging into a partnership with news-gathering citizens although there have been attempts in France and elsewhere to make this work (see Chapter 6). The Huffington Post uses unpaid amateurs, but operates more as a comment site than a news source; most of its news is repurposed or aggregated from other established organizations who can be relied upon to verify what they publish.

Virtually every example offered of audience participation in national news relates to a major breaking news story, where people who find themselves in the eye of the storm have used their mobile phones to witness events and then send them on to news organizations. The London bombings of 2005, in which four suicide bombers detonated several bombs on the London transport system during the morning rush hour, is often seen as the breakthrough moment for citizen journalism. The BBC and the *Guardian* opened up special areas for citizens on their websites, and by 10:15 am there were 1,300 independent blog posts on the subject. TV news was able to show amateur footage from inside the stations where no professional film crew could possibly have gone. It was in many ways a watershed moment in that it enabled acts of witnessing – which have always been key in any kind of live reporting – to be filmed and broadcast directly rather than being passed on in words (Allan 2006: 143–67).

The amateur footage and photographs were, of course, checked and edited by journalist 'gatekeepers' before publication. Where there are no gatekeepers, unchecked information, often no more than unsubstantiated rumour, pours out alongside verifiable facts, and it is even harder for people without time and resources to decide what to believe and what to discard. Crowdsourcing may be able to correct itself eventually, but often not before damage has been done: after the Boston bombings of 2013, events were widely reported on Twitter and then circulated on Reddit, and the storm of unverified speculation turned into a witch hunt for which Reddit was forced to apologize:

> [T]hough it started with noble intentions, some of the activity on reddit fueled online witch hunts and dangerous speculation which spiralled into very negative consequences for innocent parties. The reddit staff and the millions of people on reddit around the world deeply regret that this happened.
>
> (Hueypriest 2013)

One news organization that has taken on board the possibilities of interactivity has been the UK *Sun* but in this case it was not so much a question of the newspaper paying attention to its audience as seeing an opportunity to make use of its audience to extend its own power. The coverage related to the death of a child (known then as Baby P) who had been systematically abused by his parents when he died in August 2007. It was a tragic case and the *Sun*'s editor decided to hold the local director of children's services responsible. So she organised an online petition, which was duly signed by 1.4 million *Sun* readers, and then a demonstration calling for the director, Sharon Shoesmith, to be sacked. The government minister responsible at the time, Ed Balls, was so alarmed that he not only dismissed her but went further and stopped Shoesmith from claiming her pension. The ministerial decision has since been overturned by the courts, and the *Sun* has removed the famous petition from its website (Greenslade 2012), but the incident demonstrated that audience involvement is not necessarily spontaneous and that audiences can quite easily be manipulated.

So far the rhetoric of engagement has not had the expected effect on news coverage. Journalists dealing with a massive increase in incoming information, alongside increased workloads and lowered staffing levels (see Chapter 4), are often too pressured to embrace a new relationship with people they fear might be taking their jobs (Witschge and Nygren 2009). Indeed, research in 2008 into the work of journalists found that it was becoming harder for sources to make contact with them (Fenton 2010b, Phillips 2010a). Very few stories were being found online and few journalists paid much attention to the voices of their audiences. Many news stories did not (and still do not) even have comments enabled. Where journalists used the web, it was to track information from existing sources or to trace people using their personal details (Phillips 2010a). Research by Alfred Hermida corroborated this: 'Newsrooms struggled to handle the unsolicited emails, with a lot of the material getting lost' (2011: 620).

What audiences want

Mainstream news sites, afraid of being outpaced by Twitter, may be tempted to discard their own gatekeeping role and join in the speculation – as many of them did following the Boston bombings. But evidence suggests that this is not what audiences want: while they may pick up rumours on Twitter, they then turn to trusted sources for verification. Visualization of the tweets around the death of Bin Laden demonstrate that people using Twitter still search for authoritative sources – very often trusted journalists (Filloux 2011).

Journalists who have access to the means of authentication are starting to find a new place in the rumour mill of the Internet. In 2012, the singer Whitney Houston died. News of this was tweeted within half an hour of her death by a friend of one of the hotel staff. But people didn't believe the rumours, as this commentator points out:

> It's important to remember that while social media occasionally gets it right, it can't always be relied on for accurate news. If we believed every rumour that circulated on Twitter, then Bill Cosby has died more than four times. So obviously, we need the *real* news teams to come in and confirm or quash whatever rumour happens to be viral at the time.
>
> (Big Foot Digital 2012)

Hermida suggests that journalists and news organizations are 'reluctant to let audiences set the news agenda' (2011: 620). Fear of litigation and concern about errors – or even attempts at manipulation – are good reasons why news organizations might be reluctant to cede power to their audiences. Even OhmyNews, which is committed to helping citizens report news, often has to send trained journalists to re-interview witnesses, just to ensure that a report can be verified (Joyce 2007: 7). But another reason is that there seems little evidence the audience actually wants to set the news agenda.

Swedish research (Larsson 2011) looked at the characteristics of web users and divided them into five groups: the Bystander, the Prosumer, the Lurker, the Filter and the Critic. Lurkers and Bystanders are fairly passive consumers of material online. Only the Prosumer and the Critic (predominantly male) actively engage online, while Filters (predominantly female) are primarily engaged in passing information on to others. Applying this research to quantitative studies of news consumers is instructive. A US study found that while 37 per cent of users had 'contributed to the creation of news', their involvement was mostly indirect: 25 per cent were 'Critics', they had commented on a news story. Filters were also pretty active: 17 per cent have posted a link on a social networking site; 11 per cent have tagged content; 3 per cent have tweeted about news. Of the total user base, only 9 per cent could be described as Prosumers who have created their own original news material or opinion piece (Purcell *et al.* 2010).

The US numbers are higher than those found in most other countries. Research into UK behaviour for the Reuters institute (Newman 2012) found that only 25 per cent engage with news online, and they are half as likely to comment as their peers in the USA. The most interactive country is Brazil, where around 37 per cent comment on news stories via social media in an average week and 44 per cent are likely to share a news item. Japan is the least likely to comment on news at 7 per cent (Newman 2012). Research for the BBC asked people how they felt about getting involved in the news process, and found that Prosumers were thin on the ground in the UK:

> If a respondent was faced with a large fire and knew the emergency services had been called, only 5 per cent would contact the media to let them know what was going on. A further 14 per cent would take a photo but only 6 per cent would send the photo to a news organisation, and the remaining 8 per cent would take a photo but not send it to a news organisation.
>
> (Wardle and Williams 2008)

The *Guardian* released figures for its comments in November 2012. The website had 70.6 million unique users that month, and it published 600,000 comments, but 40 per cent of them were posted by only 2,600 prolific commentators. That means that less than 1 per cent of visitors ever interact, and only 1 per cent of *them* interact regularly. This is a huge increase on the number of letters (about 200–300 per day) but still not evidence of an overwhelming demand from readers to 'join in' (Elliott 2012).

The *Guardian* also experimented with a 'newsdesk live blog', which attempted to draw readers into suggesting news items for the day. It was halted after a few weeks because 'people just weren't that interested in our broader daily agenda' (private communication, 2013). The 'Reality Check' blog fared better – one topic chosen first thing in the morning and then researched and written on a live blog to which readers are invited to contribute information. Comments are enabled and actively trawled for useful material from well-connected readers, while the writer digs up additional information and interrogates experts. After a hopeful start, Reality Check dwindled; by 2013, it was an occasional rather than a regular item.

As the OhmyNews case demonstrates, even when citizens are invited to contribute, the majority seem to feel more comfortable with lifestyle and opinion pieces than with reporting. This is also where their contributions are most likely to be used by mainstream news organizations. In research comparing Swedish and UK online news organizations, comments were more likely to be sought in 'popular culture oriented' and 'personal/everyday life oriented' contexts rather than in the context of news and information (Jönsson and Örnebring 2011). Hermida (2011) found a similar pattern, with photographs of dogs being the most popular offering in Canadian research, while at *USA Today* many of the pictures offered were of weather and travel.

Even comment threads end up being edited – at the very minimum to ensure that they are not libellous. Where sites care about the quality of contributions, intervention of some kind is inevitable. At the *Guardian*'s 'Comment is Free' (CiF), a selected group of contributors were initially allowed direct access to the site. Posts were read briefly for legal issues and published almost immediately. As an early contributor, I enjoyed the freedom of being able to comment, almost instantly and to a very substantial audience, on the day's news. But CiF also became a victim of its own success. Three years later, in the summer of 2009, the system was changed so that contributors had to 'pitch' their comments to an editor who would also check the copy before uploading it (private communication, 2009).[2] This change absolutely exemplifies the problem faced by organizations encouraging audience interaction. You can restrict involvement and allow instant and relatively unfettered access, or you can open up access and institute controls in order to deal with the flow of material. The interactive audience will be, in the end, only the audience the gatekeeper chooses to interact with.

Living in a bubble

Where there is a problem, innovative capitalism will find a solution – but it just might not have the results that anyone expected. At the turn of the century, search engines obligingly moved in to help audiences find what they were looking for in the mass of material with which they were now being presented. Google, the pre-eminent example, wrapped itself in the language of net activism, with its cuddly catch phrase 'Don't be Evil.' The use of mathematical algorithms was touted as the best and indeed the purest way to bring audiences together with sources of information in ways that followed the 'wisdom of crowds' rather than the voice of the expert.

In reality, algorithms point us to the most popular items. Sometimes popularity is a very useful guide, but it can also signify that a very large number of people have made the same safe decisions and then been followed by very large numbers of other people doing exactly the same. They may do this because they too want to make the popular choice, or just because the most popular choice is always easy to see, up there at the top of the Google rankings. The sheer audience size of popular newspapers, and the enormous reach of television news, gave them power over what most people could see or hear. Online, however, the same names are at the top of Google's rankings – propelled there because they are names people recognize in the confusion of what they see online and then kept there as their 'popularity' is confirmed. As Matthew Hindman found in *The Myth of Digital Democracy*, 'the Internet is not eliminating exclusivity in political life; instead, it is shifting the bar of exclusivity from the *production* to the *filtering* of political information' (2009: 13).

The Daily Kos and the Drudge Report, with high numbers of loyal readers, are the exceptions to the rule that legacy media triumph. As Hindman shows, search engines favour those organizations that are already big and make them bigger. The Pew Research Center found 'Among news sites that attract 500,000 monthly visitors or more, the top 10 per cent of the most popular sites attract half the traffic' (2010b). Search engines also do well for very small, niche, organizations that depend on web search to be found at all but again search directs audiences to the biggest fish even in very small ponds. Squeezed out are the middle-sized organizations (very often those with a less populist agenda). Add to this the way in which online advertising follows popularity, and small organizations which might thrive on a bookstand – with perhaps one hundred other titles – get lost on the web where the majority of searchers rarely stray beyond the top search offerings.

> Online speech follows winners-take-all patterns. Paradoxically, the extreme 'openness' of the Internet has fuelled the creation of new political elites. The Internet's successes at democratizing politics are real. Yet the medium's failure in this regard are less acknowledged and ultimately just as profound.
>
> (Hindman 2009: 4)

One of the ways in which the search engines have tried to improve their effectiveness has been to 'personalize' search. This means that they look at your age, gender and occupation, plus what you are already reading or choosing and try to refine your search so that you are more likely to come up with the things you actually want to read or watch. In doing so they hope to solve one of the other dreams of early net enthusiasts. Experiments at the MIT Media Lab in the early days of the Internet suggested a new model of news in which all the information we need in the world would come to us, tailored for use (Hapgood 1995). No more buying a newspaper with a sports section just to use it to line the cat-litter tray; the 'Daily Me' would tailor news to our own personal tastes and deliver it wherever we are. The idea was that the audience would select the subjects that were of interest and a personalized newspaper would arrive electronically, to be printed out at home. We would all have instant access to news and information that matters to us.

There have been a number of attempts to realize this dream. First, Really Simple Syndication (RSS) allowed us to follow the sites or blogs we preferred directly. Then Google allowed us to set up news feeds and alerts to any items in our field. Pretty soon personalized aggregators like Flipboard arrived, but they had to be set up and maintained. Now a Daily Me has arrived that is completely automated; it is called Facebook. In a 2010 study of North Americans' news reading habits, 75 per cent said that they received news forwarded via Facebook or email (Purcell *et al.* 2010). In a UK study (Newman 2012), 55 per cent had shared news via Facebook, with 33 per cent sharing news on email. Younger people especially are more likely to use social media than search to find news.

Research in 2012 (Newman and Levy 2013) found that Facebook was already becoming a very important source of referrals for serious newspapers in the UK. Helping them along were the group Anders Olof Larsson calls 'Filters' (Larsson 2011), who actively engage online by bringing news items to the attention of their friends or organizations. The development of Facebook news apps, which automatically post on your profile for every link you click, made it hard *not* to see what your Facebook friends were reading; overnight, it was possible to become a 'filter' merely by signing up and reading a website. The *Guardian* saw its referrals via Facebook rocket: in the first month the new app drove more traffic to guardian.co.uk than did Google (Filloux 2012a). This sharing of news fits well with the Daily Me concept. According to the Newman report, 78 per cent of people who click on news links regularly say they are more likely to click if they know the person who sent it (Newman 2012: 47). Since friends share interests, sharing news is a simple way for time-poor audiences to keep up to date with events that are important to them.

At the same time as these apps began to spread, however, big changes were happening in the code. Where previously Facebook had all been about stuff you did yourself – sending messages and pictures to your mates and seeing what they were up to – the company was now following Google's approach of collecting private data and working out how to 'monetize' online activity. Mostly this is all about finding out what you like and making sure that advertisers can target your needs more accurately. But in trying to work out how to be one jump ahead of its users, Facebook was doing something else: it was deciding which of your Facebook friends should show up in your news feed (Pariser 2011).

By prioritizing news from people in whom you seem to have most interest, Facebook also prioritizes news that more closely accords with your interests. The same is true of your Google searches. If two different people use the same search terms in Google, they will almost certainly get different results. This inflection in the direction of your major interests is then added, on Facebook, to an already existing bias in what sort of material gets shared. Jonah Berger looked at the kind of news that spreads online and found that 'the more positive an article, the more likely it was to be shared' (Berger 2013). He reasons that this is because 'when you share a story with your friends and peers, you care a lot more how they react. You don't want them to think of you as a Debbie Downer.'

It makes sense that people would use an intimate medium like Facebook to pass on 'feel-good' messages. But, in a world in which large numbers of young people get most of their information via social networks, what does this mean for audiences as citizens rather than consumers? Eli Pariser found to his dismay that

Facebook was censoring his news feed to ensure that he only got the kind of material he tended to agree with:

> Politically I lean to the left, but I like to hear what conservatives are thinking and I have gone out of my way to befriend a few and add them as Facebook connections. I wanted to see what links they would post, read their comments, and learn a bit from them .... But their links never turned up in my Top News feed.
>
> (2011: 5)

Of course, from the point of view of efficiency, this makes sense. As information grows online, we all look for ways of screening out the rubbish so that we are searching for what we actually want. But the side effects are alarming. As we tailor our input, we automatically (and unconsciously) exclude opposing views to ours, screening out all that information which would in the past have been delivered to our doorsteps with the milk. We may not have been interested in the football scores, but we were bound to know who won the game, because it was there on the back page of a shared newspaper. As technical changes online give us the tools to search more effectively for the particular lawnmower that is suitable for our kind of lawn, it systematically shields us from any inconvenient information about the world around us.

Audiences and news

Looking back at the theories of audience engagement mentioned at the start of this chapter, it is clear that there is not now, and has never been, one single audience. Engaged citizens and passive consumers are as much a part of the mix as they have ever been. While some of the more enthusiastic assumptions about a complete change in the relationship between audience and journalist have not been borne out in practice, there have been appreciable changes in the way in which audiences interact with news organizations and use news products. Those who are already interested in news and the world around them have unprecedented opportunities to question the hegemonic assumptions of the major news organizations. It is now possible to move from a news story and search for alternative points of view, or to check assumptions made by journalists, at the click of a mouse.

At the same time, the sheer amount of available information has led to new ways of processing it and therefore new sites of ideological influence. For people who are time-poor it is now very easy indeed to close down options and tune in only to that which appears to be of direct relevance. Online organizations such as Google and Facebook are jockeying for the opportunity to deliver ever more 'relevant' information, finely tuned to immediate needs. Those organizations that achieve this stand to make vast fortunes from advertisers, who once depended on paying news organizations to get their messages across but now have direct and uninterrupted access to your eyes, your ears, and above all to your pocket. 'Personalization', as we have seen, has its own dangers. Enthusiasts for data sharing and personalization might like to remember what Adorno had to say near the start of this chapter: 'The customer is not king, as the culture industry would have us believe, not its subject but its object' (Adorno 1961: 55). Or, as blue_beetle would have it: 'If you're not paying for it, you're not the customer; you're the product being sold' (Lewis 2010).

Notes

1 Interview with Ellie Slee for her MA thesis, August 2013.
2 This was the subject of a private email exchange with Georgina Henry, then editor of Comment is Free, in June 2009.

Chapter 6

The business of journalism in the digital age

In the previous chapters we have looked at ideology and power and how they manifest themselves via the routines, practices and ownership structures of the news business. In this chapter we are going to 'open the box' and look at how that business works and how it is adapting to a future in which the funding model that has supported it for most of two centuries can no longer be relied upon to keep it afloat. In doing so we are going to look at the way certain discourses have arisen to make the decisions taken by news organizations appear natural. These discourses relate to: the power of technology, the failure of journalism, the behaviour of audiences, the innate power of innovation and the primacy of private enterprise in allowing innovation.

I am using discourse here in the way that Michel Foucault (Hall 2001) employs it to describe how 'truths' are established so that they are no longer examined but taken for granted in such a way that certain structures and ways of doing things then flow from them. This approach allows us to examine structures in the making and to understand that the future of journalism is by no means a truth waiting to be uncovered but a range of different possibilities (discourses) that are still in the process of being shaped. The future of news in the online environment will in time emerge as a dominant discourse takes hold about how it should be funded. At that point it will have become a part of what we see as 'common sense': people will simply stop thinking about whether things could have worked another way. As part of this process certain myths are constructed and then possibly discarded. We will start by examining them and the way they feed into the discourses about the news business.

Myth one: technology killed the news audience

The idea that society is re-shaped by technology and that human beings are somehow powerless against it has accompanied virtually every major change from the printing press to electricity and the telegraph. Such 'technologically determinist' assumptions infuse Marshall McLuhan's concept of the 'global village' (1962), the 'techno-utopian' ideas of Nicholas Negroponte in *Being Digital* (1995) and the free-market utopianism of Jeff Jarvis in *What Would Google Do?* (2009a).

In the more recent manifestations of this approach we are lead to believe that the Internet has changed everything for modern journalism (which is regularly lumped together as though all of it were exactly the same), that mainstream journalism has outlived its usefulness and that audiences are deserting it in droves. This comment by Ryan Holmes, CEO of HootSuite (Gassée 2013) is fairly typical of this approach: 'Big newspapers, in particular, have proven startlingly inept at delivering timely, relevant news to the people they serve. So, naturally, readers have gone elsewhere, to myriad online sources that better cater to their interests.'

However the evidence tells us that 'elsewhere' looks very familiar. When people do want to find out what is in the news, they increasingly go online, and they may use Twitter to take them there, but they are not deserting legacy news providers. They are reading or viewing them online where the biggest newspapers have proven particularly good at 'delivering timely relevant news' (Nielsen 2012: 5). Indeed big newspapers have bigger audiences than they have ever had (Nielsen 2012: 18). Even those who are reading blogs are also still reading 'dinosaur' news. A Pew report (2010a) found that over 99 per cent of the links on blogs studied came from just four sources: the BBC, CNN, the *New York Times* and the *Washington Post*.

The confusion has arisen because of the tendency by some analysts to conflate platforms and sources. Consuming news is just one of the activities we now do online in addition to shopping, reading books, watching films, playing games, gambling and chatting with friends. The difference is that we used to do those things in different locations. Now we can do them all in the same place. In that larger context we would expect news consumption to be a minority activity and indeed it is. Nevertheless evidence also seems to suggest that, at least among those who are interested in news, consumption is rising rather than falling (Pew 2012a, Newman and Levy 2013).

The sharp uptake of smartphones and tablets is also changing news consumption. In 2012, 50 per cent of US adults owned a tablet or smartphone and 66 per cent of users accessed news on them. Four in ten mobile news consumers said they were getting more news now than they used to do before mobile and 73 per cent of these used their devices to read longer articles, not just headlines (Pew 2012a). Increasing numbers of people use their social media feeds both for news and for chat, but nearly 60 per cent of those who are interested in news are following journalists and legacy news organizations (Mitchell *et al.* 2013a). Nevertheless, in spite of this shift in behaviour, researchers from McKinsey found that 92 per cent of the time people spend actually consuming news (as opposed to finding news) was either via radio, TV or newspapers. Online may be good for catching up but it is not the preferred platform for in depth consumption (Edmonds 2013).

In 2013, television remained the major source of news in developed countries although, since the introduction of cable and satellite, TV watching has become more fragmented and in urban Brazil more people access news online than on

TV. However, in the UK, Finland and France (all countries with publicly funded broadcasting), the top three broadcasters still have over 40 per cent of the news audience and in Brazil, privately run Globo is still the major source of broadcast news. In the USA, India and Germany, television audiences are more fragmented (Newman and Levy 2013: 15).

Although more people are going online, the 'legacy' media has by no means been displaced. In the UK 'Traditional media providers account for 10 of the top 15 online providers of news (eight newspaper groups plus the BBC and Sky), with the remainder predominantly being news aggregators rather than alternative sources of news' (Ofcom 2012: 8). In the USA, the top news sites (aside from aggregators) are a mix of TV and newspapers including: CNN, MSNBC, the *New York Times* and the *Washington Post*.[1] Research in Sweden indicates that newspaper reading as a habit has not gone away but has merely been displaced onto the web (Bergström and Wadbring 2008). In France and Germany, online brands are more fragmented but it is still usually the major legacy providers that are sought out, rather than new entrants. In a nine-country survey, only in Japan were legacy news providers no longer the 'go-to' source for news. Here people are going to aggregators, who for serious news stories, aggregate largely from legacy providers (Newman and Levy 2013: 57–59).

Technologies change but the human activity of gathering, analysing and disseminating information continues to be maintained across all platforms, by journalists, adapting as it has always done, from the time of pigeon post, through the telegraph, radio and then television. It seems reasonable to assume on this evidence that audiences are moving to follow journalism, rather than the other way around.

Myth two: the web guarantees diversity

The idea of the Internet as a democratic form of communication is inseparable from its origins as a network for sharing. According to Tim Berners-Lee, the originator of the World Wide Web, 'The goal of the Web is to serve humanity' (Berners-Lee 2010). Its origins lent credence to a powerful anti-authoritarian discourse in which it was seen as inherently flexible and democratic. This has then been set against a monolithic concept of mainstream journalism, which is constructed as both anti-technology and undemocratic (Anderson 2006, Shirky 2008, Beckett 2008, Jarvis 2009a). However, although the web was established to be capable of facilitating democracy in the way it has been developed, it cannot create democracy and very soon a combination of innovative and opportunistic business initiatives ensured that it moved in another direction.

Chapter 2 'News Interrupted' referred to the way in which the Internet tends to overemphasize the most popular sites. News aggregators and search engines choose their stories via a set of algorithms that are based on popularity (links and clicks) and currency. The idea is that the 'crowd' will promote the best material to the top of the search engine. Early enthusiasts assumed that this would mean that the best material was always going to be promoted by popular demand. However they had not bargained for the behaviour of big media companies who spend a lot of money on analytics so that they can get their own stories to the top of the search box. Once at the top of the list, for any given subject, they are far more likely to be chosen by searchers.

This creates what Matthew Hindman refers to as a 'winners-take-all' effect (Hindman 2009: 4), which tends to drive the audience always to the same sites. This is then added to the tendency, noted by Pierre Bourdieu (2005), for competition in the media to drive towards homogeneity. For English language news organizations, Internet choice patterns have provided opportunities for a handful of big news organizations to dominate, not just in the national context, but also internationally. Thus the UK *Daily Mail* (with its mix of gossip and scandal) now appears in the top Internet news sites compiled by a number of ratings agencies (August 2013) alongside major American news organizations such as CNN, MSNBC and the *New York Times*.

Chris Anderson, in *The Long Tail* (2006), suggests that this effect is counterbalanced by the ease with which small numbers of people can access information on non-mainstream subjects, thus rendering visible what would in the past have been invisible. He suggests that the ease of access means that the cost of catering to small disparate groups has dropped and that less popular information can now be shared across vast distances. However Hindman noticed that the 'winners-take-all' effect happens at every level of the net so that, no matter what the subject, there will always be one or two sites that dominate in every niche and attract virtually all the traffic, so that the third or fourth most popular in any range of choices may find that they get no hits at all. This tendency he refers to as 'the missing middle'. The group of publications that might well have picked up passing trade on the strength of a cover, where all newspapers and magazines are displayed equally in a store or news stand, tend not to be seen at all online and this, he suggests, is reducing the range of publications available (Hindman 2009: 129).

However, while the logic of linking means that most people are reading similar news on almost any platform (Witschge and Redden 2010, Curran *et al.* 2013), the sheer numbers visiting news sites on a casual basis suggest that many people are reading material that they might never have visited in the old days of newspaper purchasing, when everyone stuck only to their chosen publication. The liberal-leaning *Guardian* has vastly increased its readership. The newspaper, even at its peak, had a daily circulation of only around 400,000. In March 2013, it had 78.3 million unique visitors (Guardian Media Group 2013), 83 per cent of them online (Colchester and Sydney-Smith 2013: 3) and a large proportion outside the UK. Analysis of the UK news market also found that online, lower income people were more likely to access 'quality national newspapers' than to read mid-market or popular newspapers (ibid). This may be partly accounted for by the relatively low level of investment in online amongst the popular press (with the exception of the *Daily Mail*). However, for lower-income audiences seeking news online, the availability of free material seems to have changed reading habits (Colchester and Sydney-Smith 2013: 6).

While the numbers accessing news online is cause for optimism about news audiences, there is a growing concern that this may be covering a growing divide between those who are news junkies and others who have no contact with news at all. A Reuters Institute comparative report (Newman and Levy 2013) found that a third of the UK and Italian sample said that they were 'not very interested in news' (women were particularly disaffected). This survey also found that 27 per cent of younger consumers (aged 25–45) are more likely to look for news sources that 'share their point of view'. While this is neither alarming nor surprising on its own, this is also the age group most likely (44 per cent) to find news via social media. Given what we know about the propensity for social media to create 'hall of mirrors' effects (see Chapter 5) this could arguably contribute to a narrowing of political understanding and participation in public life (Mancini 2013: 105).

In the USA, with a high level of Internet penetration, and higher than average numbers of people no longer accessing legacy news providers, there is also a particularly big class divide in news consumption. Only 44 per cent of those without college education follow national news (dropping to 37 per cent for international news). This compares to 69 per cent of college graduates who regularly follow national news (Pew 2012b). This evidence is corroborated by a study of news knowledge (mentioned in Chapter 2), which also found low levels of 'hard news knowledge' among US respondents with low levels of education (Curran 2011: 57).

For those scholars, discussed in Chapter 5 'Audiences, Networks, Interaction', who see the production and dissemination of mainstream news merely as a means of maintaining the existing elite, such class divides in news knowledge might not be considered problematic. However there is no evidence that people who are disengaged from mainstream news are finding such information elsewhere and, although a deep knowledge of celebrity gossip or football might be satisfying, it is hard to see how it contributes to democracy.

Myth three: dinosaur journalists killed the industry

It is commonplace to blame the problems suffered by news organizations on old-school journalists who failed to understand the new technologies (see also Chapter 4). They are accused of reluctance to embrace participatory practices (Hermida and Thurman 2008, Heinonen 2011) or to surrender control (Gonzalez-Velez and Singer 2003); they have difficulties in moderating and controlling user-generated content (Chung 2007, Thurman 2008); and lack the necessary new skills (Brannon 2008). Worst of all they are rooted in a rigid professional culture and stick to outdated professional norms.

> Their new media ventures, therefore, are often run by the same people who, being restrained within a traditional value network (e.g. newsroom culture,

professionalism, loyalty to the old), apply to the new technology the same traditional mindset that has helped them survive and thrive well but is not at all relevant to the potential of the new technology.

(Nguyen 2008: 93)

There is no evidence that it was the behaviour of journalists in their adherence to traditional journalism cultures, or failure 'to realize the potential of new technologies' (Hermida 2012) that changed the news business. Indeed journalists were quick to embrace new technologies when they found them useful – particularly as a research tool. The problems suffered by the news business lie almost entirely in the collapse of the business framework that had been developed to support news and in the weakness of the response to that threat by news companies.

The story of news appears at first glance to be a classic case of what Clay Christensen, of Harvard Business School, referred to in *The Innovator's Dilemma* (2000). Christensen was responding to the concept of 'Creative Destruction' described by Joseph Schumpeter in *Capitalism, Socialism and Democracy*:

A process of industrial mutation – if I may use that biological term – that incessantly revolutionises the economic structure from within, incessantly destroying the old one, and incessantly creating a new one. This process of Creative Destruction is the essential fact about capitalism. It is what capitalism consists in and what every capitalist concern has got to live in.

(1943: 83)

In any given market, Christensen observed, genuinely disruptive new entrants slip in unnoticed, or derided, because what they appear to offer is typically of a much lower quality. This seemed to be what was happening to journalism in the 1990s. Online news was confined almost entirely to text which took a long time to appear on a computer screen, pictures had to be of low quality if they could be uploaded at all and video streaming was in the future. Those who moved online did so more as a novelty than as part of their core business. They wanted to be part of this change but didn't see bloggers a much of a threat.

Christensen observed that, in time, innovators improve their products and that is when they start to eat into the legacy business. Typically, the incumbents are then stuck because the profits of the legacy business don't start to fall immediately. They need to maintain what may be a highly successful business while at the same time developing a new one to take over. This is when, according to Christensen, the legacy incumbents panic and run in the wrong direction.

He recommended ways in which business might be able to respond to these disruptive threats: by setting up separate organizations where new staff can establish their own norms, rather than conforming to the 'doxa' of the old organization; allowing them to experiment with ideas that can challenge the old ways; while at the same time maintaining the old businesses for as long as they continue to bring in the majority of the money. Many of the news organizations were doing just that.

In the USA, innovation in legacy organizations was rapid. By the end of 1995, just five years after the launch of the web, 175 newspapers had launched websites. By June 1997, half the dailies in the country had web editions and two years later there were only two large newspapers that did not have a web presence (Boczkowski 2005: 8). In South Korea, OhmyNews, the first attempt in the world at a truly collaborative news venture, was launched in 2000.

The TV companies were always going to pose a problem for the legacy print organisations once they were all on the same platform. They feared that it would be hard to compete with global brands that already had massive audiences and access to unlimited high-quality video. Many of the more commercial newspapers recognized this threat and moved rapidly online in order to establish a presence in the pre-broadband era, before commercial TV had been able to do so.

In the UK, two people were particularly interested in the new possibilities: Alan Rusbridger, who became editor of the *Guardian* in 1995, and John Birt, who became Director General of the BBC in 1992. Both arrived at the top job just as the Internet was emerging and headed up organizations that were un-usual in being relatively protected from the direct force of the market. The BBC is publicly owned by and paid for by a licence fee. The *Guardian* is owned by the Scott Trust, which was designed to support the newspaper in perpetuity. It was arguably their relative protection from the market that allowed them to think first and foremost about the product, rather than the business of paying for the product.

Both moved early into producing material for the web because they believed it would prove to be the future for news and they were both also convinced that if they did not do so they would soon be overtaken by others (Wilby 2012). BBC News online was launched in 1997. The site was run by BBC insiders, hand-picked from a number of departments because they 'got' the web, but many of the journalists it employed came from the world of print journalism (Birt 2002: 473). Rusbridger launched Guardian Unlimited, which was initially quite separate from the newspaper, housed separately and employing younger jour-nalists on lower salaries. By 2008, the web and newspaper staff had been merged and by 2013, this minority-interest national player had become a global brand, read across the world with 78.3m monthly unique browsers and 'editions' in the USA and Australia (Guardian Media Group 2013).

While the *Guardian* is a commercial news organization, it is somewhat shel-tered by the Scott Trust from the harshest winds of the market, which may be why Rusbridger felt able to say to a group of journalism students, in 2010 (when the *Guardian*'s debts were calculated at £100,000 per day), that they should 'think about the journalism rather than worrying so much about the business model' (Johnson 2010). The BBC, as a publicly funded organization with a duty to inform, was ideally placed to make good the promise of the web and be a means by which 'any person could share information with anyone else, anywhere' (Berners-Lee 2010). It was in the interests of the corporation, but more particularly of its audience, to be wherever that audience wanted it to be.

For the BBC, the early move online turned out to be correct. It protected the organization from incursions by other English language advertising-funded, commercial TV companies, particularly those based in the USA, and both maintained and built up its pre-eminent position as a trusted broadcaster to the world. Birt also ensured that the BBC had an established online presence accepted before most newspapers had moved into the field. In Germany, the publicly funded broadcasters were slower to react, allowing time for newspaper owners to block them on grounds of unfair state-funded competition (Humphreys 2010).

The BBC rapidly became 'the most comprehensive content website in Europe, arguably the most innovative and respected in the world' (Birt 2002: 473). But by the time it had established its presence online it was hard for commercial competitors to do much about it. Some attempts were made to clips its wings. Educational publishers acted in concert to force the corporation to axe an innovative new platform for learners called BBC Jam (BBC Press Office 2007). But BBC news services were far too popular to close down.

Assuming the innovative disruption would come from other online news organizations (Busfield 2010), early adopters felt that they were well placed to ride out the storm. But, in terms of their own businesses, the newspapers were looking in the wrong direction. The real commercial disruption (for both newspapers and television) came not from other news providers, but from new entrants into the advertising business. Advertisers were not actually interested in news *per se*, they were only using it as a means to get to the news audience. Now they had other, cheaper ways to get to their consumers and they didn't really need news anymore. News organizations innovated their news products (some rather better than others), but their innovations turned out to be non-refundable expenses rather than radical realignments because news managements had not appreciated how the innovators would attack. If they had innovated their business models at the speed with which they innovated their journalism they might have survived in better shape.

The disrupted business model

News is expensive and in order to make it accessible to ordinary people it has (for most of the last two centuries) been supported either by political interests, wealthy individuals, state subsidy or advertising (Curran and Seaton 2003: 28, Starr 2004, McChesney and Nichols 2011). In the USA, newspapers were subsidized by a variety of forms of government support throughout the nineteenth century but these subsidies gradually disappeared. Today the news media attract a steadily dwindling degree of assistance (the lowest in the developed world) via tax breaks and the publication of government notices but it is advertising that provides the lion's share of income. In this industrialized market place, those who don't attract much advertising die, because they cannot compete with the subsidized products of the commercial press (Curran and Seaton 2003, McChesney and Nichols 2011).

It is this model that dominates commercial news markets across the world, ensuring (just as algorithms do today) that the most popular organizations attract the heaviest advertising subsidy and are therefore able to spend money on attractive content. Newspapers have never just produced serious news; people buy them for the 'funnies', the fashion and the sports. They are compendiums of quickly absorbed material available at low cost. In just the same way, cable and satellite companies cross-subsidize news, by selling it wrapped up in a bundle of more popular programming, the difference being that newspapers were developed to produce news and added the popular entertainment to subsidize them, while television was largely developed to provide entertainment and in many countries is subject to regulation to ensure that it carries news at all (Nielsen 2012: 48).

In many parts of Europe, the advertising model was recognized as a rather inefficient way of generating diversity and a variety of forms of direct and indirect public subsidy were introduced. Most countries introduced publicly funded television and, in many cases, various forms of subsidy also help newspapers. The object of such subsidy was to maintain plurality and assist democracy by protecting news (Nielsen and Linnebank 2011, Benson 2011). In Norway and Finland, newspapers are still strong and they also dominate online.

As explained in Chapter 2 'News Interrupted', in the UK and the USA, newspapers were largely left to the market. By the 1960s large numbers of cities in America and the UK had only one newspaper. These monopolies sucked up all the advertising and enjoyed high profit levels. Without competition the local and regional newspapers needed to do very little to keep the money coming in (Schlossberg 2013, McChesney and Nichols 2011). Philip Meyer, writing in the *American Journalism Review* in the mid-1990s, could see trouble ahead. He could see that circulations were dropping even as advertising revenues increased and he warned:

> That easy-money culture has led to some bad habits that still haunt the industry. If the money is going to come in no matter what kind of product you turn out, you are motivated to turn it out as cheaply as possible. If newspapers are under pressure, you can cheapen the product and raise prices at the same time. And, most important, innovation is not rewarded.
>
> (Meyer 1995)

As online news took off, there were some early attempts by the newspapers to launch their own joint advertising platforms, both in the USA (Tofel 2012) and in the UK (Oakley 2013: 63). Both failed because companies used to competing with one another for advertising were unable to agree on the best way forward and the Internet-only advertisers' brands moved faster. Craig's List provided the first broadside. It was a start-up with no commercial mission and a pretty simple idea. It offered a free listings service to anyone with a computer, thereby peeling away a very high proportion of the classified advertising that local newspapers depended upon for income. It hit the US news business very hard indeed. One estimate suggests that between 2000 and 2007 it diverted $5 billion dollars that would otherwise have gone to newspapers (Seamans and Zhu 2013). Gumtree, the Australian version, moved across the world and scooped up the UK market.

Then came another, bigger attack: first from Google and then Facebook (Phillips and Witschge 2012). Google was the classic example of a disruptive innovator. The company made no money to begin with and journalists happily used it to find information and people. Then it started not only selling ads, but also putting ads on other people's sites. The ads were very cheap and not very good to look at, so nobody worried much, but Google's gigantic scale meant that not very much for the advertiser added up to a fortune for Google. They could offer advertisements at prices that so thoroughly undercut the market that nobody else stood a chance against them (Auletta 2010). But more important than that, they could mobilize the data they collected on every individual click, and send people direct to products that they could buy.

Between 2007 and 2012, advertising spend in newspapers in the USA dropped by 42 per cent (Kilman 2013). Over 5 years there was a 23 per cent fall in Western Europe and similar falls in Australia and New Zealand. The picture was different in Asia and Latin America where, with lower levels of Internet penetration, press advertising continued to rise. Part of the problem was, of course, the world-wide recession triggered by the bank crash of 2008. News organizations were used to trimming costs as advertising dropped off and just waiting for the good times to return. But this time, there was the additional threat of new and as yet untested rivals in the advertising market. Companies panicked and started looking for ways to cut costs rather than tolerate lower returns but, as Meyer had warned back in 1995:

> The problem is that there is no smooth, non-chaotic way to get from a newspaper industry used to 20 to 40 percent margins to one that is content with 6 or 7 percent. The present owners have those margins built into their expected return on investment, which is to say their standard of living.
>
> (Meyer 1995)

On the one hand journalists were learning to embrace new technologies, but on the other they were being laid off to save money. Newspapers started to shrink and so did TV news bulletins, becoming less relevant just when they needed to be more relevant in order to fight their corner. According to the Pew Center's 2013 *State of the News Media* report, the number of US journalism jobs dropped 30 per cent in 12 years and 'on local TV sports, weather and traffic accounted on average for 40 per cent of the content produced on the newscasts studied while story lengths shrink' (Pew 2013).

The Tribune group, home of many of the big names in American newspapers, was particularly badly hit. In 2007 profits were dropping, so the company was sold to real estate entrepreneur Sam Zell. Convinced he could turn the company around, he borrowed $13 billion to do the deal, which at the time raised eyebrows because it relied on a complicated tax deal and saddled a company that needed nurturing with a pile of additional debt. When the crash came, the company had no means of paying the interest on the debt, so it went bankrupt. Zell tried to get by through cutbacks and later blamed the problems suffered by the group on 'greedy journalists' (Bercovici 2012).

A similar story occurred in the UK – and by extension in Ireland where the same companies own many of the newspapers. Attracted by the high income-levels, companies had borrowed money to buy up newspapers. Then as the crash came they had to pay back the loans, as well as provide dividends, on the back of plummeting advertising revenue (Felle 2013: 34). News organizations reacted by slashing staff and consolidating local newspapers into regional centres. Audience research (Fenton *et al.* 2010) found that people do want local news, but they would like news that is genuinely local and deals with issues that are important to them. The problem is that consolidation in the UK local and regional press has meant that increasingly news is not local (Oakley 2013: 63, Franklin 1998). A newspaper that is produced on a remote site, by a tiny staff of people who are unable to leave the office, is unlikely to be able to offer compelling coverage.

In the UK, the loss of audiences for local and regional newspapers has been precipitous. Regional circulation dropped by almost twice the European average (Chisholm 2013: 8). In 2013, only 10 per cent of the population actually read a local daily paper. This is partly because three quarters of UK daily circulation is in national newspapers, but it appears also to be a direct result of staff cutbacks that have affected content (Chisholm 2013: 8). Chris Oakley, a former UK regional newspaper editor, who was himself involved in a series of buyouts, observed looking back on this period: 'In a couple of decades, managements who have overpaid for acquisitions, over-promised to City investors and failed to recognize the threat and opportunity of the Internet have come close to destroying an industry' (Oakley 2013: 65).

In Northern Europe, local news organizations did not participate in the orgy of buyouts that characterised the Anglo-American companies and were not forced into the kind of cuts in journalism that came afterwards. They had high readership (over 50 per cent of Germans read a local newspaper) but lower profits and had never become as dependent on advertising as those in the USA and UK. In France, less than 40 per cent of newspaper income came from advertising. In the USA in 2007, the figure was nearly 90 per cent (Benson 2013:43). As a result they have survived both the advent of the Internet and the crash in reasonably good shape. In the USA, some local and regional newspapers have survived with healthy audiences and since only 6 per cent of readers read a national newspaper, there is a better chance that the decline of local news can be reversed (Chisholm 2013: 11).

If the only problem facing the old regional and local media was the decline in standards, this should have offered a huge opportunity to new, lean Internet start-ups, ready to move into local areas where the traditional press had failed. However, as media analyst Claire Enders of Enders Analysis put it: 'The income picture for local websites has turned out to be seriously challenged. They have to exist out of a very enthusiastic, activist level of engagement' (Enders 2011). A Pew Center report on non-profit local news in the USA was similarly gloomy (Mitchell *et al.* 2013b).

Myth five: information wants to be free

None of these changes in news production or consumption were built into the technology. Berners-Lee believed he was building something for the future of the world. He did not patent his work or ask for royalties. He said: 'We build it now so that those who come to it later will be able to create things that we cannot ourselves imagine' (Berners-Lee 2010). He is troubled by the way in which entrepreneurs such as Mark Zuckerberg and Steve Jobs have taken his 'mad, throbbing Web market' and tried to carve it up into 'walled gardens' (Berners-Lee 2010). His major concern is that they are controlling what people do online, but there are other worries too. These entrepreneurs took the idea of freedom to collaborate and turned it into something in which the word 'free' means something quite different.

For one group of people, including Lawrence Lessig, Henry Jenkins and indeed Berners-Lee himself, the essence of the Internet lay in its ability to allow people opportunities for creative expression. But for another group, including Larry Page and Sergey Brin of Google and Mark Zuckerberg of Facebook, its value lay in the opportunities it offered to exploit the free labour of creative, networked communities (Andrejevic 2007: 14). While promoting the idea of freedom of access, these digital entrepreneurs were at the same time promoting the idea that creative content was worth nothing and that, only by exploiting this free content, could the monetary value of the Internet actually be realised.

Neither group showed any concern for the welfare of the creative workers whose jobs were to be undermined by the sudden abundance of freely generated material. Ros Gill (2010: 250) summarises the position of creative workers thus: '[It] is characterised by risk, insecurity and contingency in which more and more of the costs of work are borne by the workers themselves.' In the context of this new discourse, the value of work produced by journalists suddenly dropped down to zero. No longer was the quality of journalism the object of the exercise of publishing; it had become, in the opinion of newspaper entrepreneur Sam Zell, a non-revenue generating overhead.[2]

Caught between one discourse that characterized journalists as simply cogs in an industry ripe for disruption and another that saw them as corrupted products of a political elite, journalists have found it very difficult to either protect their position as workers, or their importance to the democratic process. When managements collectively decided to give away their work for free (as bait to attract advertising), any protests were simply dismissed as the sound of 'dinosaurs' protesting against the inevitable onward march of technology (Witschge 2012: 99, Curran 2010a: 31).

In fact it may well be that the decision of newspapers to give away their content will turn out to be one of those historical anomalies that historians puzzle over in future years. Richard J. Tofel, now a publisher at the trust-funded investigative journalism site, ProPublica, formerly worked for the *Wall Street Journal*. He watched as newspapers moved online and believes that what happened was effectively the promulgation of a convenient myth that emerged from the heady brew of West Coast hippy-capitalism. Tofel traced the way in which a meaningless phrase: 'information wants to be free' (Brand 1987) was taken up by *Wired* magazine, by technology writers and then by the *New York Times* until it became the mantra of the new-media age. Working right at the heart of the business, he fears that the future of newspapers was 'given away' because, 'Simply put, the notion that "information wants to be free" had become Hip, and the idea that readers should pay for content as they long had in print had become Square' (Tofel 2012).

It may seem extraordinary that hard-headed business people should fall for such a slogan but the power of this idea was that it rendered those who had not 'got it' as somehow less potent, less vigorous and less innovative. For those newspaper executives who were worrying about keeping up with the operations of the new generation of technological innovators, the idea of 'free' worked well with the idea of a virtual product. It made a certain amount of sense that they could just put it all online and wait for advertising to work its magic – just as it had done for 150 years, just as it did for TV and radio. But there was nothing inherent in the technology that demanded that commercial news organizations should put their very expensive content online for free where they would allow others to profit from it.

Without the means of linking directly to existing legacy news organizations, it is doubtful that dominant web-native organizations such as the Huffington Post would have got into the general news business at all. They would have discovered very quickly that actually producing journalism is very expensive – far more expensive than simply making use (for free) of what others have produced. It is probable that niche sites would have thrived, just as they do today, but they would have done so by producing independent journalism and competing directly with specialist magazines working in the same field, rather than by plagiarising them.

They could all have held back and shored up their print operations, which even as circulations continued to shrink, were bringing in the lion's share of revenue across all markets and all countries (MC Marketing 2013). The lack of paywalls, or simple incentive-driven, one-off registration schemes, meant that newspapers were also locked out of access to readers' data. Subscriptions don't just provide direct money to pay for journalism, they also open the door to more targeted advertising, because every subscriber is providing data, not only at registration, but every time they log in to the site (or via cookies if they stay logged in).

This data is Internet gold. The more a company knows about its subscribers, the more it is able to ensure that advertising is served up in a way that targets its readers' desires, directly enlisting them to 'assist in the process of their own manipulations' (Andrejevic 2007: 15). Google and Facebook 'read' your messages looking for clues about your concerns in order to feed you 'relevant' targeted advertising. When readers pass through Google to get to news, their data is being creamed off on the way – but they are anonymous to the destination news website. Only by getting their own hands on that data could the news organizations start to re-establish their relationship with advertising.

But newspaper managements, particularly in the UK and USA, laid their bets on 'free' – often cutting staff just as they expected them to provide additional material for websites. Only the *Wall Street Journal* bucked the trend, starting free and then, a year later, in 1997, implementing a pay wall. When the wall went up, 90 per cent of the audience departed. That may have been the lesson that most resonated with the other news organizations. They moved steadily towards convergence, investing in video and continuing to give it all away free online. The rationale was that audiences online were so much larger that, even though print advertising dollars were fast becoming digital advertising dimes, they hoped to bring in the extra through scale. The figures in the US news market show just how hard that would become.

> Based on data provided by nearly 40 newspapers and interviews with executives at 13 newspaper companies, … on average, for every \$1 newspapers were gaining in digital ad revenue, they were losing \$7 in print advertising. By the end of 2012, the numbers were considerably grimmer – \$16 in print ad revenue losses for every digital dollar gained.
>
> (Jurkowitz and Mitchell 2013)

The figures in the UK were equally alarming and the *Guardian*, still convinced of its mission to produce collaborative journalism which required open access (Busfield 2010), decided that the only way to make up for the bleeding adver-tising revenue was to push hard for scale online, convinced that the astonishing upward trajectory of its audience would soon pull in enough advertising to cover the cost of its news gathering. For a while the total readership for print and online outstripped all other UK newspapers and it still has the highest online readership of the quality non-broadcast news providers (Colchester and Sydney-Smith 2013).

Unusually, the *Guardian* has done nothing to halt the decline of its print version. Over ten years its print circulation has halved to less than 200,000, while 83 per cent of its audience read online and the majority of them do not buy a newspaper (Colchester and Sydney-Smith 2013). This is at least partly because the move online has produced a product that not only duplicates what is in the paper but goes far beyond it in depth and speed of coverage. Indeed, the laggards who buy the newspaper and might then want to engage in online discussion will find that they are reading yesterday's news, and opinion and debate have passed them by. Indeed, they will find it difficult to find the article to link to should they wish to join in.

The sharp loss of print circulation and display advertising created severe financial difficulties, which the company attempted to solve by converging its newsroom and cutting staff. With mounting debts it would have gone under had it not been propped up by the Scott Trust which sold other holdings, including local newspapers, to keep it afloat. By 2013, overall digital sales were rising steadily and non-news activities such as a dating service were offsetting the loss of print advertising, but they still accounted for less than a third of total revenues.[3]

Also in the UK, the populist *Daily Mail* embraced 'free', but from a very different position. With a national print circulation of 1.5 million, the newspaper entered the online arena late and from a position of strength. Until 2006 it had barely done more than put up a *Daily Mail* page online. When it decided to invest, it ensured that the online product was not only produced separately but, in complete contrast to the *Guardian*, it was also completely different from the newspaper. Martin Clarke, the Mail Online's editor was quoted in the *New Yorker* as saying: 'We took the decision to not integrate *Mail Online*, because the *Daily Mail* was a fantastically successful newspaper, and we didn't want to do anything that was going to compromise that' (Collins 2012: 7). The Mail Online, according to a source also quoted in the *New Yorker*, 'just decided to go hell-for-leather for ratings' (ibid).

By 2010, the *Mail* had overtaken the *Guardian* to become the UK's biggest newspaper website and by some accounts the biggest in the world. It was relatively cheap to produce as it was mostly composed of recycled gossip and photographs of celebrity cellulite.[4] Though it is striking that, given the success of the site and the very high level of reader engagement, digital revenue was still only 18 per cent of total revenue in 2013 (Smith 2013). Like most newspapers in mature markets, circulation is falling, but in the case of the *Mail*, the fall has been gradual. The newspaper is a different product from the website and 40 per cent of *Mail* readers don't see the online version at all, while 29 per cent read both versions (Colchester and Sydney-Smith 2013).

The *Daily Mail* website is not draining money from the news organization, which is firmly based on servicing its paper, and it may in time start to contribute to overall profits. It is creating very high reader loyalty (many readers go back several times a day), which it is working very fast to monetize. It already has 31 million registered users.[5] The data provided by registration means that it can provide targeted advertising based on audience preferences which will attract a premium. It is embracing the Jarvis dictum: 'Cover what you do best. Link to the rest' (Jarvis 2007), though possibly not quite in the way Jarvis had imagined.

Offering the audience just what it desires may make business sense but it makes very little sense if public service journalism is the *raison d'être* of the organization. The dilemma for the *Guardian*, and all other serious newspapers, is that much as they might like to dump their print edition, go digital, and fully embrace open journalism, they cannot afford to do so because so far digital advertising shows no sign of bringing in enough money to pay for the whole news operation.

There are other dilemmas too. Scale may be attractive but, as discussed in Chapter 5 'Audiences, Networks, Interaction', it is not easy for a small group of journalists to have a direct relationship with an audience of several million. The bigger the audience gets, the more necessary it will be for journalists to use tools to screen out much of the incoming information and, as we discussed in Chapter 3 'Journalists and their Sources', that will mean that new source hierarchies are bound to develop. And there is another problem: where the dominant brand within any market stays free, then the others feel that they are forced to do the same, or lose their audience. In the pre-Internet days it was possible for small circulation publications to make enough money to cover their costs via the sale price of the product and a reasonable amount of well-targeted advertising. Today anyone can establish a blog or online news site, but only if they are prepared to work without pay and they can subsidise their love of journalism some other way. For smaller publications, the era of free will also be the era of freedom to starve, unless they can come up with an alternative means of support.

Myth six: the market will always provide

The idea that the market will spontaneously engender entrepreneurial risk-takers who will come to the rescue, armed only with self-created new technologies, is the particularly pernicious myth that sits at the heart of the debate about the future of news. It is the view often espoused by people such as James Murdoch of News Corp and academic Jeff Jarvis, of BuzzFeed, who oppose any form of government intervention:

> The future of news – and there is a future – is being built by entrepreneurs who in change see opportunity, not crisis ... In short: I say the fate of journalism is not in the hands of institutions. The fate of journalism is in the hands of entrepreneurs.
>
> (Jarvis 2009b)

He continues: 'The impact of non-market competition – both government and charity – on the tender sprouts of entrepreneurial enterprises that will grow into a new ecosystem of news is a cause for concern' (ibid).

His faith in the entrepreneurial risk-takers seems to show a lack of under-standing of just where the major technological changes that underpin the fortunes of the new media entrepreneurs actually come from. All were invented not by private enterprise but by government subsidy. Berners-Lee produced the first version of the web while working at CERN in Switzerland and went to run the World Wide Web Consortium at MIT. Touch-screen displays, GPS and voice activation also came out of government-funded projects (Mazzucato 2013: 3). It was the state that provided the long, hard funding behind the fortunes made by Google, Apple and Facebook, just as it was the state, in the form of the military, that allowed three out of four earlier telecommunications technologies to get off the ground (Marvin 1999: 58). As Mariana Mazzucato points out, it is only the state with its reserves of money that is able to underpin the huge risks and very slow rate of return that characterize any genuinely new technology.

None of this is to denigrate the role of entrepreneurs in bringing ideas to market but rather to underline the fact that significant technological change is nearly always facilitated by public spending and that, as Mazzucato suggests, a clearer understanding of this relationship could alter the terms of the debate around the relationship between private and public. It might open up the pos-sibility that the state, rather than being characterized as stifling innovation via red tape and regulation, could equally have a right to demand that innovations paid for via public funding (that is you and me) should maintain within them the trace, at least, of the public interest that produced them. The web, according to its maker, was 'built on egalitarian principles [and] because thousands of indivi-duals, universities and companies have worked, both independently and together as part of the World Wide Web Consortium, to expand its capabilities based on those principles' (Berners-Lee 2010).

What Berners-Lee had not foreseen was that he would hand to the fastest and biggest in the field the right either to buy up, or to elbow out, smaller inno-vators. Google cornered the advertising market, just as local newspapers and TV did before it, by making use of its massive scale (it provides over 90 per cent of searches in the UK (Experian Hitwise 2011) and 67 per cent in the USA (Lee 2013)) and undercutting any rivals. Where the effect of monopoly was to reduce media plurality, governments have in the past acted in a number of ways: via regulation, licensing and subsidy. The difficulty with Google is that its monopoly is not direct but indirect. It doesn't produce news but, through its search engines, it does have a near monopoly on directing people to news and, as we have seen (in Chapter 2), narrowing the choices they make and facilitating the creation of mega-news organizations while cutting off existing income streams that had formally supported small and medium-sized news enterprises.

In France, Germany and Belgium, governments have attempted to force Google into paying something back to ameliorate the damage that it has done to the business of news. France, for example, has insisted that Google put money into a fund for future innovation in news. The anonymous online response to this very small adjustment in favour of emerging online news businesses gives some flavour of the degree to which the blind belief in market forces clouds thinking.

> French government are hailing as a success a system which forces a company which is helping a dying industry to pay a fine for doing so. For any tech company to subsidize newspapers is like having HP fund the slide-rule industry, but to have a news search engine do so for driving traffic is deluded.
>
> (Anonymous comment, paidContent 2013)

To believe the myth promulgated by Google that it is actually 'helping a dying industry' is rather like believing that a bully who capsizes your boat and then suffocates you while pretending to save your life is a hero. Google is certainly not the only reason for the difficulties faced by journalism. As we have seen earlier, the greed of the news businesses themselves had a lot to answer for. Had they been leaner, fitter and more agile they would not have been so easily capsized. Nevertheless, there is a reasonable case to make that Google (and now Facebook) should be asked to pay something towards transitional funding that might help support journalism in the short term, particularly to support local journalism that has been most affected by the technical changes.

Looking for a [commercial] way out

Paying for content

One possible, and increasingly popular, new model is an old model. The example of the *Wall Street Journal* may have persuaded the first wave of news managers that free was the only way to be but, as the crisis in advertising hit, the *Wall Street Journal* suddenly looked like the one to watch, with a world-wide circulation of two million, nearly half of whom are digital subscribers. European titles such as the *Berliner Morgenpost* put up a paywall in 2009. The UK *Times* followed suit in 2010 and then so did the *New York Times*. By mid-2013, all the major Canadian newspapers had put up paywalls and more than half of US daily newspapers had implemented, or announced plans for some kind of paywall. In 2013, the *New York Times* announced that its subscriptions (on and offline) now bring in more than its advertising (Pew 2013) and it is still searchable on Google and available to casual readers, but its most loyal readership pays by subscription.

Paywalls are not just going up around the big news sites. According to a 2012 survey of European online news start-ups, the only one that was breaking even financially was the French site Mediapart, which launched as a subscription-only service. It has a modest 60,000 subscribers and is able to pay 36 journalists. It specializes in breaking big political stories, has become a 'must read' for the political elite and is followed by all the other news organisations. In the Netherlands, a similar independent news site has recently emerged. De Correspondent raised over €1 million through crowd funding. Six months later, it had 24,000 subscribers and employed a staff of seven full time and 19 freelance writers (Pfauth 2013). Both news organisations are run by experienced journalists who produce high quality material.

Mediapart was initially criticized for shutting itself off from collaboration and it was suggested that it would either collapse or be forced to go free. Its main rival, Rue 89, (also a start-up) quickly attracted more than two million monthly unique users but was unable to sustain even 26 staff members because it depended on advertising and advertising rates online are so low. It then decided to establish a monthly print magazine, containing material taken from the site, which brought in a third of its revenue, but it was finally taken over by legacy news brand *Le Nouvel Observateur* (Bruno and Nielsen 2012).

Small companies and locals might benefit from a pay-per-article arrangement. It is expensive for small publications to set up their own pay-per-view software across a plethora of different platforms, but a low-cost, friction-free arrangement (rather like a music-streaming service) could allow them to piggy-back on other better-funded publications. A number of friction-free payment services for magazines already exist. A new one, called Readly, launched in Sweden in 2013 and was about to launch in the USA and UK at the time of writing. This could well provide a help for consumer magazines, particularly in countries where casual sales, rather than subscriptions, have always been a big part of the mix. Customers pay a flat monthly fee for access to a wide range of magazines. Publishers get paid according to the number of clicks on their products. It is not hard to see a similar arrangement working for a wide range of small, campaigning publications. It wouldn't make a great deal of money, but it might keep them afloat and would almost certainly ensure that they focused on improving content rather than chasing ad sales.

Paywalls would change the online experience and many of the original evangelists for 'free' are concerned that if news sites charge, audience collaboration fostered by free websites will disappear and the age of the open Internet and open journalism will end. It would certainly change the online experience and make it harder to browse and link. But there are many imaginative ways in which technologies could be harnessed to the job of enabling diversity as well as providing funds for journalism. They just haven't been fully explored because too many people blindly followed the mantra that, 'information wants to be free'. It's time to change the tune and ask what is the best way for information to be paid for?

Promotional journalism

For organizations that already have big audiences, there are still some ways in which it is possible to stay free and make money out of scale. *Atlantic Monthly*,

Forbes magazine, the *Guardian* and many others are investing in advertising content that is variously known as: sponsored content, advertising aligned content, or brand journalism. It is a means of allowing advertisers to produce content that looks like editorial. *Forbes* advertises its BrandVoice as an opportunity for advertisers to place their copy directly onto the *Forbes* website where it will rise or fall according to audience interest. All those who have moved into this market make a big point of the fact that all this content is labelled so that it is clear that it is not actually part of the editorial, but clearly the advertisers are keen on it precisely because audiences think that it is just part of the editorial. Here is how *Forbes* presents what they are doing: 'In a digital world, publishers needed to share with marketers the tools to engage directly with a savvy audience that wanted the best information available, no matter the source' (DVorkin 2013).

The plus side is, of course, that this is the very premium advertising market that Google cannot easily enter. Promotional editorial depends for its value on the fact that it is embedded into a site that is otherwise independent and trusted. The down side is that it sales perilously close to the glass wall erected with such difficulty at the turn of the last century (see Chapter 4). While those publications experimenting with this idea may indeed be holding the ethical line and clearly separating journalism and advertising content, it is a strategy that risks undermining audience trust. Savvy audiences do indeed want the best information but they also care about its source. If it's too clearly labelled they are likely to ignore it, but by blending editorial and advertising too closely there is a real danger of polluting the very product that the strategy is attempting to save.

Live events

Multi-platform journalism is no longer just about words and picture (moving and still) print, online and mobile, it also includes live events. This approach was pioneered by *Vice* magazine which combined an advertising-funded give-away with regular music events held at the Old Blue Last, a Shoreditch pub that it acquired in 2004. The gigs were used both as a means of building audience and bringing in money. The company soon branched out into online and video as an early example of a profitable and genuinely multi-platform venture. French independent women's magazine *Causette* adopts a similar strategy of running parties to raise funds combined with a paid-for magazine. In the corporate world, live events help to fund business-to-business brands who use their editorial expertise to offer conferences, seminars and training tailored to their audiences. Media blogger Frederic Filloux sees events and conferences as a natural extension of journalism:

> The segment is crowded and success depends on a subtle combination of attendance fees vs sponsorship, but also of *editorial* content. A conference is indeed a full editorial vector that needs to be treated with the same care as any other publication, i.e, with a precise *angle*, great *casting* and first class

moderation that favors intellectual density over speakers flogging cheap sales pitches. News media are well positioned to deploy an efficient promotion for a content-rich, sustainable, conference system.

(2014)

Sustaining local news

It is at local level that the biggest funding difficulties arise. The move into voluntary or community-run online journalism has not lived up to the initial expectations. Volunteers are best able to sustain single-issue campaigning sites or micro sites covering a very small area. Google ads are little use without very high visitor numbers (which are not likely in local journalism) and in any case, what readers actually want are local advertisements that tell them about services they can reach in their own area. Google ads may be delivered locally but they rarely include local, independent businesses (Bruno and Nielsen 2012). On small publications run by part time and inexperienced journalists, few people have the time and energy to do the daily legwork and follow-up that regular journalism actually involves (Baines 2013). Nor do they have the time to do both the journalism and the hard work of selling advertising (or organising events) on which the work of journalism depends.

Attempts by larger companies to make local work online have also run into the same problems. The *Guardian* set up single-operator hyper-local sites in a handful of areas but they collapsed very quickly because they were unable to bring in enough revenue to support themselves. Patch, bought by AOL in the USA in 2009 was an attempt to support single-operator hyper-local sites with commercial backup. It was partially successful in supporting a small number of such sites but in 2013 announced that it would be cutting back because many of the sites (which only have one journalist each) are non-viable.

In the UK, Local World is experimenting with using technology to provide general news coverage on 110 local sites, and so reduce costs. Managing Director David Montgomery said: 'We will have to harvest content and publish it without human interface, which will change the role of journalists' (Hollander 2013). Even the cash-strapped rival Johnston Press feels that managing without journalists is going too far. Chief executive Ashley Highfield said: 'I don't see a world without local journalists on the ground in the community' (Hollander 2013).

Ironically it is print that has come to the rescue locally because print adverts still bring in far more than those online. Highfield, giving evidence to the House of Lords committee on media plurality said: 'I am of the view that ... we will carry on printing newspapers for many years, 20, 30, 40 years.' One reason he gave was that 'a lot of trust is given to you if you print because clearly an editing process has gone on' (Highfield 2013).

Print is also offering a helping hand to new start-ups. In the UK, a journalist, made redundant after many years in local and regional newspapers, decided to set up his own hyper-local free sheet in Bristol (Coulter 2013). Going right back to first principles, he based his funding model on providing a local service to local tradespeople. Without shareholders to worry about, this little family business is covering its costs and some more. In Hackney, East London, a local Green activist felt the need for a local paper that truly reflected local needs. The *Hackney Citizen* is a free newspaper, paid for by local advertising and distributed monthly via local cafes. In 2014, it sustained one full-time and one half-time journalist, assisted by volunteers, alongside two people selling advertising space. It stands out because it cares about the area and it is not filled with the flaccid, duty coverage of local crime but with concerns about planning, schools and the goings-on at the local council. The little one-person company that started it has now launched a second newspaper, also catering for a small local area of East London (private communication, 2014). It maintains a website but it doesn't make money from it.

Local journalism is not just about nurturing local democracy, it is also an important part of the news ecosystem. While it is easier than ever before for journalists sitting behind their computers to scour the world for news, that model is almost entirely passive and it cannot substitute for a concerned local beat reporter, who is prepared to spend time talking and listening to the people who never tweet their thoughts or take to a blog when something goes wrong. Without news journalism on the ground, at grass-roots level, it is hard for information to filter through from the periphery to the centre (see Chapter 2). Laws may be made nationally, but they are implemented locally. Without monitoring, independent of politicians, it is hard for citizens to know how new policies are working on the ground. It is the local journalists, often underpaid and almost always undervalued, who provide the daily stream of information that bubbles up from the bottom, spreading oxygen to the upper levels.

Funding a future for journalism

The discourses generated in Silicon Valley and beyond have built a vision of future journalism that enfranchises audiences at the expense of journalists and creative workers, and suggests that technology, in the hands of maverick entrepreneurs, is capable of solving the needs of democracy. It may be an enticing vision for those who believe that rugged individualism (preferably on horseback) is the preferred answer to any problem. But there are other ways that would allow the values of collaboration that Berners-Lee prizes to flourish, while at the same time providing a stable income to the journalists who collate, record and produce the news.

It seems unlikely that there will be one single answer. Television, whether watched online or on a television set, provided by public funding or via the advertising subsidy, continues to be a major provider of news. In the short term, there seems no reason to suppose that newspapers are dead either. Indeed, in many parts of the world, they are extremely healthy and they continue to employ, by a very large margin, the majority of journalists. As more people have access to mobile devices and mobile connectivity improves, it seems likely that the demand for print will fade – but not the demand for well-informed journalism.

As Lucy Küng notes in her book *Strategic Management in the Media*: 'Technological innovations tend [therefore] to supplement, rather than replace, previous technologies. The previous medium is not destroyed but progressively undermined, more often than not slipping down the food chain with lower revenues and smaller market share' (Küng 2008: 128).

The funding model for online news will need to evolve to meet future needs with a mixture of subscription, data-driven advertising, micro-payments for reading single stories, or viewing single videos (Picard 2013) and cross-subsidy via events management or digital services such as dating sites. Into this mix, we can expect to see cooperatively owned and locally controlled ventures alongside publicly funded broadcasting. Public subsidy may well be needed to help support new online ventures (such as is already available in Norway, France and Holland). Freely accessible sites will not disappear, but gradually audiences will come to understand again that good journalism is something worth paying for. As the value of journalism rises, there is a chance that diversity will also improve, providing good, well-paid employment for serious, dedicated people who think that keeping the world informed is a job worth doing. But direct payment has not covered the costs of journalism for nearly 200 years and it won't be enough. New forms of subsidy will be needed to take the place of advertising because, though information might want to be free, journalists need to be paid.

Notes

1 'Top 15 Most Popular News Websites' (August 2013): the 15 most popular news sites as derived from eBizMBA Rank, a constantly updated average of each website's Alexa Global Traffic Rank and US Traffic Rank from both Compete and Quantcast.

2 Sam Zell was recorded at a meeting in which he described the Washington bureau of the *Tribune* as 'the first unit of *Tribune* that I've talked to that doesn't generate any revenue. So all of you are overhead.' Available at www.npr.org/templates/story/story. php?storyId=89446846 (accessed 4 April 2014).

3 Guardian Media Group Annual Results 2013. Available at www.gmgplc.co.uk/press-releases/guardian-media-group-plc-gmg-today-announces-its-results-for-the-financial-year -ended-31-march-2013/ (accessed 6 September 2013).

4 According to *Daily Mail* finance director Stephen Daintith, interviewed in the *Guardian*, 'The actual investment in Mail Online has been very small, £50m cumulative over about five years' (Halliday 2013).

5 *Daily Mail* figures provided to an investors briefing in March 2013.

Chapter 7

Ethics in practice

The word 'ethics' comes from the Greek word '*ethos*' for 'character' which in turn derives from the word 'habit'. A concern for ethics implies a concern for how we behave in the world and how we develop as human beings, but it also implies that ethics arise out of habits of behaviour, which are what we think of as 'character'. To live ethically is, very broadly speaking, to take into consideration the impact of your own behaviour on others and as far as possible to live so that you enhance your own life and the lives of those around you. Attempts to find the common threads in ethical behaviour have kept generations of philosophers in business, but becoming an ethical person is not like applying for a job, there is no universal description that we can look to for guidance; it is a social construction, based on a projection of our collective assumptions about how a well-functioning adult should behave in a well-functioning society. My ethics would foreground rights over my body. Your equally firmly held ethics might not. However, the fact that ethics are socially constructed doesn't mean that they don't matter. Learning to live well with other people is an essential part of living a good life. This chapter will first consider what an ethical journalism might look like and then it will consider why it is that debates on ethics have not been central to the field of journalism studies. It will then go on to consider new approaches to ethical decision-making in the light of these debates.

Value ethics

Journalists are in the business of making and publicizing ethical decisions on a daily basis. Every story covered involves a series of choices: who to believe, what to prioritize, how to frame the narrative. Journalists take upon themselves the role of moral arbiter every time they decide whether to reveal the sins of others and hold them up to public scrutiny. Using human lives to tell moral tales is one of the ways in which human beings have always defined themselves and their cultures but, unlike the curtain-twitcher or bar-room philosopher, the stories told by journalists are amplified and broadcast to vast numbers of people, and unlike novelists, journalists use identifiable individuals to tell their stories. They have the power to do enormous harm as well as enormous good. An understanding of that power is the first step towards a recognition that it should not be used lightly. With power comes responsibility – and necessarily ethical judgement.

Since journalism is in the front line both of maintaining, and disrupting, normative values, a rule-based approach to ethics can only provide a back-stop to decision-making; a means of settling disputes about the boundaries of reasonable behaviour. But journalists working daily with human stories need something beyond boundaries and laws. Nick Couldry argued, in *Listening Beyond the Echoes* (2006), that Aristotle's approach to 'virtue ethics' would be helpful. Instead of Kantian rules of behaviour based on normative values that are imposed from without, virtue ethics relies on the 'virtues' or dispositions we internalise through experience. It demands that we ask ourselves what it means, not only to live well for ourselves, but also to live in a way that helps others live well. It is an ethics of judgement rather than an ethics of rules and as such provides a way forward for journalists who are very often faced with making practical decisions about exposing, concealing promoting or distorting information in ways which have very real consequences.[1]

Aristotle suggested that there are five particular social virtues: courage, compassion, self-love, friendship and forgiveness, but none comes automatically, each needs to be achieved through thought and experience. So for example, if a source divulges information indiscreetly, you should consider whether you have a duty to protect him or her, or a greater duty to your audience (or your editor) or indeed your own career. There is no rule that can be employed here to help you, but virtue ethics would insist on a balanced position in which the harm you might do is balanced against the good that might come from it. The decision to protect your source might demonstrate cowardice if you are merely trying to shield yourself from anger. In this case, the virtuous position would be the courageous one of saying what you believe to be true. On the other hand, if the only reason for divulging the information is to derive malicious pleasure (or allow other people to do so), then you should think again. There is no virtue in holding up another person to ridicule, but there may well be virtue if you do so out of indignation about the way that person has behaved towards others.

At the centre of this decision lies another virtue. It is the virtue of truthfulness. How do we make judgements at all if we don't know what is true? And how can we trust, or be trusted, if we don't tell the truth? In personal relationships it may be perfectly possible to agree that ethical behaviour is based on a clear policy of telling the truth about the things we have done (or failed to do) but journalists find themselves faced with a dilemma on a regular basis because it is not easy to know what is true when you are faced with a whole number of competing versions of events and have no means of verifying them through direct experience. While the argument that knowledge is both socially constructed and inherently ideological might sharpen your critical faculties, it will not help you to decide how to tell a story in the best interests of your audience. Your job is to find a way through the thickets of information, to pick apart those accounts that are merely self-serving, or partial, and to attempt to construct a narrative which is a fair and reasonable representation of events, albeit filtered through your own understanding of them as we discussed in Chapter 1 'News Defined'.

Bernard Williams, in his book *Truth and Truthfulness* (2002), unpicks some of these minefields and comes to the conclusion that the virtue of truthfulness lies in the sincerity with which we pursue accuracy. By adding the concept of 'sincerity', he suggests that a journalist (or anyone else) considers what he or she truly believes to be the case. Someone who sincerely believes in the accuracy of a statement doesn't, for example, go through an entire report, pick out the only negative statement and use that to represent the whole. Sincerity will always allow the audience to recognise the element of doubt and, where there is clearly more than one possible 'truth', will make that clear by including other opinions. But sincerity doesn't take refuge in the 'strategic ritual' of neutrality. Where the balance of evidence clearly points one way, then the ethical journalist has the courage to say so, while also including the dissenting view. Sincerity implies both the courage to draw conclusions and the humility to admit when you are proved wrong.

Roger Silverstone in *Media and Morality* (2006: 136) added to the virtues required by journalists an additional quality of 'hospitality', which could be described as an unconditional openness to others. He saw journalists as people with a very special responsibility towards strangers because, in a rapidly globalizing world, it is their job to 'make it [the world] available to us as a political and social reality'. This might seem an odd virtue to add as an essential one for journalists, but he saw that journalists have the storyteller's power either to help or harm the growing inter-connectedness of cultures. He could see the damage that can be done by the use of stories to create inter-communal disputes and felt that journalists had a particular duty to use language as a means of welcoming rather than repelling strangers. Media hospitality would, he suggests, 'ensure that ... the bodies and voices of those who might otherwise be marginalised will be seen and heard on their own terms' (2006: 136).

Marginalizing ethics

These are not complicated values and few would dispute their importance in their everyday dealings with others. This is the case, not only in the UK where, arguably, the particular characteristics of the marketplace (highly competitive but dominated by very powerful interests) mean that the debate has been most needed, but also in countries where higher ethical standards have hitherto been upheld, either because there has been less market competition, or because professional organizations have been stronger. As market forces change media structures globally, debates about ethics take on a new salience for those concerned with journalism, even though, for a variety of reasons, questions of ethical behaviour have tended to be marginalised in mainstream debates about journalism.

For political economists and sociologists, the question has seemed a diversion of little consequence because, as we discussed in Chapter 2 'News Interrupted', the structures of the media organizations that produce news are considered inimical to the possibility of individual agency. For a journalist to act ethically, he or she must be free to act according to his or her own conscience. Studies of media structures and ownership suggest that most journalists are not free actors (Bourdieu 2005). They are very heavily constrained by hierarchical editorial structures and operate most of the time under instruction from editors (Marr 2005: 235, Greenslade 2008, Yelland 2013), who in their turn are acting under instruction from proprietors, who are almost always either part of the ruling elite, using their news organizations for influence, or interested only in making money from them. However the tendency to see journalists as part of the structures under scrutiny, rather than being subject to those structural pressures, means that the potential to form protective organizations which might help them collectively to resist such pressures is insufficiently debated and it is these possibilities that we will discuss later in this chapter.

Cultural studies approaches also largely ignore ethical dilemmas as they are experienced by journalists, but in this case because their focus has been rather more on the agency of audiences than on journalists. Silverstone (2006) recognises the needs of the 'others' who are marginalized or misrepresented by journalism but he doesn't quite see the position of the journalists themselves and for John Fiske (1992), since audiences are capable of making their own 'readings' of news events and drawing their own conclusions, it is not necessary to worry about either the author of a text or its subjects. For those who have been misrepresented in the press, it is of little comfort to be told not to worry because audiences don't really believe what they read. If a news organization tells only a part of the truth and fails to provide context, audiences may have insufficient evidence with which to make such judgements.

Surprisingly perhaps, liberal pluralist approaches also have little time for the question of ethics, but in this case it is because the subject has been entirely subsumed into a debate on press freedom (Peters 2005). For liberals it is axiomatic that the news media should remain free of any controls because it is only through such freedom that the people can resist the desire of the state to control them. Liberal certainty has no time for moral scruples. In the liberal marketplace of ideas, everything can be said because only if it is said can it then be counteracted. John Milton, writing in 1644 in favour of a free press, argued that truth would always overcome falsehood and that there should be no controls on the right to publish. It is a powerful argument and it underpins most of the legal defences for press freedom that are discussed in Chapter 2. However it doesn't fully take into account the issue of relative power or of individual harm. A news organization has far greater power and influence than an individual – even in the age of Twitter – and too often freedom to publish is a weapon in the hands of the powerful rather than a means of furthering democratic debate. We will now take each of these approaches in turn and look more closely at their arguments.

Liberalism and free speech fundamentalism

The belief that ideas should be tested, to the point of destruction if necessary, and that all voices must be heard, lies at the very core of Western ideas of democracy with its roots traceable back to ancient Greece. It is the concept of the agora where people of reason were able to form their ideas, argue for them and influence the course of decision making, which underpins the Habermasian (Habermas 1996) model of the eighteenth-century idealized public sphere when, he argued, a press, freed from state control, became a channel for political debate where public opinion could be formed.

This vision of an idealized public sphere, or some version of it, is the one to which most critics refer when they consider the place of the media in the modern world. It is the ideal against which scholars measure the success or failure of the modern news media in a democracy. It underpins media legislation in democratic countries. It is a vision that asks, not merely whether people understand or are interested in what is written or said, but whether this form of communication fulfils the requirements of democracy. Does it inform? Does it represent different points of view and/or different political positions? Is it sufficiently independent of the state and its institutions to form a critique of them?

In the Western press, defence of press freedom has become almost an article of faith, often produced as the reason for invasion of privacy, and occasionally in defence of the right to insult,[2] but rarely examined in the original context of the struggle for democracy in parts of the world just emerging from the inflexible rule-bound grip of theocratic hegemony. For Milton in 1644 and John Stuart Mill 200 years later, freedom of speech was the weapon of reason (Mill 1859: 37). Jürgen Habermas writing another century later, assumed that, given favourable conditions, reason, like water, would always come through. It would prevail over dishonesty or dissembling and in doing so it would knock down the unreasonable assumptions of superstition and prejudice.

Ideas about free expression went hand in hand with notions of scientific progress. Both stem from a belief in the possibility of objective discovery. Scientific method takes as its starting point the need to measure natural phenomena in order to understand how they work. Freedom of speech takes scientific methods one step further because it underpins the right to disseminate ideas that may contradict existing norms, and freedom of the press takes its moral starting point from arguments about freedom of expression – often directly so – without taking into consideration the differences between individual freedoms and the freedom of institutions (O'Neill 2013).

In considering the importance of freedom of expression and press freedom, it is important to note that the argument in favour of it does not rest on any assumption that the press or the individual should behave morally, or indeed that they should be correct in their assumptions. The argument in favour of freedom lies entirely in the way in which information can be received and interpreted by its audiences. Freedom can never be offered only to the 'right-eous' because that would undermine the basic assumptions of all these strands of philosophy that ideas must be set free because only then can the battle of reason commence. In this 'fundamentalist' view of liberty, moral certainty lies only in the tearing down of moral boundaries. Nothing can be 'off limits' because to ban is to pre-judge. In this liberal landscape, all human beings are equal and must therefore be equally capable of arguing against that which they find offensive.

In fact there are no countries in which freedom of expression is absolute and indeed Milton did not go quite that far. He was not opposed to laws on libel or even on blasphemy, but he believed that the onus should be on the publisher to defend the position rather than to be censored in advance. The courts were after all also public and if an editor truly believed in the importance of what he (usually he) published then he should be prepared to stake his own wealth and liberty on it.

This purist liberal position is often alluded to in arguments over journalism ethics. Editor turned academic, Professor Tim Luckhurst (2012: 25) argues, in a paper published on the website of the UK Free Speech Network that, had the police only done their job properly and prosecuted all the individuals associated with phone hacking at the *News of the World*, the 'moral panic spawned by the Leveson enquiry might not have taken place'. He then goes on to absolve jour-nalists themselves of any fault in relation to phone hacking – because the police had done nothing to apply the legal penalties that already existed.

This is not a position that Milton is likely to have espoused. He believed in moral responsibility and felt that editors should be prepared to defend their own positions – he was not suggesting that they should keep on blindly pushing the boundaries until the law intervened like a parent punishing a naughty child. Most of us abide by shared rules of conduct most of the time, without looking over our shoulders to see if a police officer is watching. The idea that the only thing that went wrong was a failure on the part of the police suggests an infantile world in which everyone simply operates on the basis of their own self-interest – until they are stopped.

Of course Milton was talking about a society in which there was relative equality between contestants in the debate. In the seventeenth century, only a minority of the population was literate and only those with the means to defend themselves in court were likely to engage in such battles over truth. He was not talking about a world in which a mass circulation newspaper, read by millions, can decide to make an example of an individual or a minority group, who might have little realistic means of fighting back, in print or via the courts. In the case of a *News of the World* exposé of young drug addict Jennifer Elliot, it is hard to see what truth was being fought for and the subject of the article was given no opportunity to 'grapple' in free and open debate. Reporter Paul McMullan told a BBC Radio 4 reporter about what he had done:

> Yeah, I'd totally humiliated and destroyed her. It wasn't necessary. She didn't deserve it. She was having a bad time after her own dad had died,

and, yeah, I went a step too far. And it was based on, now, a criminal act, so you've got to question in some cases, criminal acts perpetrated by journalists aren't always justified and in this case it was not. Not only was it not justified, it was downright wrong – I sincerely regret it, and again, if there was anyone to apologise to, I would, but they're all dead – mother's dead, she's dead, father's dead. So in any way seeking atonement, I can at least say in this case we were wrong.

(McMullan 2010)

This story was based on a tip-off from a policeman who was paid for his information. So it would also have fallen into Luckhurst's definition of misconduct that should have been stopped (presumably by police action) because it was unlawful. However it is not just the fact that a policeman was bribed that should have made McMullan pause. The issue was not that he had stepped over a legal line but that he had done something unethical. He had deliberately set out to harm someone who was, in his own words: 'fragile' and he could see, in retrospect, that it was wrong and required 'atonement'. Why his editor could not see that it was wrong and refrain from printing it, he does not relate.

It is personal ethics that matters here – not the law – and too often those espousing the liberal position conflate ethics with rules and laws and fail to see that they are different. Peter Preston, former editor of the *Guardian*, argues for example, that:

once you put judgment – individual judgment according to circumstances – at the heart of your job, then rigid codes of ethics don't easily apply ... sometimes the story, the necessary story, goes beyond neat boundaries and 20 questions. The only way isn't ethics.

(Phillips 2013: 256)

Here Preston recognises that journalists need to operate in a grey area that may on occasion step outside the law but he cannot see that ethical judgement comes to the rescue of journalism, it doesn't inhibit it. Ethics are not derived from laws, they are rooted in something deeper than mere obedience. Personal ethics are quintessentially about making judgements according to circumstances. Behaviour that in one social context is used by a news organization as a marker of deviance will, in a different period or place, seem to be evidence of vulnerability, and it is indeed individual judgement that drives the decision to angle a story as evidence of moral breakdown: as evidence of the need for social support or indeed, as evidence of endurance against the odds. These judgements matter because the way in which a story is treated defines it either as a means of policing existing norms, as a plea for a more humane society, or simply as a story to be consumed as a form of 'schadenfreude'. The law cannot tell us whether it is reasonable to print a story about a young drug addict who has turned to prostitution to feed her habit, but ethical judgement might. Indeed without ethics, journalism is little more than a pernicious form of entertainment in which real lives are served up to take the place of characters in a soap opera of the damned (Phillips 2013).

Democracy requires a press that is free to criticize it and society requires news media that are prepared to defy taboo and challenge stereotypes and pre-conceptions, so it is right that news organizations are vigilant against any attempt to curb their freedoms. However, if journalists are to be allowed free-doms, above ordinary citizens, to occasionally break the law, then they should surely have to demonstrate in some way that they are acting in the public interest and not merely for private gain. The best riposte to the regulatory impulse would be to demonstrate that journalists take their ethical duties ser-iously, in the sense of doing what is right in the circumstances and weighing up each judgement at the time. A values-driven approach to ethical decision-making, as recommended by Aristotle, doesn't require rules to follow, nor a simple test of utility, but asks that each action should be judged on the basis of our own lives: 'How should each of us conduct our life so that it is a life any of us should live' (Phillips et al. 2010: 65).

The problem with the liberal approach to journalism is that it relies for its defence on an imagined state of balance in which all views have equal weight and everyone is equally capable of defending their own lives and views. As philosopher Onora O'Neill points out (O'Neill 2013), that is not the world in which journalism today takes place. In the commercial world of the media market, editors are more likely to be considering the demands of their shareholders than the demands of democracy.

Power to the people

Some cultural studies approaches may appear to end in the same place as liberal approaches but they start from a very different impulse. Where liberalism insists on freedom so that ideas can be tested, cultural approaches suggest that freedom of speech is largely irrelevant because it is in any case a fiction. Fiske writes of the deeply political nature of news. He sees the production and distribution of information as a means by which the 'power-bloc' attempts to form the knowledge and understanding of the people (Fiske 1992:49).

Looked at from this perspective, the serious newspapers that are so important to a Habermasian view of the public sphere (see Chapter 2) are not so much a place where public knowledge is debated and formed, but a means by which elite knowledge is passed off as 'common sense' disciplining the people into accepting a world view that might not be in their interests but which appears to be the only available option. However cultural studies approaches rescue the audience from the subjugation suggested by the Frankfurt school pessimists described in Chapter 2, by recognition of the resistance of the individuals who make up the audience. Here Fiske joins hands with the Internet optimists (Shirky 2008, Beckett 2008, Jenkins 2008), who see the ability to 'talk back' as evidence of an active, or interactive, audience that cannot be so easily seduced by power.

He suggests (as we discussed in Chapter 5) that the tabloid excesses are not intended to be taken seriously, that they are a parody and that they 'expose what is normally tacitly accepted to subversive laughter'. Looked at from this point of view, those who complain about the un-ethical behaviour of certain parts of the popular press are castigated as elitists who would like to ban pleasure and replace it with a dour form of dreary news-bulletin on a par with the worst excesses of Soviet propaganda. For Fiske, the importance of popular journalism lies in the scepticism with which it is received because he believes that 'tabloid stories oppose or interrogate norms' (1992: 50).

This view is taken up by Herman Wasserman who examined the rise of the South African tabloids and concluded that 'In the post-apartheid society, the tabloids provide a space where dominant post-apartheid narratives of democratic progress and the "better life for all" promised by the ANC when it came to power, can be contested' (Wasserman 2008: 792). He points out that the tabloids have come under attack from the 'journalistic establishment' who see them as 'flaunting conventional norms like objectivity, neutrality and truthtelling through their sensationalist, opinionated and seemingly far-fetched stories as well as objectifying women by publishing pictures of scantily clad or topless women and fascination with sex' (Wasserman 2006).

While it is certainly the case that tabloid or sensational news can be opposi-tional, this doesn't address the question of whether it is ethical. Tabloid jour-nalism depends for its sensationalism on personalization. It uses personal stories to provide comprehensible narratives of bigger themes. Stories of celebrities falling in and out of love, in and out of night clubs, and in and out of drug rehabilitation are arguably just a part of the public relations game played by the very rich and are exploited by news organizations to entertain the poor. It is assumed that no people were harmed in the playing of the game. But people *are* harmed and it is at that point that this cheerful collusion with the tabloid irreverence begins to wear thin.

Not all of those engaged with audience studies would agree with Fiske's approach. Mirca Madianou (2013: 198–198) turns her attention away from the audience and asks us to listen to those who are spoken about in media texts: 'the voice of the injured subject'. She argues that the ability to speak for oneself and to be allowed to give an account of oneself 'is an essential feature of what it means to be human'. She goes back to the original meaning of freedom of expression as the right of individuals to speak out and points out that, when institutions speak, they do so with far greater power so that the voices of individuals are almost always drowned out. Even sympathetic media are inclined to simplify messages in order to clarify their narratives and, in simplifying, they too often misrepresent the people they aim to serve. When the news media are unsympathetic, their simplifying narrative can do harm. For those who have been subjected to the myth-making rhetorical attack of a tabloid newspaper in full cry, the damage can be long lasting.

When Fiske suggests that tabloids interrogate disciplinary norms, he carefully chooses for his examples a series of stories in which exaggeration is used to

question normative assumptions. But tabloids use their power far more effectively to bolster normative assumptions and to invite audiences to the mediatized
equivalent of the public stocks where the deviant are held up to ridicule. This
experience can be particularly traumatic for those who are unintentionally
caught up in media scandals as the living 'personification' of behaviour that is
considered outside the bounds of those social norms that conservative news
organisations feel they have a duty to police (see more on this in Chapter 1).
Mostly it is the poor and powerless who are held up as examples of 'bad'
behaviour: those who are on benefits, who are newcomers to a country, or
whose sexuality offends the people in power. Their stories will be blown up to
sell newspapers or attract clicks and then they disappear (for more on this see
Chapter 1). But sometimes the news media turns on someone who has rather
more public profile.

It is often argued that, if people have public responsibility, or if they have
'courted publicity' they are 'fair game'. As one journalist put it to me when discussing a sacked head of children's services: 'Well she had a three figure salary.
People in positions of power should be prepared to take responsibility.' The
person under discussion was Sharon Shoesmith who, in 2008, was in charge of
child welfare, in a north London borough, when a particularly unpleasant case
of child murder came to public notice. There is no doubt that a parent who kills
a child, or is complicit in the death of a child, has transgressed the boundaries of
normative behaviour. When such deaths come to public notice they arouse great
passion. Far from questioning such norms, the press almost automatically follows
the well-trodden path of a classic 'moral panic' (Cohen 1972) in response to
these deaths.

Stanley Cohen described a moral panic thus: 'a condition, episode, person or
group of persons emerges to become defined as a threat to societal values and
interests' (Cohen 1972: 9). Erich Goode and Nachman Ben-Yehuda (1994)
established sets of stages through which media moral panics then progress: concern, hostility, consensus, disproportionality and volatility. Usually the character
that attracts the opprobrium is a marginalised young person – or group of
people (folk devils). In the stages that follow, the focus shifts to the people who
should be in charge and demands are made that 'something must be done'.
When action is taken the cycle is over and the panic subsides. In the case of
Shoesmith, the press pack, deprived of the opportunity to demand retribution
from the child's murderers, who had already been dealt with by the court,
turned their attack on another folk devil, in this case the social workers who
(in their collective opinion) had failed to save the child and they called upon the
government to act against her.

In her chapter on 'Moral Panics' in *Postmodernism and Popular Culture*, Angela
McRobbie (1994: 208) argues that the classic cycle described above in which
'folk devils' are demonised and political retribution is then demanded by the
media, has been overtaken by a more 'knowing' response in which marginal
groups play with the moral outrage expressed by the media in order to define

their own difference, and experts and pressure groups use these opportunities to recruit the mass media to their position, thus demonstrating that marginalized groups are no longer merely subject to media power, they also make use of it for their own ends. While this happens in some cases and the power of interest groups have had an impact on the way some issues are now reported, there are still many instances in which the mass media get caught up in a loop of retributive rage, often recruited by conservative political forces who see opportunities in vilifying particular people, who can be used as examples of failed (usually) progressive policies.

Individuals on welfare, teachers, nurses and social workers have all been subject to attack in the conservative press when it has been politically expedient to use them as a metaphor for the moral failures of progressive political policies. Shoesmith was a senior public servant (paid for by the taxpayer) so the people (as represented by the mass media) were characterized as having special rights to demand that she pay for her failure to prevent this child's death. Lilie Chouliaraki speaks of journalism as 'performative'. It is, she argues, about 'doing things with words, not simply about using words as facts' (2012: 268). In this case, the British newspapers, full of righteous indignation, orchestrated a concerted campaign, which was prosecuted with the ferocity of a medieval witch-hunt.

The *Sun* (owned by News International) went furthest, using audiences and online forums to gather an avenging army in order to force Shoesmith out of her job. Pursued by photographers and journalists, she was nevertheless given no chance to speak for herself, or to defend her position or her reputation, she was rendered 'voiceless'. Five years later she finally managed to win compensation for unfair dismissal, but by then her career was over and the money she was offered was little recompense for her destroyed reputation. She had been effectively 'dehumanized' by journalists in pursuit of a story.

This is not the place to debate the facts of the case. Some argue that people in her position should be prepared to take responsibility (even if that means losing their livelihood), others point to the fact that, if the head of Children's Services resigned every time a child was killed, we would have nobody left to run the services. Nor is the question about whether the press should have covered the story – it was clearly important that it should do so. It is more a matter of proportionality. This was a woman who had spent her entire life working with and for children. How much did the destruction of this woman's life aid the protection of children?

Journalists may argue in response that their job is: 'to hold power to account' and that she was clearly in a position of power in relation to this child. Cultural theorist Ian Connell (1992: 81–82) suggested that tabloid stories that deal with apparent abuses of power are 'written on behalf of the people' and are 'the expression of outrage on behalf of the "have nots"'. He might have seen the audiences of the *Sun* being gathered together as an empowering act of 'resistance' against servants of the state. However it is probably more accurate to say that they were themselves being used in a carefully orchestrated drama by the editors of a mass-market newspaper who found it expedient to embarrass the particular political elite of the moment. The sacrifice of Shoesmith provided the necessary dramatic climax to the story, it created a feeling of 'belonging' to the readers who signed the *Sun* petition to sack her, and it was a useful staging post in a campaign against a government of which the *Sun* had tired.

Certainly as discussed in Chapter 5 'Audiences, Networks, Interaction', the Internet does provide greater opportunities for audiences to interact and challenge the hegemonic narratives of journalists but, as Madianou points out (2013: 183), it has also further disempowered victims of media witch-hunts, who now find that, instead of attacks fading away with the newspaper cycle, they remain forever and continue to be equally accessible, online, for all to see. Sharon Shoesmith had her day in court but the media coverage will never go away. Less powerful individuals caught up in the attacks on the welfare or immigration systems have no effective means of being heard at all and risk being eternally frozen in the role of 'folk devil'. The destruction of reputation is like a lingering death that the subject is required to live out in public, their bodies and lives used as collateral in the battle for the moral high ground.

Mass media power doesn't disappear in a networked society, it is amplified. Individuals may publish their thoughts and opinions but it is usually necessary to be well known, or have a very good grasp of how social media can be manipulated, for an individual to make use of network effects. People without connections may speak, but they will never be heard. The mass media, on the other hand, can harness network effects to ensure an even greater audience that will swamp the small voice of the individual. Networked or collaborative journalism may go a very small way towards shifting the balance but, as long as journalism provides the gateway to the mass audience, it continues to hold the power.

Structures, power and markets

For political economists it is the ownership and structure of the press, rather than audience reception that dictates its outcomes. It is hard to escape the logic of this position. Journalists working for the competitive commercial press are indeed, more often than not, operating in a hierarchical structure in which they are expected to dance to the proprietor's tune. When the owner changes, so does the tune. As *Philadelphia Enquiry* columnist Monica Yant Kinney wrote when she heard that her newspaper had been purchased by a local business man who she had regularly criticized in print: 'I've never heard of an entrepreneur who would buy something to get beat up' (Associated Press 2012).

Richard Peppiatt was a tabloid news journalist who gave evidence at the Leveson. He admitted to the Inquiry that some stories he wrote at the *Daily Star*, where he worked, were 'wholly inaccurate, often written under pressure from superiors to distort the facts at hand'. He went on:

> It is fair to say that in a highly competitive market in which agencies are competing to get their stories used by the national press, there is an obvious

financial incentive in making your stories stand out from the crowd, and so the temptation to spin or embellish a story always exists. One obvious consequence of reporters cannibalizing the work of other journalists is that the former is often wholly unaware of the veracity of their information. Sometimes the maxim that a story is 'too good to check' comes into play, and in this manner falsehoods can easily become propagated across the media.

(Peppiatt 2011)

Peppiatt walked out of his job when he could no longer stand it and earned praise for his 'conscientious objection' from Alistair Campbell, ex-tabloid journalist and former 'spin doctor' to Prime Minister Tony Blair. Campbell feels that the state of British journalism would be improved if journalists just behaved more honorably. He said:

Journalists have to own their journalism, see it as something with codes of behaviour. So that when a news editor instructs them to harass, or write what amounts to lies, or twist the facts to suit a pre-ordained line they cannot support, they say 'No, I won't,' just as a good doctor would not knowingly prescribe the wrong drugs or a good lawyer would not knowingly misrepresent the law. It takes courage to stand up to a boss, but courage is what leads to change, and there has been too little of it bottom up, from people saying 'this is wrong, not what I came into journalism to do'.

(Campbell 2013)

But, given the structure of the British press, it is not always easy to take such a stand. In the close knit world of news media, a journalist who has an ethical difference with one news editor will probably find that his or her name has been broadcast ahead, before they have even left the building. Only those with considerable cultural capital already accrued, as well as considerable courage, can take the risk of arguing with the editor. The combination of hierarchical structures and precarious employment is, as Pierre Bourdieu observes, 'a loss of liberty, through which censorship ... can be more easily expressed' (Bourdieu 2005: 43). He might have been describing a situation rather like this:

I have spent this week reporting for XX and it has strained to breaking point every moral fibre I thought I had. They decide what a story is, then get me to find the facts that fit their narrative. This has happened on at least three occasions this week and they ignore facts or opinions which break the mould. I know this is true to an extent with every news publication, but given my political beliefs I find it quite galling. I do not want to do this for a long time, but it is too good an opportunity to turn down at the moment (not least financially). They are getting me in again next week, however they have said it will be on a week-to-week basis from thereon so I am doubtful of anything more permanent.

(Personal communication, 2012)

Or perhaps like this, 10 years earlier:

> I thought the story was appalling. I thought all along that it was a ludicrous exercise with no logic whatsoever and I felt very ashamed about it ... I talked to a senior reporter and said that I wasn't very happy about it and he said to keep my head down and say nothing. ... He said that I would lose my job if I raised it with anybody more senior than him. ... I set about planning to leave. I'd just arrived so I knew I couldn't leave straight away ... I kept my head down, I worked hard, I knew it would be at least a year before I could go. I was in a position the same as everybody who joins the [paper] from a local newspaper in that I was doing shifts on a daily basis. And it was up to them to decide whether to renew my job the next day. So if I lost my job I wouldn't be able to pay the rent or anything like that which probably isn't an excuse but there was still that thought there.
>
> (Interview with reporter, mid-market popular daily, 2002)

Both these journalists did in the end find ways of moving on to work on publications that they found more ethical, but in leaving they were in no way able to change the organizations they had left. As one of them said: 'The guy who is standing on the footplate doesn't change the direction of the train. And if you get to a position where you can change it, you've internalised so much of it that you don't necessarily want to' (Interview with reporter, mid-market popular daily, 2002).

Bourdieu described journalism as 'a weakly autonomous field' (2005: 41) in which the autonomy of an actor is tied to his or her place in the field (this is described in more detail in Chapter 4). He argued that the more commercial the publication, and the more intense the competition for audience, the less freedom journalists have to act on their own initiative or to make their own moral judgements. On mid-market and popular newspapers in the UK, young journalists are kept on rolling contracts so that every time they make a mistake they will be afraid that they won't be re-hired. Pretty soon they find themselves taking on the 'doxa' of the organization and searching out the kind of story that the news editor will like. Precarity of employment is not particular to the UK however; it was mentioned as a growing problem worldwide in a report from the International Federation of Journalists (Walters et al. 2006).

This would matter a great deal less if all journalists were free to move around the field and find their place working on publications, or in organizations, that allow them to make their own judgements. However competition in the media tends to homogenize, pulling all publications into the centre ground where they compete against each other for the largest audiences (see Chapter 2). Given these realities, much of the attention of political economists has been focused on issues of market competition and plurality. Media scholar Bob Franklin in *Newszak and News Media* said: 'Competition is the prime mover in journalism's move down market.' He suggests that a secondary factor is the 'increasingly concentrated ownership of British newspapers' (1997: 223).

Similar arguments on a more global scale are made by Edward Herman and Robert McChesney (1997), who traced ownership internationally and demonstrated the degree to which a small number of Western media companies were then moving into positions of domination in emerging economies. This view of an American 'cultural imperialism' (Schiller 1976, Saïd 1993) in which the ideas of the imperial West are implanted in the minds of people in the developing world has been contested by those who point both to the growing power of local companies and programming and the skepticism of audiences (Tomlinson 1991). However, as Daya Thussu (2009) points out, locally owned television news is in no way protected from the pressures of competition. Scandal is a currency across the world and nowhere more so than in countries like India and South Africa, where the emerging news space is fought over by competing commercial interests.

The argument for political economists has therefore been that it is the structure that needs changing to ensure that commerce is not the only, or even the major, factor in shaping the field of journalism. A more plural, representative media would, they suggest, be more responsible. There is certainly evidence to suggest that, where the state supports diversity by helping small publications, subsidizing entry jobs on new or minority publications and providing start-up capital to new ventures, it also underpins independence from the state rather than undermining it and improves ethical behaviour (Benson 2011, Hallin and Mancini 2004). A more ethical system, they maintain, can therefore only be produced by political action, it can never be a product simply of the marketplace: 'A media system, that sustains journalism of consequence is willed into existence and maintained by a people and by their representatives' (McChesney and Nichols 2011).

The arguments for public action to ensure diversity are not in themselves controversial. Most democracies have some controls in place to try and regulate markets to ensure that no one provider is capable of dominating. However, although it is clearly not in the interests of politicians to allow any proprietor to manoeuvre themselves into becoming a monopoly provider of news, there has been little action taken to prevent mergers and consolidation across the news markets. The opponents of such market regulation tend to be the owners of large media corporations (Tompkins 2003), who are wont to point towards the Internet and simply declare that plurality exists because there is a plethora of different places and sources from which audiences can choose. They argue also that any attempt to try and enforce plurality by imposing ownership caps or preventing mergers is likely to be counter-productive, given that the news media are under financial pressure and only the big beasts can survive in such a cruel media market. This argument holds little water. Consolidation in newspapers in the 1980s and 1990s was about increasing profits rather than safeguarding companies (see Chapter 6).

However action to limit the size of media organizations is never going to be enough if it is the sole instrument of regulation. Plurality of providers doesn't necessarily equate with plurality of opinion. This is why arguments about greater plurality often go hand in hand with a de-professionalizing agenda. If journalists are seen merely as instruments of powerful elites then, the logic goes, it is important to establish and fund alternative methods of providing news. Dan Hind (2010), for example, describes a vision of journalism in which practitioners publish manifestos and public funding is offered to those the public wish to promote. While there is no doubt that 'alternative' journalism has a vital function in changing the news agenda and amplifying alternative non-mainstream views (see Chapter 4) and a diversity in ownership would certainly be desirable, reform that relies on de-professionalizing journalists, as some form of ethical alternative, is not a useful way forward.

The Twitter-sphere demonstrates that amateur communicators are no more inherently ethical, and often a great deal less so, than those who are trained to do the job and do it for a living. News organizations who use untrained community reporters have found that they favour opinion over reporting and trained people are needed to re-write copy, but usually on less favourable conditions than reporters and with much less job satisfaction (see Chapters 4 and 5). Given these examples, it is hardly surprising that journalists tend to regard untrained people producing content for free as a threat to working conditions, job satisfaction and indeed to the jobs themselves. And greater job insecurity is not a means of producing more ethical actors. As Bourdieu (2005) points out, it could well have entirely the opposite effect.

Towards a practical ethics of journalism

While all three theoretical positions have strengths, they all tend to downplay the position of journalists as 'actors' in favour of structural change, audience involvement or the play of the market. Ignoring the agency of journalists and therefore marginalizing the question of personal responsibility and its problems has left a vacuum at the centre of an important debate. It is not enough to say, as does media scholar Barbie Zelizer, that 'ethical standards are all but impossible to achieve in journalism and that codes of situated ethics do not come close to reflecting all that journalism constitutes' (2013: 281). To take such a stance is to renounce any responsibility or indeed concern for the harm that can be done to individuals by a news media that is more interested in winning in the market than in the public interest. It also renounces responsibility for the journalists who so often find themselves sucked into the centre of ethical firestorms.

Journalists work under pressure. They have to deal with angry sources who feel misrepresented, and eager editors who want them to push the boundaries just that little bit further. They have to sort out the genuinely aggrieved from people who are seeking revenge and hold to account those who are trying to avoid responsibility without tarnishing those who find themselves innocently in the firing line. Every story involves a series of small decisions, each of which can have consequences for sources, for subjects and for the journalists themselves. To suggest that journalists have no need for a considered approach to ethics is to suggest that they should navigate shark-infested waters in a blindfold.

However, as the discussion above makes clear, nor is it enough simply to enjoin journalists to behave better. Individual journalists may wish to behave better, but too often the only power they have at their disposal is the power to withhold their labour. Where that is done in combination with other journalists it stands some chance of success, but acting alone, journalists have very little power against commercial media interests. The only effective way of changing the behaviour of these organizations is to use regulation in order to change the balance of power within and between them. It is only when they have a vested interest in behaving ethically that they will change and invest in systems that demonstrate they are trustworthy.

But regulation, in the hands of the state, can very easily become censorship so any form of state regulation of the media is necessarily regarded with deep suspicion. This is why attempts to bring in a form of legally based, ethical self-regulation in the UK triggered world-wide responses from editors concerned that any hint of censorship in the British press would lead to a crack-down on press freedom elsewhere (Peyrègne 2014). In fact, none of the major organizations favouring regulation in the UK suggested that it should be state controlled. All agreed that ethical regulation must be independent of the government, but also of the proprietors, because both are powerful interests capable of distorting news content.

A system of independent ethical regulation is not easy to devise because there are so many competing interests: journalists, audiences, the subjects of stories, and proprietors. In most (though not all) countries, ethics bodies provide seats for 'independents', often as a means of demonstrating that they are indeed 'independent bodies' with the public interest at heart. However, individuals who represent only themselves (as they do in the UK and Australia for example) are unlikely to have any real power, sitting alongside representatives of major organizations. Ethics councils that fail to recognize the different interests of proprietors (often represented by editors) and the journalists who work for them are also unlikely to be effective in upholding ethical behaviour. In Sweden, Denmark, Norway and Finland, journalists' trade unions appoint members to the ethics bodies. This means that they have the backing of an organization and more power to stand up to their employers when their interests diverge.

If ethical behaviour is about practices, rather than rules, then it requires opportunities for debate far beyond the confines of a single ethics committee, however well organized. It needs a framework that supports and develops ethics in practice.

Sincerity and truthfulness

The sheer complexity of the arguments over ethics and press freedom burst onto the world stage over the publication in a Danish newspaper of 'cartoons' of the Prophet Muhammad in 2005 which deeply upset the religious Muslim minority in that country and led to riots in Muslim countries elsewhere (Eide *et al.* 2009). That the debate arose in Denmark, the only country in Europe with a statutory system of ethical regulation, brings into focus the difficulty of legislating for ethical behaviour. Writing in the *Guardian* at the time, O'Neill wrote in favour of greater curbs on the freedom of the press:

> Once we take account of the power of the media, we are not likely to think that they should enjoy unconditional freedom of expression. We do not think that corporations should have unrestricted rights to invent their balance sheets, or governments to damage or destroy the reputations of individuals or institutions, or to deceive their electorates. Yet contemporary liberal readings of the right to free speech often assume that we can safely accord the same freedom of expression to the powerless and the powerful.
>
> (O'Neill 2006)

She argued then and earlier (1996) that the powers of the news media should be regulated, not just to protect the powerless, but to protect democratic accountability itself. Writing several years later, she had more fully considered the peculiar needs of the news media to be both free of state censorship, able to comment and condemn and yet responsible for actions that harm. Her later solution (2013) lies in regulating process rather than content in order to remove the possibility of censorship from ethical regulation. This raises some interesting ideas about attempts to re-balance the relative power of the subject and the audience in relation to the news organization. Her key recommendations are that material produced as news should be audited to ensure that it is: 'intelligible' and 'assessable' by audiences. It is an approach that speaks directly to the 'virtues' of sincerity, truthfulness and hospitality that were mentioned at the start of this chapter and to the development of ethical practice rather than the imposition of ethical norms.

Some of her suggestions are impractical, for example that news organizations should be obliged to make information available on relationships between journalists and sources that might constitute 'a conflict of interest' (2013: 34). The business of journalism depends on cultivating sources. Indeed, in this context, what is a relationship? At what stage does a relationship, cultivated for the purpose of work, become a conflict of interest? Should a dinner with a source be declared, a cup of coffee, a bottle of champagne? The level of transparency that might seem obvious to academics, who do not mix regularly with the subjects they write about and for whom footnotes and attribution are a form of currency, would be difficult to deliver for journalists, working on covert investigations, often at high speed. And how would such relationships be declared? Any obligation to reveal sources would instantly close down channels of information that are critical to investigative reporting and it is easy to see how useful such an obligation could become to governments and companies intent on preventing leaks.

However there are conflicts of interest that could and should be declared and an auditable duty to do so would be simple to operate and to monitor. For example, if every publication was required to publish a list of gifts and payments, the public would see which publications depend on 'freebies' for restaurant reviews and which pay their own way. This information will become even more important as news organizations stray into the field of promotions. Audiences have a right to know whether so-called 'news' is being paid for by promoters and journalists would be protected from pressure to indulge in covert promotion by the need to publish this information openly. It is certain that companies would continue to offer free tickets and bottles of perfume but at least the readers would have access to information with which to make judgements about how things are reviewed. Such an obligation would also impact bloggers who depend on free gifts but don't tell their audiences about their dependency. Publishing free gifts is neither time-consuming nor expensive and there is little reason (other than subterfuge) why it should be covered up. It would empower audiences, be useful to journalists, and would go to the heart of unethical practice.

One objection would be that such disclosure of interests would be difficult in broadcast and to some extent in printed media (particularly in the popular press). Caveats and footnotes don't work well with articles of 200 words and pages designed around pictures and banner headlines. Nor are they possible on television or radio. However the Internet has now become the live archive of the news media and it offers new opportunities because it is no longer limited by the cost of space and time.

Linking as an ethical practice

The process of linking allows unlimited possibilities to connect readers with material that they can use to verify what they read. Indeed, for early bloggers, linking was seen as a form of attribution. As Jane Singer said, 'What truth is to journalists, transparency is to bloggers' (Singer 2007: 86). However, research into linking practices by mainstream news organisations (Larsson 2013) suggests that it is very far from becoming standard practice. Most hypertext links are internal and take audiences to previous stories on the same subject rather than adding context or the means to 'assess' information (Quandt 2008: 742, Witschge and Redden 2010).

The use of linking and metadata methodologies offers new opportunities for the kind of audit envisaged by O'Neill. It can provide ways of establishing the provenance of information, offering a simple means of improving ethical accountability. With very little expenditure, it is also now possible to develop systems for recording the change history of every article (Media Standards Trust 2008), flagging up the connections to the organizations cited and linking to research material used in articles (Media Reform 2012). Journalists would still be able to write the same tightly crafted summary of a story, structure it to emphasize the angle they (or their editor) prefer and argue for the version that makes sense in the light of the evidence. But they could also be required to link to any public sources they have used and to indicate whether hotels and airlines had provided free flights and accommodation.

Of course much must remain confidential in order to protect investigative journalism and there would need to be a presumption of the right to protect sources but, just by insisting that online news sources link to their *publicly* available sources and offer information about free offers associated with particular articles, news organizations would start to provide an information trail that would be assessable by any member of the audience who cared to read it. This would not be a huge leap for news organizations. Journalists routinely make notes of their online sources so that they can easily retrieve them in the future. It would not be arduous to include these links in their copy.

In an ideal world, these levels of assessability would simply be seen as in the interests of good journalism and news organizations would link as a matter of course. It is clear from existing research that audiences are concerned about the trustworthiness of their news sources (Newman and Levy 2013: 59). So it is in the interests of news organisations that wish to present themselves as trustworthy to develop systems of transparency that would increase trust, but it would be entirely feasible to develop a system of ethical audit, similar to financial auditing, that would simply ensure that such systems were in place and being used on a regular basis. When organizations are held accountable for their practices, by their audiences or their peers, they tend to bring in reliable systems to ensure compliance because it is in their interests to do so.

Hospitality and the right of reply

While assessibility would help to maintain the virtue of truthfulness, it would not help with some of the most difficult ethical dilemmas described in this chapter. The power of the mass media would still retain the power to define the narrative. As Madianou recounts in her work on the 'injured subject', one of the hardest things to bear is voicelessness. To hear yourself spoken about, without any ability to speak back, has a corrosive effect. But one thing could be changed. In this case the statutory right of reply – a right that goes to the heart of the virtue of hospitality.

Just as the protection of anonymity allows some people to say things that they would never dream of saying if they were identifiable, so the power of the big news corporations protects and indeed encourages behaviour that individuals would find untenable in their private lives. Knowing that people have the right to speak back helps to break-down the fortress walls, allowing journalists and editors to feel the pain of those they have hurt.

Such a right has been 'commended' by the Council of Europe and is already provided in France, Germany, Denmark, Belgium, Norway, Sweden, Finland, Greece, Austria, Ireland, Switzerland and South Korea (Fielden 2012: 4,

Youm 2008). The Finnish Freedom of Expression Act enshrines a right of reply in a law that positively upholds freedom of expression, demonstrating that the freedom of expression afforded to the press does not trump the freedom of expression afforded to the individual. Journalists in these countries manage to operate in the knowledge that their subjects have rights and, in most cases, the practice is to ensure that opposing voices are heard within the original article in order to ensure that later corrections are not required. The obligation to offer 'balance' is also mandatory in the UK broadcasting sector.

In the USA, there is no right of reply, just a presumption of professionalism and the rule of the courts. In the UK, editors have long argued against allowing an automatic right of reply on the grounds that it would undermine the freedom of the press, create endless arguments with disgruntled sources and spoil the look and lay-out of their newspapers (Media Reform 2012:10). Under the existing UK complaints system, run by the (soon to be replaced) Press Complaints Commission, an apology or correction is sometimes recommended and is usually complied with, but the complaints system is slow and there is no obligation to make such corrections either prominent or even comprehensible. Often they occur so long after the original transgression that the audiences may have little idea of the injury that is being corrected (Media Standards Trust 2011). Of course, complainants have the right to use the courts – but the cost and effort required to take court action is usually prohibitive for those who are not wealthy. And for those who are most powerless, the barriers to simply being heard are insurmountable.

As all news converges online, arguments about lack of space and time for opposing voices are no longer relevant. The Internet offers a new opportunity for news organizations to engage with those they are reporting on and to offer them space in which to reply beneath any item without requiring expensive changes to layout or taking up space required for new stories. Some might argue that such space is already there in the 'comments'. But those who are genuinely aggrieved require more consideration than to be allowed to appear in the middle of hundreds of comments, many of which may be hostile. It would be easy to separate out a 'rebuttal' space from run-of-the-mill comments, so that people who feel aggrieved can make themselves heard.

By offering people the opportunity to speak, the doors would be opened to more voices and the power would be tipped towards the subjects of news stories. Once such a right became the norm then those who are too frightened to speak in their own defence might gradually start to come forward. Where journalists do sincerely believe in the truth of what they have written, they would be able to stand by their stories. Theirs would still be the dominant narrative, but they would now have to write more carefully in the knowledge that their subjects can speak back. Journalists who are unsure of the truth of their stories would feel the need to take that extra step to verify their sources, rather than be left open to instant contradiction. Journalists would still have the power to define the debate, but not to overwhelm all other possible arguments. True freedom of expression should aim for alternative arguments within, not merely between, publications.

Regulation of process to improve accountability would undoubtedly empower those journalists who genuinely wish to write responsible stories based on what they sincerely believe to be the best interpretation of the facts. It does not require expensive court systems or judgements. It is virtue ethics in action, changing the process of journalism from the inside. Where the walls of the news fortress are penetrated by the subjects of their stories, journalists would be confronted daily with the need to accommodate alternative versions of events. Some will argue that this would result in dull or less challenging journalism. But it might equally result in a more vibrant, argumentative journalism and a more engaged, trusting and informed audience.

By harnessing technology to the needs of better journalism, rather than using it only to find ways of producing cheaper journalism, some of the promises of a networked and more democratically accountable journalism could start to emerge. But this can only happen if the needs of journalists, for better representation and more power, as workers within the media system, are taken seriously. Ethics bodies or legislation that speak only to the power of media owners and take no account of the needs of media workers, will never change journalism for the better.

Notes

1 For a discussion of the difference between these approaches to ethics, see Couldry 2006.
2 For a discussion of this see the discussion of the Muhammad cartoons affair in which most European news organizations were more interested in the right to publish than the possible harm done to those who have no equivalent right to reply (Eide *et al.* 2009).

References

Adorno, T. W. (1961) 'Culture Industry Reconsidered', reprinted in W. Brooker and D. Jermyn (eds) (2003) *The Audience Studies Reader*, London: Routledge.

Albuquerque, A. de (2012) 'On Models and Margins', in D. C. Hallin and P. Mancini (eds) *Comparing Media Systems Beyond the Western World*, Cambridge: Cambridge University Press.

Al Jazeera (2012) 'About Us: Facts and Figures', *AlJazeera.com*. Available HTTP: www.aljazeera.com/aboutus/ (accessed 16 July 2012).

Allan, S. (2006) *Online News*, Maidenhead: Open University Press.

Allern, S. (2002) 'Journalistic and Commercial News Values: News Organizations as Patrons of an Institution and Market Actors', *Nordicom Review*, 23(1–2): 137–52.

Andén-Papadopoulos, K. and Pantti, M. (2013) 'Re-imagining Crisis Reporting: Professional Ideology of Journalists and Citizen Eyewitness Images', *Journalism*, 14: 960–77.

Anderson, A. (1991) 'Source Strategies and the Communication of Environmental Affairs', *Media, Culture and Society*, 13: 459–76.

Anderson, C. (2006) *The Long Tail: Why the Future of Business is Selling Less of More*, New York: Hyperion.

Anderson, C. and Wolff, M. (2010) 'The Web is Dead. Long Live the Internet', *Wired*. Available HTTP: http://bit.ly/bvRGG0 (accessed 2 July 2012).

Anderson, C. W. (2011) 'Between Creative and Quantified Audiences: Web Metrics and Changing Patterns of Newswork in Local US Newsrooms', *Journalism*, 12(5): 550–66.

Andrejevic, M. (2007) *iSpy: Surveillance and Power in the Interactive Era*, Lawrence: University Press of Kansas.

Anonymous (2013) Comment to 'In Settlement with French publishers, Google Promises $82 million Fund and Advertising Help', *paidContent*. Available HTTP: http://paidcontent.org/2013/02/01/in-settlement-with-french-publishers-google-promises-82-million-fund-and-advertising-help/ (accessed 9 September 2013).

Arendt, H. [1968] (2006) *Between Past and Future*, London: Penguin.

Asquith, I. (1975) 'Advertising and the Press in the Late Eighteenth and Early Nineteenth Centuries: James Perry and the Morning Chronicle 1790–1821', *The Historical Journal*, 18(4): 703–24.

Associated Press (2012) 'Philadelphia Inquirer Sold to Political Figures', *Politico*. Available HTTP: www.politico.com/news/stories/0412/74754.html (accessed 26 August 2013).

Auletta, K. (2010) *Googled: The End of the World as We Know It*, New York: Penguin Books.

Avilés, J.A.G. and Carvajal, M. (2008) 'Integrated and Cross-Media Newsroom Convergence: Two Models of Multimedia News Production – The Cases of Novotécnica and La Verdad Multimedia in Spain', *Convergence*, 14: 221–39.

Bærug, J. R. and Harro-Loit, H. (2011) 'Journalism Embracing Advertising As Traditional Journalism Discourse Becomes Marginal', *Journalism Practice*, 6(2): 172–86.

Baines, D. (2013) 'Reclaiming the Streets?', in N. Fowler, J. Mair and I. Reeves (eds) *What Do We Mean by Local?* Bury St Edmunds: Arima Publishing.

Bauman, Z. (2011) *Liquid Modernity*, Cambridge, MA: Polity Press.

Baumberg, B., Bell, K. and Gaffney, D. (2012) 'Benefits Stigma in Britain', *Turn2us*, Available HTTP: www.turn2us.org.uk/PDF/Benefits%20Stigma%20in%20Britain.pdf (accessed 30 July 2013).

BBC Press Office (2007) 'BBC Jam to Be Suspended', *Press Release*, BBC Press Office. Available HTTP: www.bbc.co.uk/pressoffice/pressreleases/stories/2007/03_march/14/jam.shtml (accessed 25 February 2014).

Beckett, C. (2008) *SuperMedia: Saving Journalism so it Can Save the World*, Malden: Wiley-Blackwell.

Benhabib, S. (1992) 'Models of Public Space: Hannah Arendt, the Liberal Tradition, and Jürgen Habermas', in C. Calhoun (ed.) *Habermas and the Public Sphere*, Cambridge, MA: MIT Press.

Benson, R. (2006) 'News Media as a "Journalistic Field": What Bourdieu Adds to New Institutionalism and Vice Versa', *Political Communication*, 23: 187–202, 2006.

Benson, R. (2011) 'Public Funding and Journalistic Independence: What Does Research Tell Us?' in R. W. McChesney and V. Pickard (eds.) *Will the Last Reporter Please Turn Out the Lights?* New York: The New Press.

Benson, R. (2013) *Shaping Immigration News: A French-American Comparison*, Cambridge, Cambridge University Press.

Benson, R. and Neveu, E. (2005) *Bourdieu and the Journalistic Field*, Cambridge, MA: Polity Press.

Benson, R. and Powers, M. (2011) *Public Media and Political Independence*, Free Press Policy Report, Washington D.C.: Free Press.

Bercovici, J. (2012) 'Sam Zell Blames Tribune Failure on "Greedy" Journalists', *Forbes*. Available HTTP: www.forbes.com/sites/jeff bercovici/2012/02/22/delusional-sam-zell-blames-tribune-failure-on-greedy-journalists/ (accessed 28 August 2013).

Berger, D. (2007) 'Constructing Crime, Framing Disaster: Hurricane Katrina, Mass Incarceration, and the Crisis of Journalistic Authority', paper presented at the annual meeting of the NCA 93rd Annual Convention, TBA, Chicago, IL, 15 November 2007.

Berger, J. (2013) *Contagious: Why Things Catch On*, New York: Simon & Schuster.

Bergström, A. and Wadbring, I. (2008) 'The Contribution of Free Dailies and News on the Web – Is Readership Strictly Decreasing among Young People?', paper presented at Nordic Media in Theory and Practice Conference at University College London (UCL), 7–8 November 2008. Available HTTP: https://reutersinstitute.politics.ox.ac.uk/fileadmin/documents/nordic_media_papers/Bergstrom_Wadbring.pdf (accessed 27 August 2013).

Berkowitz, D. (1997) *Social Meanings of News: A Text-Reader*, Sage: London.

Berkowitz, D. and TerKeurst, J. V. (2006) 'Community as Interpretive Community: Rethinking the Journalist-Source Relationship', *Journal of Communication*, 49(3): 125–36.

Berners-Lee, T. (2010) 'Long Live the Web: A Call for Continued Open Standards and Neutrality', *Scientific American*. Available HTTP: www.scientificamerican.com/article.cfm?id=long-live-the-web&print=yes (accessed 9 September 2013).

Bew, R. (1998) 'The Role of the Freelancer in Local Journalism', in B. Franklin (ed.) *Local Journalism and Local Media: Making the Local News*, London: Routledge.

Big Foot Digital (2012) 'Viral Outbreaks on Twitter Spread to News Sources', *Big Foot Media*. Available HTTP: www.bigfootdigital.co.uk/tag/rumours/ (accessed 4 February 2014).

Bird, S. E. (2003) *The Audience in Everyday Life: Living in a Media World*, New York: Routledge.

Bird, S. E. and Dardenne, R. W. (2009) 'Rethinking News and Myth as Storytelling', in K. Wahl-Jorgensen and T. Hanitzsch (eds) *The Handbook of Journalism Studies*, Abingdon: Routledge.

Birt, J. (2002) *The Harder Path*, London: Little, Brown Book Group.

Boczkowski, P. J. (2005) *Digitizing the News: Innovation in Online Newspapers*, Cambridge, MA: MIT Press.

Boczkowski, P. J. (2010) *News at Work: Imitation in an Age of Information Abundance*, Chicago and London: The University of Chicago Press.

Boorstin, D. J. (1962) *The Image: A Guide to Pseudo-Events in America*, New York: Atheneum.

Bourdieu, P. [1972] (1977) *Outline of a Theory of Practice*, Vol. 16, Cambridge: Cambridge University Press.

Bourdieu, P. (1984) *Distinction: A Social Critique of the Judgement of Taste*, London: Routledge.

Bourdieu, P. (1986) 'The Forms of Capital', in J. G. Richardson (ed.) *Handbook of Theory and Research for the Sociology of Education*, New York: Greenwood Press.

Bourdieu, P. (1988) *Homo Academicus*, Cambridge, MA: Polity Press.

Bourdieu, P. (1989) 'Social Space and Symbolic Power', *Sociological Theory*, 7(1): 14–25.

Bourdieu, P. (1990) *In Other Words: Essays Towards a Reflexive Sociology*, Stanford: Stanford University Press.

Bourdieu, P. (1996) *The Rules of Art*, Cambridge, UK: Polity.

Bourdieu, P. (1998) *On Television*, New York: The New Press.

Bourdieu, P. (2005) 'The Political Field, the Social Science Field and the Journalistic Field' in R. Benson and E. Neveu (eds) *Bourdieu and the Journalistic Field*, Cambridge, MA: Polity Press.

Bourdieu, P. and Wacquant, L. (1992) *An Invitation to Reflexive Sociology*, Chicago: University of Chicago Press.

Brand, S. (1987) *The Media Lab: Inventing the Future at MIT*, New York: Viking.

Brannon, J. (2008) 'Maximize the Medium: Assessing Obstacles to Performing Multimedia Journalism in Three US Newsrooms', in C. Paterson and D. Domingo (eds) *Making Online News: The Ethnography of New Media Production*, New York: Peter Lang.

Broersma, M. (2013) 'A Fractured Paradigm: Journalism, Hoaxes and the Challenge of Trust', in C. Peters and M. Broersma (eds) *Rethinking Journalism: Trust and Participation in a Transformed News Landscape*, London: Routledge.

Broersma, M. and Graham, T. (2013) 'Twitter As A News Source', *Journalism Practice*, 7(4): 446–64.

Bruno, N. (2011) *Tweet First, Verify Later? How Real-Time Information is Changing the Coverage of Worldwide Crisis Events*, Oxford: Reuters Institute for the Study of Journalism. Available HTTP: https://reutersinstitute.politics.ox.ac.uk/fileadmin/documents/Publications/

fellows–papers/2010–11/TWEET_FIRST_VERIFY_LATER.pdf (accessed 4 February 2014).

Bruno, N. and Nielsen, R. K. (2012) *Survival is Success: Journalistic Online Start-Ups in Western Europe*, Oxford: Reuters Institute for the Study of Journalism. Available HTTP: https://reutersinstitute.politics.ox.ac.uk/fileadmin/documents/Publications/Challenges/Survival_is_Success,pdf (accessed 12 January 2014).

Busfield, S. (2010) 'Guardian Editor Hits Back at Paywalls', *The Guardian*. Available HTTP: www.theguardian.com/media/2010/jan/25/guardian-editor-paywalls (accessed 4 September 2013).

Campbell, A. (2013) 'Why Journalism, and Why it Matters in a World of Flux', *CRASSH Humanitas Lecture*. Available HTTP: www.crassh.cam.ac.uk/events/25150 (accessed 4 February 2014).

Carey, J. W. (2000) 'Some Personal Notes on US Journalism Education', *Journalism*, 1(1): 12–23.

Cathcart, B. (2000) *The Case of Stephen Lawrence*, London: Penguin.

Chalaby, J. K. (1996) 'Journalism as an Anglo-American Invention: A Comparison of the Development of French and Anglo-American Journalism, 1830s–1920s', *European Journal of Communication*, 11(3): 303–9.

Champagne, P. (2005) 'The "Double Dependency": The Journalistic Field Between Politics and Markets', in R. D. Benson and E. Neveu (eds) *Bourdieu and the Journalistic Field*, Cambridge, MA: Polity Press.

Chaudhary, A. and Gabriëls, H. (1974) 'Comparative News Judgment of Indian and American Journalists', *International Communication Gazette*, 20: 233–48.

Chisholm, J. (2013) 'The Industry in Context and How We Can Rediscover It', in N. Fowler, J. Mair and I. Reeves (eds) *What Do We Mean by Local?* Bury St Edmunds: Arima Publishing.

Chouliaraki, L. (2012) 'Re-Mediation, Inter-Mediation, Trans-Mediation', *Journalism Studies*, 14(2): 267–83.

Christensen, C. (2000) *The Innovator's Dilemma: When New Technologies Cause Great Firms to Fail*, St. Paul, MN: Highbridge Company.

Chung, D. S. (2007) 'Profits and Perils: Online News Producers' Perceptions of Interactivity and Uses of Interactive Features', *Convergence*, 13(1): 43–61.

Cision (2011) '2011 Social Journalism Study: Perceptions and Use of Social Media among European Journalists in 2011 – Germany, Sweden, Finland and United Kingdom', *Cision*. Available HTTP: www.academia.edu/1074499/Perceptions_and_use_of_Social_Media_among_European_Journalists_in_2011–Germany_Sweden_Finland_and_United_Kingdom (accessed 4 February 2014).

Coddington, M. (2013) 'This Week in Review: Censorship in the UK, and Al Jazeera America's Promise and Problems', *Nieman Journalism Lab*. Available HTTP: www.niemanlab.org/2013/08/this-week-in-review-censorship-in-the-u-k-and-al-jazeera-americas-promise-and-problems/ (accessed 25 August 2013).

Cohen, S. (1972) *Folk Devils and Moral Panics*, London: Routledge.

Colchester, J. and Sydney-Smith, M. (2013) *National Newspapers: Print and Digital Audiences*, London: Enders Analysis.

Collins, L. (2012) 'Mail Supremacy', *The New Yorker*. Available HTTP: www.newyorker.com/reporting/2012/04/02/120402fa_fact_collins (accessed 12 January 2014).

Connell, I. (1992) 'Personalities in the Popular Media', in P. Dahlgren and C. Sparks (eds) *Journalism and Popular Culture*, London: Sage.

Copps, M. J. (2014) 'From the Desk of a Former FCC Commissioner', *Columbia Journalism Review*. Available at HTTP: www.cjr.org/essay/from_the_desk_of_a_former_fcc.php (accessed 18 February 2014).

Couldry, N. (2006) 'Towards a Global Media Ethics', in *Listening Beyond the Echoes: Media, Ethics and Agency in an Uncertain World*, Boulder: Paradigm.

Couldry, N. (2010) 'New Online News Sources and Writer-Gatherers', in N. Fenton (ed.) *New Media, Old News*, London: Sage.

Coulter, R. (2013) 'How Filton's New Voice can be a Business Model for Hyperlocal Journalism', in N. Fowler, J. Mair and I. Reeves (eds) *What Do We Mean by Local?* Bury St Edmunds: Arima Publishing.

Crawford, S. P. (2012) 'Is Google a Monopoly? Wrong Question', *Bloomberg*. Available HTTP: www.bloomberg.com/news/2012-07-08/is-google-a-monopoly-wrong-question.html (accessed 29 August 2012).

Crouse, T. (1973) *The Boys on the Bus*, New York: Random House.

Cullen, D. (2009) *Columbine*, New York: Hachette.

Currah, A. (2009) *What's Happening to Our News? An Investigation into the Likely Impact of the Digital Revolution on the Economics of News Publishing in the UK*, Oxford: Reuters Institute for the Study of Journalism.

Curran, J. (2010a) 'Technology Foretold', in N. Fenton (ed.) *New Media, Old News*, London: Sage.

Curran, J. (2010b) 'Entertaining Democracy' in J. Curran (ed.) Media and Society, Bloomsbury, 2010.

Curran, J. (2011) *Media and Democracy*, Oxford: Routledge.

Curran, J. and Seaton, J. (2003) *Power Without Responsibility: The Press, Broadcasting, and New Media in Britain*, Oxford: Routledge.

Curran, J. and Seaton, J. (2010) *Power Without Responsibility: The Press, Broadcasting, and New Media in Britain*, Oxford: Routledge.Curran, J., Coen, S., Aalberg, T. and Iyengar, S. (2011) in Curran, J. (2011) *Media and Democracy*, Oxford: Routledge.

Curran, J., Coen, S., Aalberg, T., Hayashi, K., Jones, P. K., Splendore, S., Papathanassopoulos, S., Rowe, D. and Tiffen, R. (2013) 'Internet Revolution Revisited: A Comparative Study of Online News', *Media, Culture & Society*, 35(7): 880–97.

Cushion, S. (2012) *The Democratic Value of News: Why Public Service Media Matter*, Basingstoke: Palgrave Macmillan.

Dale, I. (2012) 'Paying Cash for Stories: A Demeaning Trade', *iaindale.com*. No longer available HTTP (accessed 4 September 2012).

Davies, N. (2008) *Flat Earth News*, London: Vintage.

Davis, A. (2002) *Public Relations Democracy*, Manchester: Manchester University Press.

DCMS (2010) 'Future for Local and Regional Media', *Culture, Media and Sport Committee*, Fourth Report. London: House of Commons.

De Certeau, M. (1984) 'Reading as Poaching', in *The Practice of Everyday Life*, Berkeley: University of California Press.

Di Tella, R. and Franceschelli, T. (2009) *Government Advertising and Media Coverage of Scandals*, NBER Working Paper Series, Cambridge, National Bureau of Economic Research. Available HTTP: www.nber.org/papers/w15402.pdf (accessed 18 February 2014).

Deuze, M. (2007) *Media Work*, Cambridge, UK: Polity.

Deuze, M. (2010) *Managing Media Work*, London: Sage.

Deuze, M. and Fortunati, L. (2011) 'Journalism Without Journalists: On the Power Shift from Journalists to Employers and Audiences', in G. Meikle and G. Redden (eds) *News Online: Transformations and Continuities*, Basingstoke: Palgrave Macmillan.

Dick, M. (2013) *Search: Theory and Practice in Journalism Online*, Basingstoke: Palgrave Macmillan.

Donsbach, W. and Patterson, T. E. (1992) 'Journalists' Roles and Newsroom Practices: A Cross-national Comparison', paper presented at 42nd Conference of the International Communications Association, Miami, Florida, 21–25 May.

Donsbach, W. and Patterson, T. E. (2004) 'Political News Journalists: Partisanship, Professionalism, and Political Roles in Five Countries', in F. Esser and B. Pfetsch (eds), *Comparing Political Communication: Theories, Cases, and Challenges*, Cambridge: Cambridge University Press.

Dowell, B. (2011) 'Private Eye is 50? Surely Shome Mistake', *The Guardian*. Available HTTP: www.theguardian.com/media/2011/sep/11/private-eye-50 (accessed 4 February 2014).

Dreher, T. (2009) 'Eavesdropping with Permission: The Politics of Listening for Safer Speaking Spaces', *Borderlands*, 8: 1–21.

Du Plessis, D. (2006) 'House of the Rising Sun', *CPQ* (January): 46–50.

DVorkin, L. (2013) 'Inside Forbes: Journalism Requires New Models for Both Editorial and Ads', *Forbes*. Available HTTP: www.forbes.com/sites/lewisdvorkin/2013/03/04/inside-forbes-journalism-requires-new-models-for-both-editorial-and-ads/ (accessed 6 February 2014).

Edmonds, R. (2013) 'New Research Finds 92 percent of Time Spent on News Consumption is Still on Legacy Platforms', *Poynter*. Available HTTP: www.poynter.org/latest-news/business-news/the-biz-blog/212550/new-research-finds-92-percent-of-news-consumption-is-still-on-legacy-platforms/ (accessed 27 August 2013).

Eide, E., Kunelius, R. and Phillips, A. (2009) *Transnational Media Events: The Mohammed Cartoons and the Imagined Clash of Civilizations*, Göteborg: Göteborg University and NORDICOM.

Elliott, C. (2012) 'The Readers' Editor on ... the Switch to a "Nesting" System on Comment Threads', *The Guardian*. Available HTTP: http://bit.ly/179MH3o (accessed 19 August 2013).

Elmer-Dewitt, P. (1994) 'Battle for the Soul of the Internet', *Time*, 144 (4): 50–57.

Emery, E., Emery, M. and Roberts, N. (1996) *The Press and America*, Englewood Cliffs, NJ: Prentice-Hall.

Enders, C. (2011) 'The Future of Local Media in the UK', *Westminster Forum*. Available HTTP: www.westminsterforumprojects.co.uk/forums/showpublications.php?pid=257 (accessed 12 January 2014).

Entman, R. M. (1993) 'Framing: Toward Clarification of a Fractured Paradigm', *Journal of Communication*, 43(4): 51–58.

Ericson, R., Baranek, P. and Chan, J. (1989) *Negotiating Control: A Study of News Sources*, Toronto: University of Toronto Press.

Experian Hitwise (2011) 'Google Increases Market Share of UK Searches', *Experian*. Available HTTP: www.hitwise.com/uk/press-centre/press-releases/google-increases-market-share-of-uk-searches (accessed 27 February 2014).

Felle, T. (2013) 'From Boom to Bust: Irish Local Newspapers Post-Celtic Tiger', in J. Mair, N. Fowler and I. Reeves (eds) *What Do We Mean by Local?* Bury St Edmunds: Arima Publishing.

Fenton, N. (2010a) *New Media, Old News*, London: Sage.

Fenton, N. (2010b) 'NGOs, New Media and the Mainstream News: News from Everywhere', in *New Media, Old News*, London: Sage.

Fenton, N. and Witschge, T. (2011) 'Comment is Free, Facts are Sacred: Journalistic Ethics in a Changing Mediascape', in G. Meikle and G. Redden (eds) *News Online: Transformation and Continuity*, Basingstoke: Palgrave Macmillan.

Fenton, N., Freedman, D., Metykova, M. and Schlosberg, J. (2010) 'Meeting the News Needs of Local Communities', *Media Trust*. Available HTTP: www.mediatrust.org/uploads/128255497549240/original.pdf (accessed 14 January 2014).

Fielden, L. (2012) *Regulating the Press: A Comparative Study of International Press Councils*, Oxford: Reuters Institute for the Study of Journalism.

Figenschou, T. U. (2013) *Al Jazeera and the Global Media Landscape: The South is Talking Back*. Abingdon and New York: Routledge.

Filloux, F. (2011) 'Lessons from the Bin Laden Coverage', *The Monday Note*. Available HTTP: http://bit.ly/kABVOb (accessed 4 February 2014).

Filloux, F. (2012a) 'The Sharing Mirage', *The Monday Note*. Available HTTP: www.mondaynote.com/2012/03/26/the-sharing-mirage/ (accessed 30 March 2012).

Filloux, F. (2012b) 'Transfer of Value', *The Monday Note*. Available HTTP: www.mondaynote.com/2012/07/08/transfer-of-value/ (accessed 4 February 2014).

Filloux, F. (2014) 'News Media Revenue Matrix: The Bird's Eye View', *The Monday Note*. Available HTTP: www.mondaynote.com/2014/02/23/news-media-revenue-matrix-the-birds-eye-view/ (accessed 27 February 2014).

Fishman, M. (1980) *Manufacturing the News*, Austin: University of Texas Press.

Fiske, J. (1990) *Understanding Popular Culture*, London and New York: Routledge.

Fiske, J. (1992) 'Popularity and the Politics of Information', in P. Dahlgren and C. Sparks (eds) *Journalism and Popular Culture*, London: Sage.

Fiske, J. (1996) *Media Matters, Race and Gender in US Politics*, Minnesota: University of Minnesota Press.

Foucault, M. (1981) 'The Order of Discourse', in R. Young (ed.) *Untying The Text: A Post-Structuralist Reader*, Boston: Routledge.

Fowler, M. S. and Brenner, D. L. (1982) *A Marketplace Approach to Broadcast Regulation*, Austin: Texas Law Review Publications.

Franklin, B. (1997) *Newszak and News Media*, London: Bloomsbury.

Franklin, B. (1998) *Local Journalism and Local Media: Making the Local News*, London: Routledge.

Franklin, B. and Carlson, M. (2011) *Journalists, Sources, and Credibility: New Perspectives*, London: Routledge.

Fraser, N. (1992) 'Rethinking the Public Sphere: A Contribution to the Critique of Actually Existing Democracy', in C. Calhoun (ed.) *Habermas and the Public Sphere*, Cambridge, MA: MIT Press.

Freedman, D. (2012) 'Web 2.0 and the Death of the Blockbuster Economy', in J. Curran, N. Fenton and D. Freedman (eds) *Misunderstanding the Internet*, London: Routledge.

Freedom House (2012) 'Freedom of the Press 2012', *Freedom House*. Available HTTP: http://bit.ly/In8haS/ (accessed 2 August 2012).

Friend, C. and Singer, J. B. (2007) *Online Journalism Ethics: Traditions and Transitions*, Armonk, NY: M. E. Sharpe.

Galloway, M. (2010) 'Foreword', in A. Fenyoe *The World Online: How UK Citizens Use the Internet to Find out About the Wider World*, International Broadcasting Trust. Available

HTTP: http://celebrityanddevelopment.files.wordpress.com/2012/06/2010-uk-citize ns-use-of-internet.pdf (accessed 4 February 2014).

Galtung, J. and Ruge, M. H. (1965) 'The Structure of Foreign News', *Journal of Peace Research*, 2(1): 64–90.

Gandy, O. H. (1982) *Beyond Agenda Setting: Information Subsidies and Public Policies*, New York: Ablex.

Gans, H. J. (1979) *Deciding What's News: A Study of CBS Evening News, NBC Nightly News, Newsweek, and Time*, Evanston, IL: Northwestern University Press.

Garnham, N. (2000) *Emancipation, the Media, and Modernity: Arguments about the Media and Social Theory*, Oxford: Oxford University Press.

Gassée, J. L. (2013) 'Culture War: Jeff Bezos and The Washington Post', *Monday Note*. Available HTTP: www.mondaynote.com/2013/08/11/culture-war-bezos-and-the-washington-post/ (accessed 27 August 2013).

Gieber, W. (1964) 'News Is What Newspapermen Make It', in L. A. Dexter and D. M. White (eds) *People, Society and Mass Communications*, New York: Free Press.

Gilad and Devin (2011) 'Breaking Bin Laden: Visualizing the Power of a Single Tweet', *Social Flow*. Available HTTP: http://blog.socialflow.com/post/5246404319/breaking-bin-laden-visualizing-the-power-of-a-single (accessed 17 February 2014).

Gill, R. (2010) '"Life is a Pitch": Managing the Self in New Media Work', in M. Deuze (ed.) *Managing Media Work*, London: Sage.

Gillespie, M. (2003) 'Television, Ethnicity and Cultural Change', in W. Brooker and D. Jermyn (eds) *The Audience Studies Reader*, London: Routledge.

Gillmor, D. (2006) *We the Media: Grassroots Journalism by the People, for the People*, Sebastopol, CA: O'Reilly.

Gilmour, I. (1993) *Dancing with Dogma*, London: Simon & Schuster.

Gitlin, T. (1980) *The Whole World is Watching*, Berkeley: University of California Press.

Goffman, E. (1974) *Frame Analysis: An Essay on the Organization of Experience*, Lebanon, NH: Northeastern University Press.

Golding, P. and Elliot, P. (1979) *Making the News*. London: Longman.

Golding, P. and Elliot, P. (1996) 'News Values and News Production', in P. Marris and S. Thornham (eds) *Media Studies: A Reader*, Edinburgh: Edinburgh University Press.

Gonzalez-Velez, M. and Singer, J. B. (2003) 'Envisioning the Caucus Community: Online Newspaper Editors Conceptualize their Political Roles', *Political Communication*, 20: 433–45.

Goode, E. and Ben-Yehuda, N. (1994) *Moral Panics: the Social Construction of Deviance*, Oxford: Blackwell.

Gov.uk (2012) 'Victims Statistics', *Statistics on Race and the Criminal Justice System 2012*. Available HTTP: www.gov.uk/government/publications/statistics-on-race-and-the-criminal-justice-system-2012 (accessed 17 February 2014).

Grade, M. (2004) 'Building Public Value', BBC Press Office. Available HTTP: http://bbc.in/1fAnktf (accessed 24 September 2012).

Gramsci, A. (1971) *Selections from the Prison Notebooks*, London: Lawrence and Wishart.

Greenslade, R. (2008) 'Minutes of Examination of Witnesses', *Parliamentary Select Committee on Communications*. Available HTTP: www.publications.parliament.uk/pa/ld200708/ldselect/ldcomuni/122/8012307.htm (accessed 24 January 2013).

Greenslade, R. (2009) 'Controlling Interest', *The Guardian*. Available HTTP: www.theguardian.com/media/2009/jul/27/newspaper-owners-editorial-control (accessed 4 February 2014).

Greenslade, R. (2012) 'The Sun Changes its Stance, yet again, over the Baby P Case', *The Guardian*. Available HTTP: www.theguardian.com/media/greenslade/2012/aug/02/sun-baby-p (accessed 1 August 2013).

Guardian Media Group (2013) 'GMG Annual Review'. Available HTTP: www.gmgannualreview2013.co.uk (accessed 9 September 2013).

Guskin, E. (2013) '5 Facts about Ethnic and Gender Diversity in US Newsrooms', *Pew Research Center*. Available HTTP: www.pewresearch.org/fact-tank/2013/07/18/5-facts-about-ethnic-and-gender-diversity-in-u-s-newsrooms/ (accessed 16 February 2014).

Habermas, J. (1989) *The Structural Transformation of the Public Sphere: Inquiry into a Category of Bourgeois Society*, Cambridge: Polity Press.

Habermas, J. (1994) 'Three Normative Models of Democracy', in *Constellations*, 1(1): 1–10.

Habermas, J. (1996) 'The Public Sphere', in P. Marris and S. Thornham (eds) *Media Studies: A Reader*, Edinburgh: Edinburgh University Press.

Hall, S. (1973) *Encoding and Decoding in the Television Discourse*, Birmingham: Centre for Cultural Studies, University of Birmingham.

Hall, S. (2001) 'Foucault: Power Knowledge and Discourse', in M. Wetherell, S. Taylor and S. Yates (eds) *Discourse Theory and Practice: A Reader*, London: Sage.

Hall, S., Critcher, C., Jefferson, T., Clarke, J. and Roberts, B. (1978) *Policing the Crisis: Mugging, the State, and Law and Order*, London: Macmillan.

Hall, S., Critcher, C., Jefferson, T., Clarke, J. and Roberts, B. (1996) 'The Social Production of News', in P. Marris and S. Thornham (eds) *Media Studies: A Reader*, Edinburgh: Edinburgh University Press.

Halliday, J. (2013) 'Mail Online to Ramp up Growth by Hiring New Staff', *The Guardian*. Available HTTP: www.theguardian.com/media/2013/jul/17/mail-online-growth-new-staff (accessed 31 August 2013).

Hallin, D. C. (1986) *The 'Uncensored War': The Media and Vietnam*, Oxford: Oxford University Press.

Hallin, D. C. and Mancini, P. (2004) *Comparing Media Systems: Three Models of Media and Politics*, Cambridge: Cambridge University Press.

Hallin, D. C. and Mancini, P. (2012) *Comparing Media Systems Beyond the Western World*, Cambridge: Cambridge University Press.

Hamilton, J. T. (2004) *All the News That's Fit to Sell: How the Market Transforms Information Into News*, Princeton: Princeton University Press.

Hapgood, F. (1995) 'The Media Lab at 10', *Wired Magazine*. Available HTTP: www.wired.com/wired/archive/3.11/media.html (accessed 4 February 2014).

Harcup, T. and O'Neill, D. (2001) 'What is News? Galtung and Ruge Revisited', *Journalism Studies*, 2(2): 261–80.

Heinonen, A. (2011) 'The Journalists' Relationships with Users: New Dimensions to Conventional Roles', in J. B. Singer, A. Hermida, D. Domingo, A. Heinonen, S. Paulussen, T. Quandt, Z. Reich and M. Vujnovic (eds) *Participatory Journalism: Guarding Open Gates at Online Newspapers*, Chichester: Wiley-Blackwell.

Herman, E. and McChesney, R. (1997) *The Global Media: The New Missionaries of Global Capitalism*. Oxford: Blackwell.

Hermida, A. (2011) 'Mechanisms of Participation: How Audience Options Shape the Conversation', in J. B. Singer, A. Hermida, D. Domingo, A. Heinonen, S. Paulussen, T. Quandt, Z. Reich and M. Vujnovic (eds) *Participatory Journalism: Guarding Open Gates at Online Newspapers*, Chichester: Wiley-Blackwell [Kindle edition].

Hermida, A. (2012) 'Tweets and Truth: Journalism as a Discipline of Collaborative Verification', *Journalism Practice*, 6(5–6): 659–68.

Hermida, A. and Thurman, N. (2008) 'A Clash of Cultures: The Integration of User-generated Content Within Professional Journalistic Frameworks at British Newspaper Websites', *Journalism Practice*, 2(3): 343–56.

Highfield, A. (2013) Evidence to the Select Committee on Media Plurality, House of Lords Evidence Session 12. Available HTTP: www.parliament.uk/documents/lords-committees/communications/Mediaplurality/ucCOMMS291013ev12.pdf (accessed 5 November 2013).

Himelboim, I. and Limor, Y. (2008) 'Media Perception of Freedom of the Press: A Comparative International Analysis of 242 Codes of Ethics', *Journalism*, 9(3): 235–65.

Hind, D. (2010) *The Return of the Public*, London: Verso.

Hindman, M. (2009) *The Myth of Digital Democracy*, Princeton: Princeton University Press.

Hollander, G. (2013) 'Local World's David Montgomery: "We Will Harvest Content and Publish it without Human Interface"', *Press Gazette*. Available HTTP: www.pressgazette.co.uk/david-montgomery-we-will-harvest-content-and-publish-it-without-human-interface (accessed 16 September 2013).

Howard, P. N. and Hussain, M. M. (2011) 'The Role of Digital Media', *Journal of Democracy*, 22(3): 35–48.

Hueypriest (2013) 'Reflections on the Recent Boston Crisis', blog.reddit. Available HTTP: http://bit.ly/11y8qhb (accessed 4 February 2014).

Humphreys, P. (2010) 'EU State Aid Rules, Public Service Broadcasters' Online Media Engagement and Public Value Tests: The German and UK Cases Compared', *Interactions: Studies in Communication & Culture*, 1(2): 171–84.

Ireland, J. (2014) 'Tony Abbott Blasts National Broadcaster: ABC Takes "Everyone's Side but Australia's"', *Sydney Morning Herald*. Available HTTP: www.smh.com.au/federal-politics/political-news/tony-abbott-blasts-national-broadcaster-abc-takes-everyones-side-but-australias-20140129-31lt8.html (accessed 4 February 2014).

Jacobs, R. N. (1996) 'Producing the News, Producing the Crisis: Narrativity, Television and Newswork', *Media Culture and Society*, 18(3): 373–97.

Jarvis, J. (2006) 'Networked Journalism', *BuzzMachine*. Available HTTP: http://bit.ly/JJG38k (accessed 3 April 2013).

Jarvis, J. (2007) 'New Rule: Cover What You Do Best. Link to the Rest', *BuzzMachine*. Available HTTP: http://buzzmachine.com/2007/02/22/new-rule-cover-what-you-do-best-link-to-the-rest/ (accessed 6 September 2013).

Jarvis, J. (2009a) *What Would Google Do?* London: HarperCollins.

Jarvis, J. (2009b) 'The Future for Journalism Will Always Embrace Change', *The Guardian*. Available HTTP: www.theguardian.com/media/pda/2009/nov/02/journalism-in-crisis-debate (accessed 16 September 2013).

Jefferson, T. (1787) Letters to Carrington, in J. P. Boyd (1950) *The Papers of Thomas Jefferson*, Princeton: Princeton University Press.

Jenkins, H. (2008) *Convergence Culture: Where Old and New Media Collide*, New York: New York University Press.

Johnson, M. (2010) 'Alan Rusbridger Rules out Pay Walls at the Guardian', *Journalism.co.uk*. Available HTTP: www.journalism.co.uk/news/alan-rusbridger-rules-out-pay-walls-at-the-guardian/s2/a537204/ (accessed 4 September 2013).

Jönsson, A. M. and Örnebring, H. (2011) 'User-generated Content and the News', *Journalism Practice*, 5(2): 127–44.

Joyce, M. (2007) 'The Citizen Journalism Web Site "OhmyNews" and the 2002 South Korean Presidential Election', *Internet & Democracy Case Study Series*, Harvard, MA: Berkman Centre for Internet and Society.

Jurkowitz, M. and Hitlin, P. (2013) 'Citizen Eyewitnesses Provide Majority of Top Online News Videos in Oklahoma Tornado Disaster', *Pew Research Center*. Available HTTP: www.pewresearch.org/fact-tank/2013/05/22/citizen-eyewitnesses-provide-majority-of-top-online-news-videos-in-oklahoma-tornado-disaster/ (accessed 27 August 2013).

Jurkowitz, M. and Mitchell, A. (2013) 'Newspapers Turning Ideas into Dollars', *PewResearch Journalism Project*. Available HTTP: www.journalism.org/analysis_report/about_re port_1 (accessed 29 August 2013).

Karmasnack (2012) 'Search Engine Market Share', *Karmasnack*. Available HTTP: http://bit.ly/14l3PVI (accessed 10 August 2012).

Kent, R. (1979) *Aunt Agony Advises: Problem Pages through the Ages*, London: W.H. Allen.

Kevin, D. (2003) *Europe in the Media: A Comparison of Reporting, Representation and Rhetoric in National Media Systems in Europe*, London: Laurence Erlbaum Associates.

Kieve, J. (1973) *The Electric Telegraph: A Social and Economic History*, Newton Abbott: David and Charles.

Kilman, L. (2012) 'World Press Trends: Newspaper Audience Rise, Digital Revenues Yet to Follow', *WAN-INFRA*. Available HTTP: www.wan-ifra.org/press-releases/2012/09/03/world-press-trends-newspaper-audience-rise-digital-revenues-yet-to-follow (accessed 11 April 2013).

Kilman, L. (2013) 'World Press Trends: Increasing Audience Engagement is Future for News Media', *WAN-IFRA*. Available HTTP: www.wan-ifra.org/press-releases/2013/06/02/world-press-trends-increasing-audience-engagement-is-future-for-news-media (accessed 29 August 2013).

Knight Foundation (2013) 'Finding a Foothold: How NonProfit News Ventures Seek Sustainability', *Knight Foundation*. Available HTTP: www.knightfoundation.org/features/nonprofitnews/ (accessed 12 January 2014).

Konow Lund, M. T. and Puijk, R. (2012) 'Rolling News as Disruptive Change: A Managerial Perspective on TV 2 and VG in Norway', *Nordicom Review*, 33(1): 67–81.

Kovach, B. and Rosenstiel, T. (2007) *The Elements of Journalism: What News People Should Know and the Public Should Expect*, New York: Three Rivers Press.

Küng, L. (2008) *Strategic Management in the Media: Theory to Practice*, Los Angeles: Sage.

Larsson, A. O. (2011) 'Interactive to Me – Interactive to You? A Study of Use and Appreciation of Interactivity on Swedish Newspaper Websites', *New Media & Society*, 13(7): 1180–97.

Larsson, A. O. (2013) 'Staying In or Going Out?', *Journalism Practice*, 7(6): 738–54.

Lazarsfeld, P., Berelson, B. and Gaudet, H. (1948) *The People's Choice: How the Voter Makes Up His Mind in a Presidential Campaign*, New York, Columbia University Press.

Lee, J. (2013) 'Google's Search Market Share Shoots Back to 67%', *Search Engine Watch*. Available HTTP: http://searchenginewatch.com/article/2289560/Googles-Search-Market-Share-Shoots-Back-to-67 (accessed 27 February 2014).

Lee-Wright, P. (2012) 'Journalists' Work Recrafted', in P. Lee-Wright, A. Phillips and T. Witschge (ed.) *Changing Journalism*, London: Routledge.

Lee-Wright, P. and Phillips, A. (2012) 'Doing it All in a Multi-Skilled Universe', in P. Lee-Wright, A. Phillips and T. Witschge (eds) *Changing Journalism*, London: Routledge.

Leveson, B. (2012) 'An Inquiry into the Culture, Practices and Ethics of the Press', *The Stationary Office*. Available HTTP: www.official-documents.gov.uk/document/hc1213/hc07/0780/0780.asp (accessed 4 February 2014).

Lewis, J., Williams, A. and Franklin, B. (2008) 'A Compromised Fourth Estate? UK News Journalism, Public Relations and News Sources', in *Journalism Studies*, 9(1): 1–20.

Lewis, A., a.k.a. blue_beetle (2010) Comment to 'User-driven Discontent', *Metafilter*. Available HTTP: http://bit.ly/cY3Xu6 (accessed 4 February 2014).

Lewis, T. (2013) 'YouTube Superstars: The Generation Taking on TV – and Winning', *The Observer*. Available HTTP: www.theguardian.com/technology/2013/apr/07/youtube-superstars-new-generation-bloggers (accessed 4 February 2014).

Liebes, T. and Katz, E. (1990) *The Export of Meaning: Cross-Cultural Readings of Dallas*, Oxford: Oxford University Press.

Lippmann, W. (1922) *Public Opinion*, New York: Macmillan.

Lloyd, J. (2004) *What The Media are Doing To Our Politics*, London: Constable & Robinson.

Lloyd, J. (2011) *Scandal! News International and the Rights of Journalism*, Oxford: Reuters Institute Study of Journalism.

Luckhurst, T. (2012) *Responsibility Without Power: Lord Justice Leveson's Constitutional Dilemma*, Bury St Edmonds: Abramis Press.

Lule, J. (2001) *Daily News, Eternal Stories: The Mythological Role of Journalism*, New York: Guilford Press.

Lyon, S. (2012) 'Detecting the Truth in Photos: How a News Service Verifies Images and Videos', *Nieman Reports*, 66 (2): 7–9.

MacAskill, E. (2013) 'NSA Paid Millions to Cover Prism Compliance Costs for Tech Companies', *The Guardian*. Available HTTP: www.theguardian.com/world/2013/aug/23/nsa-prism-costs-tech-companies-paid (accessed 17 September 2013).

McChesney, R. W. (2000) *Rich Media, Poor Democracy: Communications Politics in Dubious Times*, New York: The New Press.

McChesney, R. W. and Nichols, J. (2011) *The Death and Life of American Journalism: The Media Revolution That Will Begin the World Again*, Philadelphia: Nation Books.

MacGregor, P. (2007) 'Tracking the Online Audience', *Journalism Studies*, 8(2): 280–98.

McLuhan, M. (1962) *The Gutenberg Galaxy: The Making of Typographic Man*, Toronto: The University of Toronto Press.

McMullan, P. (2010) 'Interviewed by John Minel, Ex News of the World Journalist Admits "Destroying" Suicide Victim He Wrote About & Paying Police', repeated July 2011, *World at One*, BBC Radio 4. Available HTTP: www.youtube.com/watch?v=lb9cnlbzhgk&feature=youtube_gdata_player (accessed 13 November 2013).

McMullan, P. (2011) Evidence to the Leveson Inquiry. Available HTTP: www.levesoninquiry.org.uk/wp-content/uploads/2011/11/Transcript-of-Afternoon-Hearing-29-November-2011.txt (accessed 4 February 2014).

McRobbie, A. (1994) *Postmodernism and Popular Culture*, London: Routledge.

Madianou, Mirca (2013) 'Ethics of Mediation and the Voice of the Injured Subject', in N. Couldry, M. Madianou and A. Pinchevski (eds) *Ethics of Media*, London: Palgrave Macmillan.

Mancini, P. (2013) 'Partiality and Polarisation of News' in D. Levy and N. Newman (eds) *Digital News Report 2013*, Oxford: Reuters Institute for the Study of Journalism. Available HTTP: https://reutersinstitute.politics.ox.ac.uk/fileadmin/documents/Publications/Working_Papers/Digital_News_Report_2013.pdf (accessed 14 January 2014).

Manning, P. (2001) *News and News Sources: A Critical Introduction*, London: Sage.

Marr, A. (2005) *My Trade: A Short History of British Journalism*, London: Pan Books.

Marvin, C. (1999) 'When Old Technologies Were New: Implementing the Future', in H. Mackay and T. O'Sullivan *The Media Reader: Continuity and Transformation*, London: Sage.

Marx, K. (1847) 'Wage, Labour and Capital', Marx/Engels Internet Archive (marxists.org) 1993, 1999. Available HTTP: www.marxists.org/archive/marx/works/1847/wage-labour/ (accessed 9 December 2013).

Marx, K. and Engels, F. [1845] (1970) *The German Ideology*, New York: International Publishers.

Mazzucato, M. (2013) *The Entrepreneurial State: Debunking Public vs. Private Sector Myths*, London: Anthem Press.

MC Marketing (2013) 'New Revenue Sources Help Offset Decline in Newspaper Ad Spend', *World Association of Newspapers*. Available HTTP: www.marketingcharts.com/wp/print/new-revenue-sources-help-offset-decline-in-newspaper-ad-spend-28492/ (accessed 4 September 2013).

Media Reform (2012) 'Part 2 – Ethical Practice: A New Settlement for British News Publishing'. Available HTTP: www.mediareform.org.uk/wp-content/uploads/2013/04/Submission-to-Module-4-of-the-Leveson-Inquiry.pdf (accessed 28 November 2013).

Media Standards Trust (2008) 'Transparency Initiative'. Available HTTP: http://mediastandardstrust.org/projects/transparency-initiative/background/ (accessed 4 February 2014).

Media Standards Trust (2011) 'PCC Statistics: A Critical Analysis by the Media Standards Trust'. Available HTTP: http://mediastandardstrust.org/wp-content/uploads/downloads/2012/02/PCC-Statistics.pdf (accessed 20 January 2014).

Meyer, P. (1995) 'Learning to Love Lower Profits', *American Journalism Review*. Available HTTP: www.ajr.org/article.asp?id=1461 (accessed 28 August 2013).

Meyer, T. and Hinchman, L. (2002) *Media Democracy: How the Media Colonize Politics*, Oxford: Polity.

Mill, J. S. [1859] (2005) *On Liberty*, New York: Cosimo Classics.

Milne, C. and Taylor, A. (2006) 'South Africa: Research Findings and Conclusions', *African Media Development Initiative*. Available HTTP: http://bit.ly/1505EpI (accessed 4 February 2014).

Milton, J. [1644] (1918) *Areopagitica*, Cambridge: Cambridge University Press.

Mitchell, A., Holcomb, J. and Page, D. (2013a) 'News Use Across Social Media Platforms', Pew Research Center, Available HTTP: www.journalism.org/files/2013/11/News-Use-Across-Social-Media-Platforms1.pdf (accessed 21 January 2014).

Mitchell, A., Jurkowitz, H., Holcomb, J., Enda, J. and Anderson, M. (2013b) 'Nonprofit Journalism: A Growing but Fragile Part of the US News System', *PewResearch Journalism Project*. Available HTTP: www.journalism.org/2013/06/10/nonprofit-journalism/ (accessed 12 October 2013).

Molphy, J. (2012) 'Feminism Rules, OK! Err, or not Apparently … ', *Grazia*. Available HTTP: http://bit.ly/SbtiXX (accessed 4 February 2014).

Moore, M. (2010) *Shrinking World: The Decline of International Reporting in the British Press*, The Media Standards Trust. Available HTTP: http://mediastandardstrust.org/publications/shrinking-world-the-decline-of-international-reporting-in-the-british-press/ (accessed 4 February 2014).

Morley, D. (1980) 'The Nationwide Audience', in W. Brooker and D. Jermyn (eds) (2003) *The Audience Studies Reader*, London: Routledge.

Murdoch, J. (2009) MacTaggart Memorial Lecture, delivered at Edinburgh International Television Festival. Available HTTP: http://image.guardian.co.uk/sysfiles/Media/documents/2009/08/28/James MurdochMacTaggartLecture.pdf (accessed 4 February 2014).

Murdoch, R. (1989) MacTaggart Memorial Lecture, delivered at Edinburgh International Television Festival. Available HTTP: www.geitf.co.uk/sites/default/files/geitf/GEITF_MacTaggart_1989_Rupert_Murdoch.pdf (accessed 4 February 2014).

Negroponte, N. (1995) *Being Digital*, London: Coronet.

Nerone, J (2009) 'The Death and Rebirth of Working Class Journalism', *Journalism*, 10(3): 353–55.

Newman, N. (2011) *Mainstream Media and the Distribution of News in the Age of Social Discovery*, Oxford: Reuters Institute for the Study of Journalism. Available HTTP: http://bit.ly/YcolTt (accessed 4 February 2014).

Newman, N. (2012) *Reuters Institute Digital News Report 2012: Tracking the Future of News*, Oxford: Reuters Institute for the Study of Journalism.

Newman, N. and Levy, D. (2013) *Reuters Institute Digital News Report 2013: Tracking the Future of News*, Oxford: Reuters Institute for the Study of Journalism. Available HTTP: http://bit.ly/12WYcga (accessed 4 February 2014).

Nguyen, A. (2008) 'Facing "the Fabulous Monster": The Traditional Media's Fear-driven Innovation Culture in the Development of Online News', *Journalism Studies*, 9(1): 91–104.

Nguyen, A. (2011) 'Marrying the Professional to the Amateur: Strategies and Implications of the OhmyNews Model', in G. Meikle and G. Redden (eds) *News Online: Transformations and Continuities*, Basingstoke: Palgrave Macmillan.

Nielsen, R. K. (2012) *Ten Years that Shook the Media World*, Oxford: Reuters Institute for the Study of Journalism.

Nielsen, R. K. and Linnebank, G. (2011) *Public Support for the Media: A Six-Country Overview of Direct and Indirect Subsidies*. Available HTTP: https://reutersinstitute.politics.ox.ac.uk/fileadmin/documents/Publications/Working_Papers/Public_support_for_Media.pdf (accessed 13 January 2014).

Nordvision (2005) 'Public Service Broadcasting in the Nordic Countries'. Available HTTP: http://bit.ly/160nU21 (accessed 4 February 2014).

Nossek, H. (2004) 'Our News and their News: The Role of National Identity in the Coverage of Foreign News', *Journalism*, 5(3): 343–68.

NSPCC (2013) 'Child Homicides Statistics', Inform. Available HTTP: www.nspcc.org.uk/Inform/research/statistics/child_homicide_statistics_wda48747.html (accessed 16 February 2014).

Oakley, C. (2013) 'The Men who Killed the Regional Newspaper Industry', in J. Mair, N. Fowler and I. Reeves (eds) *What Do We Mean by Local?*, Bury St Edmunds: Arima Publishing.

O'Connor, C. and O'Neill, D. (2008) 'The Passive Journalist: How Sources Dominate the Local News', *Journalism Practice*, 2(3): 487–500.

Ofcom (2007) 'New News, Future News'. Available HTTP: http://stakeholders.ofcom.org.uk/market-data-research/other/tv-research/newnews/ (accessed 4 February 2014).

Ofcom (2012) 'Annex 4, News Consumption in the UK: Annex to Ofcom's Advice to the Secretary of State for Culture, Olympics, Media and Sport'. Available HTTP: http://stakeholders.ofcom.org.uk/binaries/consultations/measuring-plurality/statement/Annex4.pdf (accessed 27 August 2013).

Oliver, L. (2010) 'Trinity Mirror Wants MEN Staff to Move to Oldham in Deal with GMG', *Journalism.co.uk.* Available HTTP: www.journalism.co.uk/news/trinity-mirror-wants-men-staff-to-move-to-oldham-in-deal-with-gmg/s2/a537511/ (accessed 23 August 2013).

O'Neill, O. (1996) *Towards Justice and Virtue: A Constructive Account of Practical Reasoning*, Cambridge: Cambridge University Press.

O'Neill, O. (2006) 'A Right to Offend?', *The Guardian*. Available HTTP: www.theguardian.com/media/2006/feb/13/mondaymediasection7 (accessed 17 February 2014).

O'Neill, O. (2013) 'Media Freedoms and Media Standards', in N. Couldry, M. Madianou and A. Pinchevski (eds) *Ethics of Media*, London: Palgrave Macmillan.

Örnebring, H. (2012) 'Reassessing Journalism as a Profession', in S. Allan (ed.) *The Routledge Companion to News and Journalism*, London: Routledge.

Örnebring, H. (2013) 'Anything You Can Do, I Can do Better? Professional Journalists on Citizen Journalism in Six European Countries', *International Communication Gazette*, 75(1): 35–53.

Paper Cuts (2012) Available HTTP: http://newspaperlayoffs.com/ (accessed 4 February 2014).

Pariser, E. (2011) *The Filter Bubble: What the Internet is Hiding from You*, New York: Viking.

Patmore, A. (1993) *Marge: The Authorised Biography*, London: Warner.

Peachey, P. and Burrell, I. (2012) 'How the Press Ignored the Lawrence Story – Then Used it to Change Britain', *The Independent*. Available HTTP: www.independent.co.uk/news/media/press/how-the-press-ignored-the-lawrence-story–then-used-it-to-change-britain-6284645.html (accessed 31 July 2013).

Peppiatt, R. (2011) Evidence to the Leveson Inquiry. Available HTTP: www.levesoninquiry.org.uk/wp-content/uploads/2011/11/Witness-Statement-of-Richard-Peppiatt.pdf (accessed 21 January 2014).

Peters, J. D. (2005) *Courting the Abyss: Free Speech and the Liberal Tradition*, Chicago: University of Chicago Press.

Petley, J. (2011) 'Rules, Recycling, Filters and Conspiracies: Nick Davies and the Propaganda Model', in B. Franklin and M. Carlson (eds) *Journalists, Sources, and Credibility: New Perspectives*, London: Routledge.

Pew (2006) 'Principles of Journalism', *PewResearch Journalism Project*. Available HTTP: www.journalism.org/resources/principles (accessed 26 August 2013).

Pew (2009) 'The State of the News Media Report 2009', *Project for Excellence in Journalism*. Available HTTP: http://stateofthemedia.org/2009/ (accessed 31 July 2014).

Pew (2010a) 'A Year in the News 2010', *Project for Excellence in Journalism*. Available HTTP: http://stateofthemedia.org/2011/mobile-survey/a-year-in-news-narrative/ (accessed 21 January 2014).

Pew (2010b) 'Nielsen Analysis', *The State of the News Media*. Available HTTP: http://bit.ly/hHiCOB (accessed 4 February 2014).

Pew (2012a) 'The Future of Mobile News: The Explosion in Mobile Audiences and a Close Look at What it Means for News', *Project for Excellence in Journalism*. Available HTTP: http://cdn.economistgroup.com/leanback/wp-content/uploads/2012/09/TABLET-2012-REPORT-PEW-and-ECONOMIST.pdf (accessed 27 August 2013).

Pew (2012b) 'The State of the News Media Report 2012', *Project for Excellence in Journalism*. Available HTTP: http://stateofthemedia.org/overview-2012/ (accessed 16 July 2012).

Pew (2013) 'Overview: The State of the Media 2013', *Project for Excellence in Journalism*. Available HTTP: http://stateofthemedia.org/2013/overview-5/ (accessed 30 August 2013).

Peyrègne, V. (2014) 'World's Press Examines UK Press Freedom', *WAN-IFRA*. Available HTTP: www.wan-ifra.org/press-releases/2014/01/17/world-s-press-examines-uk-press-freedom (accessed 20 January 2014).

Pfauth, E. (2013) 'How We Turned a World Record in Journalism Crowd-funding into an Actual Publication'. Available HTTP: https://medium.com/de-correspondent/2a06e298afe1 (accessed 18 February 2014).

Phillips, A. (2007a) 'The Alternative Press', in K. Coyer, T. Dowmunt, A. Fountain (eds) *The Alternative Media Handbook*, London: Routledge.

Phillips, A. (2007b) *Good Writing for Journalists*, London: Sage.

Phillips, A. (2008) 'Advice Columnists', in B. Franklin (ed.) *Pulling Newspapers Apart*, London: Routledge.

Phillips, A. (2010a) 'Old Sources, New Bottles', in N. Fenton (ed.) *New Media, Old News*, London: Sage.

Phillips, A. (2010b) 'Transparency and the New Ethics of Journalism', Journalism Practice, 4(3): 373–82.

Phillips, A. (2012a) 'Faster and Shallower', in P. Lee-Wright, A. Phillips and T. Witschge (eds) *Changing Journalism*, London: Routledge.

Phillips, A. (2012b) 'Transparency and Ethics', in P. Lee-Wright, A. Phillips and T. Witschge (eds) *Changing Journalism*, London: Routledge.

Phillips, A. (2012c) 'Sociability, Speed and Quality in the Changing News Environment', *Journalism Practice*, 6(5–6): 669–79.

Phillips, A. (2013) 'Journalism Ethics and the Impact of Competition', in N. Couldry, M. Madianou and A. Pinchevski (eds) *Ethics of Media*, London: Palgrave Macmillan.

Phillips, A. and Witschge, T. (2012) 'The Changing Business of News', in P. Lee-Wright, A. Phillips and T. Witschge (eds) *Changing Journalism*, London: Routledge.

Phillips, A., Couldry, N. and Freedman, D. (2010) 'An Ethical Deficit? Accountability, Norms and the Material Conditions of Contemporary Journalism', in N. Fenton (ed.) *New Media, Old News*. London: Sage.

Phillips, A., Singer J. B., Vlad, T. and Becker, L. B. (2009) 'Implications of Technological Change for Journalists' Tasks and Skills', *Journal of Media Business Studies*, 6(1): 61–85.

Picard, R. G. (2013) 'The Bottom Line: Do and Will Consumers Pay for Digital News?', in N. Newman and D.A.L. Levy (eds) *Reuters Institute Digital News Report 2013*, Oxford: Reuters Institute for Journalism.

Powell, W. W. and DiMaggio, P. J. (1991), *The New Institutionalism in Organizational Analysis*, Chicago: University of Chicago Press.

Press Association (2013) 'Chicago Sun-Times Lays off Entire Photography Staff', *The Guardian*. Available HTTP: www.theguardian.com/media/2013/may/30/chicago-sun-times-photography-staff (accessed 4 February 2014).

Purcell, K., Rainie, L., Mitchell, A., Rosenstiel, T. and Olmstead, K. (2010) 'Understanding the Participatory News Consumer: How Internet and Cell Phone Users have Turned News into a Social Experience', *PewResearch Internet Project*. Available HTTP: www.pewinternet.org/Reports/2010/Online-News.aspx (accessed 2 May 2014).

Quandt, T. (2008) '(No) News On The World Wide Web?', *Journalism Studies*, 9(5): 717–38.

Ramesh, R. (2013) 'Stafford's A&E set for Closure as Anger Grows at "Crucifixion of a Good Hospital"', *The Guardian*. Available HTTP: www.theguardian.com/society/2013/jul/28/staffords-hospital-closure-anger-grows (accessed 1 August 2013).

Rantanen, T. (2009) *When News Was New*, Chichester: Wiley-Blackwell.

Rao, U. (2010) 'Empowerment through Local News Making', in S. E. Bird (ed.) *The Anthropology of News and Journalism: Global Perspectives*, Bloomington: Indiana University Press.

Ray, T. (2011) 'The "Story" of Digital Excess in Revolutions of the Arab Spring', *Journal of Media Practice*, 12(2): 189–96.

Reich, Z. (2006) 'The Process Model Of News Initiative: Sources Lead First, Reporters Thereafter', *Journalism Studies*, 7(4): 497–514.

Reich, Z. (2011) 'Source Credibility as a Journalists Work Tool', in B. Franklin and M. Carlson (eds) *Journalists, Sources, and Credibility: New Perspectives*, London: Routledge.

Riggins, S. H. (1997) 'The Rhetoric of Othering', in S. H. Riggins (ed.), *The Language and Politics of Exclusion: Others in Discourse*, Thousand Oaks, CA: Sage.

Robinson, S. (2009) '"If You Had Been with Us": Mainstream Press and Citizen Journalists Jockey for Authority over the Collective Memory of Hurricane Katrina', *New Media Society*, 11(4): 795–814.

Robison, A. (2012) 'Working with Brands: Building Relationships Beyond Reviews and Giveaways', *Independent Fashion Bloggers*. Available HTTP: http://heartifb.com/2012/12/20/working-with-brands-building-relationships-beyond-reviews-giveaways/ (accessed 4 February 2014).

Rosen, J. (2006) 'The People Formally Known as the Audience', *PressThink*. Available HTTP: http://bit.ly/dbrHm1 (accessed 4 February 2014).

Russell, A. (2011) *Networked: A Contemporary History of News in Transition*, Cambridge, MA: Polity Press.

Saïd, E. (1993) *Culture and Imperialism*, New York: Pantheon Books.

Sainath, P. (2010) 'Advertising, Bollywood, Corporate Power', *The Hindu*. Available HTTP: http://bit.ly/aPNorM (accessed 19 September 2012).

Saltzis, K. and Dickinson, R. (2008) 'Inside the Changing Newsroom: Journalists' Responses to Media Convergence', *Aslib Proceedings*, 60(3): 216–28.

Schiller, H. I. [1969] (1992) *Mass Communications and American Empire*, Boulder, CO: Westview Press.

Schiller, H. I. (1976) *Communication and Cultural Domination*, Armonk, NY: M. E. Sharpe.

Schiller, H. I. (1996) *Information Inequality*, London: Routledge.

Schlesinger, P. (1987) *Putting 'Reality' Together: BBC News*, London: Methuen.

Schlesinger, P. and Tumber, H. (1994) *Reporting Crime: The Media Politics of Criminal Justice*, Oxford: Clarendon Press.

Schlossberg, J. (2013) 'Co-opting the Discourse of Crisis: Reassessing Market Failure in the Local News Sector', in J. Mair, N. Fowler and I. Reeves (eds) *What Do We Mean by Local?* Bury St Edmunds: Arima Publishing.

Schudson, M. (1995) *The Power of News*, Cambridge, MA: Harvard University Press.

Schudson, M. (2005) 'The US Model of Journalism: Exception or Exemplar?', in H. de Burgh (ed.) *Making Journalists: Diverse Models, Global Issues*, London: Routledge.

Schumpeter, J. A. (1943) *Capitalism, Socialism and Democracy*, New York: Harper.

Seamans, R. and Zhu, F. (2013) 'Responses to Entry in Multi-Sided Markets: The Impact of Craigslist on Local Newspapers'. Available HTTP: www.gc.cuny.edu/CUNY_GC/media/CUNY-Graduate-Center/PDF/Programs/Economics/Course%20Schedules/Seminar%20Sp.2013/seamans_zhu_craigslist(1).pdf (accessed 4 February 2014).

Shattuc, J. (1997) *The Talking Cure: TV Talk Shows and Women*, New York: Routledge.

Shirky, C. (2008) *Here Comes Everybody*, New York: Penguin.

Sigal, L. V. (1973) *Reporters and Officials: Organization and Politics of Newsmaking*, Lexington, MA: D. C. Heath.

Silverstone, R. (1988) 'Television Myth and Culture', in J. C. Carey *Media Myths and Narratives: Television and the Press*, London: Sage.

Silverstone, R. (2006) *Media and Morality: On the Rise of the Mediapolis*, Cambridge, MA: Polity Press.

Singer, J. B. (2004) 'More than Ink-Stained Wretches: The Resocialization of Print Journalists in Converged Newsrooms', *Journalism & Mass Communication Quarterly*, 81(4): 838–56.

Singer, J. B. (2007) 'Contested Autonomy: Professional and Popular Claims on Journalistic Norms', *Journalism Studies*, 8(1): 79–95.

Skillset (2001) 'Skills for Tomorrow's Media: The Report of the Skillset/DCMS Audio Visual Industries Training Group'. Available HTTP: www.skillset.org/uploads/pdf/asset_184.pdf?1 (accessed 4 February 2014).

Smith, P. (2013) 'Behind the Business Model of MailOnline, the Biggest Newspaper Site in the World', *The Media Briefing*. Available HTTP: www.themediabriefing.com/article/mail-online-biggest-news-site (accessed 30 August 2013).

Sparks, C. (1992) 'Popular Journalism: Theory and Practice', in P. Dahlgren and C. Sparks (eds) *Journalism and Popular Culture*, London: Sage.

Splichal, S. and Sparks, C. (1994) *Journalists for the 21st Century*, New York: Ablex.

Spivak, G. C. (1985) 'The Rani of Sirmur: An Essay in Reading the Archives', *History and Theory*, 24(3): 247–72.

Spuldar, R. (2013) 'Brazil's Mídia Ninja Covers Demonstrations from the Inside', *Index on Censorship*. Available HTTP: www.indexoncensorship.org/2013/08/brazils-midia-ninja-covers-demonstrations-from-the-inside/ (accessed 30 August 2013).

Starr, P. (2004) *The Creation of the Media: Political Origins of Modern Communications*, New York: Basic Books.

Steenveld, L. and Strelitz, L. (2010) 'Trash or Popular Journalism? The Case of South Africa's Daily Sun', *Journalism*, 11(5): 531–47.

Stein, S. (2012) 'Obama on Trayvon Martin Case: "If I Had a Son, He'd Look Like Trayvon"', *Huffington Post*. Available HTTP: www.huffingtonpost.com/2012/03/23/obama-trayvon-martin_n_1375083.html (accessed 1 August 2013).

Stephenson, H. and Mory, P. (1990) *Journalism Training in Europe*, Paris: Commission of the European Community and European Journalism Training Association.

Tameling, K. and Broersma, M. (2013) 'De-converging the Newsroom: Strategies for Newsroom Change and their Influence on Journalism Practice', *International Communication Gazette*, 75(1): 19–34.

Tapscott, D. and Williams, A. D. (2006) *Wikinomics*, New York: Portfolio.

Thanki, A. and McKay, S. (2005) *Why Ethnic Minority Workers Leave London's Print Journalism Sector*, Final Report for the Commssion for Racial Equality, London: Working Lives Research Institute. Available HTTP: http://workinglives.org/fms/MRSite/Research/wlri/Photo%20gallery/Why%20ethnic%20minorities%20leave%20London%27s%20print%20industries.pdf (accessed 16 February 2014).

Thompson, H. (2013) 'The How Not To Public Relations Guide', *Twelve Thirty Eight*. Available HTTP: www.1238kmh.com/PRBuzz.htm (accessed 4 February 2014).

Thompson, J. B. (1995) *The Media and Modernity: A Social Theory of the Media*, Stanford, CA: Stanford University Press.

Thurman, N. (2008) 'Forums for Citizen Journalists? Adoption of User Generated Content Initiatives by Online News Media', *New Media and Society*, 10(1): 139–57.

Thurman, N. and Walters, A. (2013) 'Live Blogging – Digital Journalism's Pivotal Platform?' *Digital Journalism*, 1(1): 82–101.

Thussu, D. (2000) *International Communication: Continuity and Change*, London: Bloomsbury Academic.

Thussu, D. (2009) *News As Entertainment*, London: Sage.

Tofel, R. J. (2012) *Why American Newspapers Gave Away the Future*, Now and Then Reader [Kindle edition].

Toffler, A. (1980) *The Third Wave*, New York: Bantam Books.

Tomlinson, J. (1991) *Cultural Imperialism: A Critical Introduction*, London: Continuum.

Tompkins, A. (2003) 'Ownership Caps and Fuzzy Media Maths', *Poynter*. Available HTTP: www.poynter.org/uncategorized/11761/ownership-caps-and-fuzzy-media-math/ (accessed 20 January 2014).

Trammell, K. D. and Keshelashvili, A. (2005) 'Examining the New Influencers: A Self-Presentation Study of A-List Blogs', *Journalism & Mass Communication Quarterly*, 82(4): 968–82.

Tuchman, G. (1972) 'Objectivity as a Strategic Ritual', *The American Journal of Sociology*, 77(4): 660–67.

Tuchman, G. (1978) *Making News: A Study in the Construction of Reality*, New York: Free Press.

Tunstall, J. (1993) *Television Producers*, London and New York: Routledge.

Turner, D. (2012) 'Inside the BBC's Verification Hub: Technology and Human Intervention Are Key', *Nieman Reports*, 66(2): 10–13.

Turvill, W. (2013) 'The Accused: At Least 61 UK Journalists Arrested since April 2011', *Press Gazette*. Available HTTP: www.pressgazette.co.uk/accused-least-59-uk-journalists-arrested-april-2011 (accessed 25 August 2013).

Ursell, G. (2012) 'Changing Times, Changing Identities: A Case Study of British Journalists', in T. Elgard Jensen and A. Westenholz (eds) Identity in the Age of the New Economy: Life in Temporary and Scattered Work Practices. Cheltenham: Edward Elgar Publishers.

Van Dijk, T. A. (2009) 'News Discourse and Ideology', in K. Wahl-Jorgensen and T. Hanitzsch (eds) *The Handbook of Journalism Studies*, Abingdon: Routledge.

Vidal, M. (2013) 'At Least 45 Killed as Train Derails in Spain', *Reuters*. Available HTTP: www.reuters.com/article/2013/07/24/us-spain-train-idUSBRE96N17 R20130724 (accessed 4 February 2014).

Vike-Freiberga,V., Däubler-Gmelin, H. and Hammersley, B. (2013) 'A Free and Pluralistic Media to Sustain European Democracy', *The Report of the High Level Group on Media Freedom and Pluralism, European Commission*. Available HTTP: http://ec.europa.eu/digital-agenda/en/high-level-group-media-freedom-and-pluralism (accessed 17 February 2014).

Wallace, S. (2013) 'The Complexities of Convergence: Multiskilled Journalists Working in BBC Regional Multimedia Newsrooms', *The International Communication Gazette*, 75(1): 99–117.

Walters, E., Dobbie, M. and Warren, C. (2006) 'The Changing Nature of Work: A Global Survey and Case Study of Atypical Work in the Media Industry', *The International Federation of Journalists*. Available HTTP: www.ifj.org/assets/docs/068/112/3fbf944–95ebe70.pdf (accessed 4 February 2014).

Wardle, C. and Williams, A. (2008) 'ugc@thebbc: Understanding its Impact upon Contributors, Non-contributors and BBC News', Research Report. Available at www.bbc.co.uk/blogs/knowledgeexchange/cardiffone.pdf (accessed 17 February 2014).

Wasserman, H. (2006) 'Tackles and Sidesteps: Normative Maintenance and Paradigm Repair in Mainstream Media Reactions to Tabloid Journalism', *Communicare*, 25(1): 59–80.

Wasserman, H. (2008) 'Attack of the Killer Newspapers!', *Journalism Studies*, 9(5): 786–97.

Weaver, D. H. (1998) *The Global Journalist: News People Around the World*, Cresskill, NJ: Hampton Press.

Weaver, D. H. (2005) 'Who Are Journalists?', in H. DeBurgh (ed.) *Making Journalists*, London: Routledge.

Weber, M. (1947) *The Theory of Social and Economic Organization*, New York: Free Press.

Webster, J. G. (2011) 'The Duality of Media: A Structurational Theory of Public Attention', *Communication Theory*, 21(1): 43–66.

Wells, K. (2005) 'The Nomads of Esplanade', *Wall Street Journal*. Available HTTP: http://on.wsj.com/1aiDTwB/ (accessed 16 July 2012).

White, D. M. (1950) 'The Gatekeeper: A Case Study in the Selection of News', *Journalism Quarterly*, 27(3): 383–90.

Wilby, P (2012) 'Alan Rusbridger: The Quiet Evangelist', *New Statesman*. Available HTTP: www.newstatesman.com/media/media/2012/05/guardian-editor-alan-rusbridger-peter-wilby (accessed 6 February 2014).

Williams, A. and Franklin, B. (2007) *Turning Around the Tanker: Implementing Trinity Mirror's Online Strategy*, Cardiff: Cardiff University.

Williams, B. (2002) *Truth and Truthfulness: An Essay in Genealogy*, Princeton: Princeton University Press.

Williams, K. (2005) *European Media Studies*, Oxford: Oxford University Press.

Williams, R. (1977) *Marxism and Literature*, Oxford: Oxford University Press.

Witschge, T. (2012) 'The Tyranny of Technology' in P. Lee-Wright, A. Phillips and T. Witschge (eds) *Changing Journalism*, London: Routledge.

Witschge, T. and Nygren, G. (2009) 'Journalism: A Profession under Pressure?', *Journal of Media Business Studies*, 6(1): 37–59.

Witschge, T. and Redden, J. (2010) 'A New News Order? Online News Content Examined', in N. Fenton (ed.) *New Media Old News: Journalism and Democracy in the Digital Age*, London: Sage.

Woyke, E. (2009) 'The Struggles of OhMyNews', *Forbes*. Available HTTP: http://onforb.es/18vZagE (accessed 13 July 2012).

Yapp, R. (2005) 'We Feared for our Lives in the Hell of the Superdome', *Daily Mail*. Available HTTP: http://dailym.ai/1dPM8lr/ (accessed 4 August 2013).

Yelland, D. (2013) 'Leveson Anniversary Lecture, 29th November 2013', *Media Standards Trust*. Available HTTP: http://mediastandardstrust.org/mst-news/david-yellands-leveson-anniversary-lecture-29th-november-2013-full-text/ (accessed 30 November 2013).

Youm, K. H. (2008) 'The Right of Reply and Freedom of the Press: An International and Comparative Perspective', *The George Washington Law Review*, 76(4): 1017–64.

Younge, G. (2005) 'Murder and Rape – Fact or Fiction?', *The Guardian*. Available HTTP: http://bit.ly/1dPVWMh/ (accessed 21 July 2012).

Zelizer, B. (2013) 'When Practice is Undercut by Ethics', in N. Couldry, M. Madianou and A. Pinchevski (eds) *Ethics of Media*, London: Palgrave Macmillan.

Zhao, Y. (2012) 'Understanding China's Media System in a World Historical Context', in D. Hallin and P. Mancini (eds) *Comparing Media Systems Beyond the Western World*, Cambridge: Cambridge University Press.

Zogby International (2008) 'Newsroom Barometer 2008: Main Results, the Integrated Newsroom Will be the Norm', *WAN-INFRA*. Available HTTP: www.editorsweblog.org/2008/05/06/1-newsroom-barometer-2008-main-results-the-integrated-newsroom-will-be-the-norm (accessed 18 January 2014).

Index